Oh, Baby, I Love It!

Oh, Baby, I Love It!

Baseball Summers • Hot Pennant Races • Grand Salamis • Jellylegs • El Swervos Dingers and Dunkers etc • etc etc

by Tim McCarver
with Ray Robinson

Villard Books New York 1987

Library of Congress Cataloging-in-Publication Data

McCarver, Tim.
  Oh, baby, I love it!

    1. McCarver, Tim.   2. Baseball
players—United States—Biography.
3. Sportscasters—United States—Biography.
I. Robinson, Ray.   II. Title.
GV 865.M25A3 1987   796.357′092′4 [B]   86–40381
ISBN 0–394–55691–7

Designed by Quinn Hall

Manufactured in the United States of America

9 8 7 6 5 4 3 2

FIRST EDITION

*To Anne, whose love, loyalty
and patience have carried us
through the ups and downs
of the long seasons—T.McC.*

*To Phyllis, who learned
as much about baseball
as I did during the gestation
of this book, and Penrod,
my Norfolk terrier, who was
my constant companion
when I wasn't trailing
after Tim—R.R.*

Acknowledgments

I'd like to thank Jay Horwitz, the Mets' PR director, for his many kindnesses that made life easier; Rick Cerrone, formerly of the Baseball Commissioner's Office, for always picking up his phone; Peter Gethers, our editor, for his enthusiasm and belief in this project; Marty Appel, for obligingly fielding nit-picking questions; Bob Witten, for the use of his Xerox machine, which was always handled quickly and with a smile by that ultimate Mets fan, Marianna Sorshek; Bob Rosen and Sterling Lord, for being excellent agents and gentlemen.

Contents

1 ◆ Roots of a Ballplayer 3

2 ◆ The Loneliness of a Long-Distance
Catcher 20

3 ◆ Three Pitchers: Carlton, Gibson,
Gooden 49

4 ◆ Catchers and Pitchers 74

5 ◆ That Old Devil Pressure 96

6 ◆ Where Have All the Pep Talks Gone? 107

7 ◆ The Not-So-Gentle Art of Managing 117

8 ◆ I Love—and Hate—It: Likes, Dislikes,
Pet Peeves, and Gratuitous Opinions 127

9 ◆ Baseball Realities—Good and Bad 141

10 ◆ After the Ball Is Over 153

11 ◆ A Long Season in a Small Booth 160

Mets 1986: Living It 186

A Glossary of Pitches 243

Oh, Baby, I Love It!

1

Roots of a Ballplayer

You know, I always thought it was
pretty wonderful to be a ballplayer.
—BOB O'FARRELL,
CATCHER 1915–1935,
from *The Glory of Their Times*

With the glorious advantage of almost thirty years of hind-sight, I can now see that on my first day in the big leagues I was given a clear sign that while I might turn out to be a pretty good ballplayer, I *definitely* had a future in broadcasting.

From where I sat that September day in 1959, I could gaze into the Milwaukee Braves' home-team dugout and get a clear view of the peaceful black face and muscular forearms of my boyhood hero, Henry Aaron.

Already a celebrated performer after a half dozen years with Milwaukee, Aaron had earned a special place in my young mind and heart—along with Willie Mays, Monte Irvin, and my new teammate, Stan Musial, whom I revered. Each one of these men had meant something special to me while I was growing to manhood in steamy central and south Memphis, Tennessee, those rough strips of city above the Mississippi River.

So when Hank came to bat for the first time that day, I leaped from my perch in the Cardinals' dugout and did what I always did when I listened to the Braves play the Cards.

"Come on, Henry!" I yelled. *"Come on, Henry!"*

The action seemed natural to me, but some of my team-mates weren't amused. Glares from guys like Alex Grammas, Gene Green, Kenny Boyer, Bill White, Joe Cunningham, and Manager Solly Hemus reminded me of where I was, what I had just done, and what uniform I was wearing. And if the glares weren't enough to put an end to my gaucherie, their snarls and comments made their message even more emphatic: I was a baseball Benedict Arnold. Pointedly, but with a bit of amuse-ment, they restrained me from making more of a damned seventeen-year-old fool of myself than I already had.

"Around here, kid, we root for *our* guys, not theirs," one Card judiciously reminded me.

This is how life in the big leagues began for me. Now I can laugh when I think about that indoctrination. In retrospect, it's amusing. Hey, I got caught up in the moment, I was a fan, and I *loved* Henry Aaron. At the time it happened, it was an em-barrassment that reddened my face and certainly shut my mouth—for a while, at least. I learned my first lesson the hard way.

As the game progressed that day, Solly Hemus suggested to me that I might be getting a time at bat.

"If Cunningham gets on, you bat, Stan," the manager re-marked to Musial. Then, looking over at me, Hemus said, "If Cunningham doesn't get on, you bat, Tim."

Cunningham didn't get on, so there I was, younger than Musial's own son, picking up a bat and advancing to the plate. As I stepped in to face Don McMahon, a veteran right-handed relief pitcher with a commanding fastball, my knees literally shook with fear. I settled myself nervously at the left side of the plate while McMahon peered—he appeared bigger than life—at me and his catcher, Del Crandall.

Before I knew it, I had two strikes on me. Then, with relief, I flied out to right field. I hit a curveball—and it was not a good curveball—but I was secretly proud that my bat had even touched the ball in my first try as a Cardinal and a Na-tional Leaguer.

Who caught the fly? Hank Aaron.

. . .

I was born James Timothy McCarver in Memphis, Tennessee, city of the blues and Boss Crump, on October 16, 1941. Just eleven days before my arrival and less than two months before Pearl Harbor detonated into World War II, a Brooklyn Dodgers catcher named Mickey Owen made his classic mistake: he let a third-strike, ninth-inning pitch from Hugh Casey get away from him in the fourth game of the World Series, costing Brooklyn the game against the Yankees. To Dodger fans this was almost as serious as the Japanese attack.

Like Mickey Owen, I became a catcher, too, but unlike Mickey I never became a household word. Of course, I don't think I want to be associated with the particular part of the house they used when they referred to Mickey in those days.

I grew up in a tough, run-down neighborhood, where some of the rough-talking kids in the area went straight from high school into prison. I don't want to build the impression that I was Horatio Alger going from rags to riches—or from nothing to extreme poverty, as Groucho Marx once said. But by any legitimate social measurement the McCarvers of Lamar Terrace rated a smidgen less than lower middle class.

My three brothers, Grover, Pat, and Dan, and my sister, Marilyn, five years older than I—I was next to youngest—were raised in a strict Catholic environment. In an ethnically mixed neighborhood, we were distinctly a minority family. Tennessee was only 6 percent Catholic. Also, only some sixteen years before I was born, Tennessee had been the scene of the Scopes trial, which put those celebrated lawyers William Jennings Bryan and Clarence Darrow arguing about evolution on opposite sides of the courtroom. Protestant fundamentalists always ruled the roost in our state, so I think I learned something about bias at an early age—enough to know you don't go around picking on other people if they're of a different color or religious belief.

I've always been a staunch advocate of the theory that a man is presumed innocent until proven guilty, but I'm afraid that many of my buddies from Lamarr Terrace such as Jumbo and Herbie probably belonged behind bars. Another friend, Bobby, went to Humes High in Memphis, which was where Elvis Presley also went to high school. In 1964, after the Cards won the World Series, I was asked to go to Nashville to toss the first ball up in a Harlem Globetrotters exhibition game. At halftime, the warden from the state prison there came up to me and said that the best athlete they had ever had on the grounds wanted to say hello to me. He then passed along greetings from my old pal Bobby. "What an athlete," I said. "Yeah," the warden agreed. "We're gonna hate to see him go." For the record, Marvelous Marv Throneberry, Casey Stengel's favorite on the Mets, especially when he was trudging and tumbling out triples, also came out of Memphis.

When I run into people from my hometown these days, they invariably ask me, "What's so-and-so doing?" and half kiddingly I answer, "Oh, one-to-five."

If these kids were rough, I was no sweet pea, either. Don't rate me as a delinquent. I wasn't that. Because my father was a policeman, I was afraid to break the law. But on a delinquency scale of one to ten, maybe I would have come in at around five or six. One of the McCarver neighbors, Mr. Maugham (no relation to Somerset), once took my father aside when I couldn't have been more than seven years old and warned him: "If your son don't change his ways and start controlling himself, he's going to wind up squattin' in the electric chair."

Well, I wound up squattin' behind home plate for twenty-one years, but I'm not crowing about it. To be blunt, I was probably lucky to emerge as a halfway decent citizen, considering that I was constantly sprawling and brawling all over the place. I'd spend a good deal of my time throwing punches around, then end the week by eating the Mrs. Paul's fish sticks that my mother served us every Friday along with soggy French fries. To this day, I cannot eat a Mrs. Paul's fish stick.

My Dad, G. E. "Ed" McCarver, had been a good athlete in his younger days. At least, that's what he told us. Tough and ruggedly honest, he pounded a beat in Memphis until he became a lieutenant on the police force. His top salary was $417 a month, not a helluva lot to feed five kids on. Later, he opened up shop as a private detective. We nicknamed him Sam Spade. He retired in 1964. His logic was that he could then spend more time watching me play ball.

When I was a little kid, my mother, Alice, used to make the sign of the cross on my back before I went out to play ball. She loved to hum "Alice Blue Gown" as she went about her chores. I was quite close to my mother—she died at the age of sixty-seven—but, as I look back on it, I'm afraid she lived vicariously through me and my athletic exploits. Although it saddens me to say it, and I find it kind of painful to reflect upon, that's not an uncommon phenomenon for parents with children who become professional athletes. It used to make me mad because I sometimes felt the only thing my parents cared about was whether or not I went three-for-four. It doesn't make me mad anymore. I understand it now, and that's simply the way it was. However, even though I might be rationalizing, I am glad that I have two daughters. I know that I can't put the same kind of athletic pressure on them that I might on a son.

I was a dues-paying roughneck, but I was able to channel most of that aggressiveness into sports. I'd often wander around the neighborhood, always carrying a baseball glove, hoping that someone would invite me to play in a pickup game. My two older brothers, in the tradition of many older brothers, didn't pay much attention to me. They were good athletes, but they didn't want me to play with them. I mean, I didn't even know whether I batted right-handed or left-handed. Just to be different, my sister Marilyn said, "Why be like all the rest of the kids on the block?" So she started me batting left-handed, even though I do everything else right-handed.

Marilyn, who was a tomboy first class, happened to be an outstanding athlete. She used to crush me daily playing tackle football. She hit like a linebacker. When she was thirteen, my mother made her stop playing, which I couldn't understand and was kind of bitter about. I didn't find out until years later that it was because Marilyn had started having her period. Marilyn played softball, she bowled, and she was always available to hit grounders to me. The legend around the McCarver family is that I broke so many windows playing for Marilyn's team that they stopped using baseballs and began substituting tennis balls in their games.

At eight I began playing ball for the Oliver Finnie Co.

Little League team—our nickname was the Candy Kids—and by the time I was ten years old I was playing with the Bemis Bag Company under Joe Etzberger, a guy who had won many amateur championships in Memphis. It was Joe who turned me into a catcher. To this day I don't know if I should thank the man!

At about the time I started playing Little League ball, we moved to our first house, which was in South Memphis. I transferred to St. Thomas Grammar School. But whenever there was a ball game at the local minor-league ballpark, Russwood Park, I'd run over there and sell peanuts and popcorn for a half cent a bag.

The most popular street game in Memphis in those days was cork ball, which I played for hours with my buddy Louie Truemper. We would take a thermos cork or jug cork, weight it down a bit with a penny on each end, and then stick tape around it to make a ball. The bat we used was an old broomstick. I was already batting left-handed in cork ball, thanks to the diligent efforts of my sister, Marilyn.

I got an early start on my announcing career while playing cork ball, imitating Harry Caray on the play-by-play. Harry was something of a hero in our house, alongside Aaron, Irvin, Mays, Musial, and two guys named Jabbo Jablonski and Rip Repulski. Jablonski came out of Chicago and played third base for the Cards in 1953 and 1954. Repulski hit twenty-three homers for the Cards in 1955. I guess I liked Rip and Jabbo because their names had those alliterative rings.

The Cards, with their ballpark just three hundred miles or so away in St. Louis, were always the preferred ballclub in my house. "This is the Cardinal baseball network," Harry Caray would intone, as his voice traveled over 124 stations in fourteen southwestern and midwestern states. He was a fun-loving guy and a nonconformist who used to screech "Holy cow!" over the airwaves long before Phil Rizzuto made it his signature. Harry still hasn't lost his enthusiasm for baseball. He always called himself "a fan with a mike in front of my face." In recent years he's been the resident optimist in the Chicago Cubs' booth. He just finished his forty-second year in broadcasting.

I guess it was unusual for a kid from Memphis to have

black men like Irvin and Aaron as heroes. But I accepted that fact without ever questioning it or trying to figure it out. I accepted it, just as I accepted the fact that there were no blacks in my segregated grammar school or at Christian Brothers High School, which I attended after St. Thomas on an athletic scholarship worth about $180 a year.

Christian Brothers, in addition to providing me with a place to play baseball, football, and basketball, was a first-rate educational institution, but I wasn't a great student. Brother Alberto handed me a flat F in my second-year algebra course. The fact that I had a hard time staying awake in his course probably contributed to my problem. I used to get up at three-thirty every morning to deliver newspapers, plus I was playing four separate sports—track and the three majors. It was hard to stay awake for math. But I always thought that if I liked something I'd do well in it.

I did develop an appreciation for reading and for books, and the interest has never left me.

Despite the name of the school, Christian Brothers also gave me a chance to know a lot of Jewish kids whose folks sent them there because they thought it was a good school. Along the way (but not at school) I met a kid named Avron Fogelman, and we played against each other in Little League. Avron wound up as a baseball executive and is owner today, with Ewing Kauffman, of the Kansas City Royals. I have Avron to thank for officially affixing my name to the Memphis Chicks' home stadium a few years ago.

At Christian Brothers I played bang-'em-up, hard-nosed football and became a twelve-letter man, all told, in sports. Eventually I had at least forty colleges knocking on my door and wanting to talk about football scholarships.

Kentucky, Alabama, and Tennessee all wanted me. In 1958 I visited South Bend, Indiana, to watch Notre Dame play Purdue. I sat on the bench next to Moose Krause, the famous athletic director of the Irish, who had given me ten bucks of expense money to cover my trip.

"Don't tell anyone I gave it to you," Moose whispered. Today that would barely keep an athletic aspirant in bubble gum. Moose wanted me to come to Notre Dame and to play baseball and football once I got there. The scholarship offer made it imperative that I play both sports, but football was clearly my first love.

In those years there were also loads of baseball scouts haunting Christian Brothers' ball field. Our football coach, Tom Nix, took note of this and tipped off my father that it might be wise for me to give up football in my senior year to concentrate on baseball. I couldn't get paid for playing football, and baseball offered the opportunity to go directly into professional sports and receive an immediate signing bonus. *Immediate* was the operative word there. Coach Nix thought a football injury would hurt my chances of getting that signing money.

But I said "No way" and continued to play football. I loved the contact. And got plenty of it.

General Bob Neyland, formerly the long-time football coach at the University of Tennessee and then the athletic director, had apparently scouted me a few times, and he came away saying the nicest things. He told me I was "the best blocking lineman" he'd ever seen in a high school game anywhere. That's a lot of praise (what's the proper collective there —a mouthful or a throatful?), and it got me to thinking about the general's university seriously, since he had also offered me a grant-in-aid. He was also really nice to my parents, bringing them up to see a couple of games. It was all very enticing and flattering.

But it was baseball that got my final vote. Money was the deciding factor, plain and simple. But I've got to note here that while cash was the immediate lure and the thing that got me into the game, I eventually reached a point where I would have played for nothing.

Anyway, I got some good offers from sixteen or so ballclubs, then boiled those offers down to a final three: the Yankees, the Cards, and the San Francisco Giants.

At first it looked as if I'd wind up with the New York Yankees. Those were the days, don't forget, when the Yankees still dominated the sport, with Mickey Mantle and Yogi Berra and that lovably cocky left-hander Whitey Ford. Casey Stengel was double-talking the Yankees to one pennant after another, and Mickey seemed to have a lock on the American League's annual Most Valuable Player award. They were giants in the land, man, and what kid wouldn't want to play for them?

Bill Dickey, the great Yankee catcher of the 1930s who had once roomed with Lou Gehrig, had been feverishly pursuing me while scouting for the Yankees. He hung around my house so much it's a wonder my father didn't hand him the mortgage note.

Dickey had been a bruising backstop in his day. Many people may not remember how hang-tough Bill was: One day in 1932 he broke the jaw of Carl Reynolds of the Washington Senators in a one-punch unscheduled bout at home plate after Reynolds knocked the ball out of Bill's mitt while scoring. (Dickey was heavily fined and suspended, but the battered Reynolds was out for six weeks with a jaw that had to be wired.)

If Dickey had a boxer's solid punch, he was something of a cagey politician, too. For instance, he knew that we were Catholic, so one Friday night he caught a mess of catfish and brought them to my mother. It was probably the first time in history that catfish were ever used as a bribe!

"If you sign with the Yanks," Bill assured me, "I'll take you along with me on a two-week fishing trip. We'll talk about catching inside and out."

So there it was: the Yankees, Cards, and San Francisco Giants going to the wire in their bidding for me, a kid just seventeen years old in a pair of baggy flannels and the crewcut that they gave to marine recruits at Parris Island.

Dickey's original bid on behalf of the Yanks was $50,000. Hugh Poland, representing the Giants, went to $58,000. When Dickey heard that the Giants went to that level, his offer was upped to $60,000.

But ultimately it was the Cards, through scout Buddy Lewis, and St. Louis's farm director, Walter Shannon, who decided to make the clinching bid of $75,000 for me. Buddy had had a pretty good track record for signing young talent. Previously he'd put Vinegar Bend Mizell's signature on a Cards contract, even before Vinegar bothered to pitch with his shoes on. Buddy told me he'd actually signed Vinegar Bend down at the local swimming hole in Alabama, where Mizell grew up. (Mizell did wear shoes when he served in the U.S. Congress many years later!)

To this day I have some feelings of guilt about how I dealt with Bill. I had promised him that whatever offer I received from the Cards, I'd immediately call him at his hotel in Memphis and tell him about it. When the final and firm Cards' offer was put on the table, I never did call Bill. Let's say I've been quasihaunted by this dereliction of duty ever since. Though I've never regretted choosing the Cards, I'm sorry about how I handled it with Bill. I tell myself I was only seventeen years old and had no agent—only advice from my father. Bill apparently hasn't held any major grudges, though. After I committed myself to the Cards, he actually presented me with a new pair of shoes and a catcher's mitt.

Lewis, Shannon, and just about every McCarver in Memphis, including, of course, my mother and father, were present at the contract signing. It took place in the dining room of Will Carruthers, a Memphis sportswriter who for many years had been a close friend of the family. It's strange to think that I didn't even think Will liked me very much after he had first spotted me when he managed a team in the Memphis Rotary League. Shows you how wrong you can sometimes be about people. I never realized, either, that every time Will wrote a story about me in the papers he was helping to boost the price that someone might be willing to pay for me—someone like the Cards, for example.

Actually, there was no real bargaining, as I recall it, for the Cards were determined to get me. They were also determined that $75,000 was as high as they'd go. In my heart, I was equally determined to play for them. So when they said "Take it or leave it," there was no further haggling. Leaning on Will's drop-leaf dining table, Dad just signed for me on the dotted line. He had to sign because I wasn't twenty-one yet.

Will Carruthers promised me that when I got married, he'd make a wedding gift of the historic dining room table in his house, and he kept his promise. When Anne and I were married five years later, in 1964, he did present it to us—and it was even well polished. In every respect, Will was a man of his word.

When the contract was signed, sealed, and delivered—at 1:45 A.M. on June 15, 1959, at 282 Eastland Drive—there were no Hollywood kliegs focused on the event. It didn't rate up there with Appomattox or Versailles or Geneva. For that matter, it didn't even compare to Ruppert's Brewery in New York City, where, during the darkest days of the Depression, Babe Ruth negotiated his meaty contract.

In my case, the bonus money ($75,000) from the Cards was more cash than my father had ever made in his life—total. That plus my guaranteed annual salary of $6,000 per year for five years added up to a nice, Christmassy package.

Sure, I was excited and thrilled about that contract. I'd have been a pretty cold-blooded kid if I hadn't gotten chills thinking of all that money coming in to me and my family. As important, though, I was thrilled at the opportunity to become a successor to so many other able catchers who won their credentials in Redbird uniforms: Bob O'Farrell, who once caught for Grover Cleveland Alexander and was behind the bat the day Tony Lazzeri was struck out by Alex with the bases loaded in the 1926 World Series; Gus Mancuso, who went on to catch such great pitchers as Carl Hubbell and Hal Schumacher of the Giants; Jimmy Wilson, the catcher on Pepper Martin's 1931 Series team; Bill DeLancey, the ill-fated young man who caught for the Gashouse Gang and was forced to leave baseball because of tuberculosis; Walker Cooper, who was the Card catcher when I was born; and what's that guy's name? Oh yes, Joe Garagiola.

After the signing I gave $15,000 of my bonus money to my family to pay off their mortgage. I also gave them money to build a den and bought them a 1959 Pontiac. As for me, AT&T got some of my investment money.

Suddenly here I was, after walking around in the same two pairs of pants for over a year and getting up at three-thirty in the morning to sell papers, coming into big money. At least to me and my family it was big money. No more shiny pants with the seats worn out.

I was confident enough to feel that I'd be playing with the Cards immediately after signing, but Hal Smith, the Cards' regular catcher for several years, didn't go into a dead faint when they told him of my imminent arrival. So the Cards assigned me to Keokuk, in the Class D Midwest League, where I batted .360 in sixty-five games. I also committed fourteen errors, so I didn't get *too* cocky about my future.

From Keokuk the Cards sent me that same season to Rochester in the International League, where, in seventeen games, I hit .357 and showed distinct improvement in the fielding department. The fact that I didn't hit a single home run in seventy at bats sobered me up to the fact that I wasn't about to become an overnight threat to the Babe or Ralph Kiner in the distance department.

The Cards were keeping close tabs on me, as they did with all of their prospects, especially those who had been handed some of that golden ointment. By early September the front office in St. Louis, using the mysterious and wonderful system of modern communications, had put in a hurry-up call for me to come up to the parent club.

Now nobody, to this day—friend, foe, or disinterested observer—has ever accused me of being any kind of fashion plate. Even with my newfound wealth I didn't make any best-dressed lists as a ballplayer, even among catchers.

When I arrived at the Cards' team bus for the first time I was nervous enough. I didn't know these guys, and I wanted to impress them because I'd always heard the phrase "dress like a big leaguer." No one ever told me what that meant, so I tried to figure it out for myself. I think their first look at me must have made them think I came out of a nineteenth-century London poorhouse. If they didn't have that much imagination, they might have thought I'd emerged from the stock company of *Tobacco Road.* In short, I was one roaring sartorial mess, Memphis's contribution to the old clothes business, a sight for any ballplayer's bloodshot eyes. Years later I did come to understand what it means to dress like a big leaguer. It means slacks, Ban-Lon, and a sport coat.

When Mickey Mantle came out of Commerce, Oklahoma, and presented himself and all of his worldly goods to Manager Casey Stengel in 1951, eyewitness observers insist he had hay coming out of his ears and a cardboard suitcase clutched in his hand. Well, I wasn't that skyscraper-shy, and I wasn't that much of a country boy. But by the reckoning of my teammates I was the quintessential busher—or "Bush," as Bob Nieman called me every day he looked at me in 1960, my second year with the Cards.

Nieman, something of a burly guy with a .292 lifetime batting average, took in my appearance on that first trip—brown wing tip shoes, yellow socks, gray pants, plaid Madras sport coat, godawful-color belt, the whole thing worth maybe a dollar and a half—and blurted out, "That's the worst-looking fucking outfit I've ever seen, bar none." Then he roared, "Whaddya say, Bush?!"

And he wasn't talking about our owner, Gussie Busch, either.

Not more than a year later, as I started to make some minor progress with my wardrobe, Nieman came close to apologizing for his treatment of me.

"Hell, Bush," he said, "I once called Brooks Robinson bush, and look where he is today."

It was all right. I'd come to like the nickname. In fact, I was mildly offended when my teammates didn't use it.

One guy who wasn't ever bush, even when he first came up to the Cards in 1941 as an outfielder converted from a pitcher, was Stan "the Man" Musial.

This is as good a place as any in this book to talk about Stan.

Musial was thirty-eight years old when I arrived with the team. He had just gone through his first subpar year, with a .255 average. But you never could tell from Stan's behavior or demeanor that things weren't going well for him. In many ways he exemplified that great Card team.

Today a statue of Musial stands outside gate seven at Busch Stadium. It's only fitting that he has been sculpted into a monument, for he has become, since the day of his retirement in September 1963, a true monument—to decency, character, and performance. The inscription on the side of the marble pedestal says it all: "Here stands baseball's perfect warrior . . . here stands baseball's perfect knight."

I can still see Stan in that inimitable peeking-around-the-corner left-handed stance. I played in Stan's final game, and although I wasn't around for his first one in 1941, I'm certain his stance never changed in those twenty-one years. Neither did his smile or his talent.

Do you want one of the most remarkable statistics in baseball, maybe in all of sports? Stan had 3,630 hits in his career: 1,815 at home, 1,815 on the road. Man, talk about consistency!

The alchemy of that thing called charisma might never have actually touched Musial, as it did Willie Mays and Babe Ruth. (As one writer noted, "General Lee had it, General Grant didn't.") But Stan always had the respect and affection of several generations of baseball fans. He still does.

It always seemed ironic to me that Musial, with one of the sunniest dispositions I've ever encountered, should have been born in the coal town of Donora, Pennsylvania, where the skies were always as dark as the inside of an umpire's pockets.

Many stories are told about Stan, and there isn't a single one I've heard that tarnishes the mythic figure. But one of the funniest stories has to be related here, mainly because it presents Stan somewhat out of character.

In 1961, a couple of years before Stan retired, the Cards were playing the Los Angeles Dodgers in LA. That venerable scoutmaster Leo Durocher was then serving under Walter Alston as a coach, and he didn't believe in keeping quiet about it. With Durocher every day was a "hollerday" (as poet Ogden Nash would have put it). This particular day wasn't any different.

As the Dodgers took a commanding 9–1 lead, Durocher, not widely known for being a particularly gracious winner, strutted back and forth in the Los Angeles dugout. Waving his arms in what could only be interpreted as a put-down and spewing his well-rehearsed obscenities at us, he was, indeed, an obnoxious figure.

Stan, along with the other Cards watching Durocher's performance, was more than a little annoyed. Stan usually took such things in stride—with a twinkle in his eye and his typical lopsided smile—but this day was different. He was fed up with Durocher's endless caterwauling. Walking to the steps of the dugout, Stan peered over at Durocher. Then he pointed his index finger at him.

"You're up and strutting now," he yelled, "but just you wait. We'll get you, you *prick!*"

I'm not certain that Durocher heard it, and I don't think he would have cared anyhow. But the Cards heard it to a man. And you want me to tell you something? They loved it! It's always nice to find out that some saints just ain't.

(Whenever I think about Leo Durocher, I think about Stan's rebuke. I also think of that funny story about two New York journalists. For want of anything better to do, the writers challenged each other to write down on a slip of paper the names of the three "most evil men in history." After they scribbled their choices, they compared them. Both had selected Hitler and Stalin for the one-two positions. And their third choice was the same, too: Walter O'Malley, the man who took the Dodgers out of Brooklyn! I tell this anecdote here because I have a feeling a lot of people might have penciled in Durocher for the number-three slot. Not me, however. I like the guy.)

The impact of a man like Musial on a bunch of ballplayers can't ever be exaggerated. Year in and year out, it was more than his seven batting titles that made an impression on his teammates. Those who spent time around him recognized that he was a person of good character and decency. He tried to lead by example. He wasn't much of a talker, a special pleader, or a clubhouse lawyer. He was just a good man.

Sometimes the respect for and feeling about Stan reached such proportions that his teammates actually felt that with Stan around nothing bad could happen to them. I'm referring here specifically to the possible dangers inherent in travel, by both air and bus. With Stan on board, everybody felt we'd make it to the next destination. With Stan on the plane nothing could possibly happen to the craft or to us. Silly? Superstitious? Sure, but that's the effect Stan had on his teammates.

I remember one time—and this story often gets credited as a Yogi Berra story, but I was there; it was Stan—when the Cards went from Philly to St. Louis on a prop job. Ordinarily this would have been about a four-and-a-half-hour trip. When we got on the plane, Walt "Moose" Moryn, a big outfielder who struck me as being as rational as anyone else, said he didn't "feel very comfortable" about the trip because Stan hadn't gotten on the plane with us. He had an appointment in New York and couldn't make the trip.

About a quarter of the way to St. Louis, one of the props suddenly stopped working properly. The plane had to turn around and go back to Philly. As we disembarked, somewhat weary and more than a little concerned, Moryn kept shaking his head.

"If Stan had been here, nothing like this would have happened," he said. Sounds crazy? But Moryn believed it, and so did the other guys.

About the only thing Stan seemed incapable of doing was teaching others to hit as well as he did. If you asked him for advice, as teammates often did (players on rival teams would approach him, too), he'd be generous with his time, but his teaching technique was often flawed. He would try to illustrate. "Well, here's how I do it," he would say, invariably assuming that corkscrew stance, the one that could drive pitchers into speedy retirement.

I once heard him tell a rookie the secret of hitting. "If I want to hit a grounder," Stan said, "I hit the top third of the baseball. If I want to hit a line drive, I hit the middle third. If I want to hit a fly ball, I hit the bottom third."

Faced with such intelligence, the rookie probably wished he had adopted another professional sport.

Stan didn't realize that it did little good to show others how *he* did it. That was beside the point: it's what he could tell *others* to do. He never seemed to be able to do that, although he always tried his damnedest.

They used to tell the story about how Chuck Connors, who turned out to be a better television actor than a major-league hitter. Connors was frustrated by his lack of progress when he played briefly for the Brooklyn Dodgers in 1949 and the Chicago Cubs in 1951. He wanted desperately to survive in the big leagues, so he discussed his problems with his Cub teammates.

"There's only one guy to go to," they said. "That's Musial. He'll help if he can."

So the next time the Cubs came in to Chicago, Chuck, determined to improve, introduced himself to Musial. Would

Stan take a few seconds to watch him in batting practice? Connors asked. You know the answer.

Stan watched, then took Chuck aside and talked to him. The lesson went on for the better part of a half hour, with Stan using the technique of how *he* did it, not how others should do it.

Years later, Connors, then star of "The Rifleman," recalled the lesson with fondness. "I was a bum of a hitter, just not cut out for the majors," said Connors. "But how could I ever forget Stan's kindness? When he finished watching me and talking to me, Stan slapped me on the back and told me to keep swinging."

Stan's respect for others is something that Bill White, now a broadcaster for the Yankees, has always been willing to pinpoint in his appraisal of the man. White is a black man with a keen appreciation of the social struggle that took place in baseball, even while he was playing.

"I never hesitated to ask Stan about hitting," he once said. "He's helpful to anyone who asks him. More important, I guess, is his cooperative attitude toward anyone—white or black—who approaches him. It doesn't make any difference to him. He's that kind of man. He's always congenial, always ready to share."

The late Kenny Boyer, the third baseman for the Cards and once the team's captain, remarked about Musial: "He's living proof that nice guys don't have to finish last."

I'll never forget the day that the "nice guy" let Leo Durocher have it. Talk about memorable moments in baseball!

The Loneliness of a Long-Distance Catcher

> You gotta have a catcher. If you don't have a catcher, you'll have all passed balls.
>
> —CASEY STENGEL

With Bill James and other sabermetricians around these days, it's surprising nobody has bothered to calculate one of the more salient statistics relating to ballplayers: how much time they spend alone.

Bill James should apply himself to this Euclidean problem: How many seconds, minutes, hours, days, and weeks do players spend alone in hotels, restaurants, lobbies, bathrooms, airports, bars, and anyplace else you can think of? (I was about to add the time they spend alone in museums and libraries, but that wouldn't be too hard to figure out.) David Brenner, the comedian, once cracked: "I've spent so much time in hotel rooms that I even dial nine when I'm at home." That goes for me, too. Some joke, huh?

Did you ever try to figure out where jokes originate in this land? You hear a joke in the clubhouse in Shea Stadium one night. The next thing you know you're picking it up in Los Angeles—or Atlanta or Chicago—in a matter of hours. It's truly one of the wonders of our civilization. More remarkable than fast food is the fast joke, or the *fast-moving* joke.

Now about living alone and being alone. I've never quite agreed with that player who once told me he didn't like living with himself. "When I'm alone, I'm in bad company," he mumbled sadly. Well, I understand the problems of being alone and being lonely, and I'll admit that it doesn't go easy for many guys, but I'm one of the luckier ones. Over more than twenty-seven years of playing and announcing I've learned how to cope with it.

For instance, being alone in New York, as I've been for the past few years, can be a pleasure for some of us. E. B. White once wrote that "on any person who desires such queer prizes, New York will bestow the gift of loneliness and the gift of privacy."

If you want to choose a symbol of baseball life on the road —maybe a symbol, generally, of the solitary life—take a peek at any ballplayer's refrigerator if he's dumb enough to let you into his hotel room.

Take a look at the scarcities and excesses of my own refrigerator in almost any city on the circuit at any time. You must remember, I'm a married man, but here I am, living as a bachelor and trying to tend to my own needs without a wife around to spoil me or cater to me (feminists, please note!).

It was never too easy for Anne to accept our constant separations over the long seasons. She says, "I've learned to accept it logically but not emotionally." Ballplayers' marriages inevitably experience strains; ours was no different. The kids, Kathy and Kelly, would often wonder, sometimes out loud, why Daddy was away so much. "That's what Daddy does," Anne would try to tell them.

Sure, there were times when I had pangs of guilt about this existence. But if you're going to live a ballplayer's life, you've got to come to grips with the fact that you're different, that you do without things that are normal in other families. It also means that when you're with your wife and kids you try to make it quality time.

Open my refrigerator and what do you see?

There are two six-packs of beer, three quarts of Tropicana orange juice, two bottles of white wine, two bottles of water, and five shriveled-up grapes that are stuck tenaciously to the shelves. There are also three quarters of a mangy-looking orange, half a lemon, and a humidor full of cigars.

That empty fridge may give you a pretty good idea of why some guys get overdedicated to the game. They can't wait to get to the ballpark each day because that's where they belong. That's where their friends are, where their life is. Sure, baseball's a masculine society—what do the psychiatrists call it, male bonding?—but baseball buddyship, baseball talk, and baseball thinking can fill the endless empty hours. Life on the road would be desperately lonely without it. A New York sportswriter once said, rather lugubriously, that the road can make a bum out of anyone.

Some guys in the game happen to be more self-sufficient than others. Maybe I fit into that category. You have to like yourself in order to be able to cope with all the free time you're going to spend by yourself. My ability to be by myself, enjoy myself, and be happy by myself has stood me in good stead over the years.

Springtime in baseball can be the loneliest and most unsettling time of the year even for veteran players. But it can also be a learning process. So can the seemingly endless business of travel. If ever a guy could use a good butler or servant, that's the time, brother. Packing, unpacking, packing, unpacking, living out of a suitcase, rushing to airports, rushing to buses, always making sure you haven't left anything behind. (Do I leave that battered orange or that bottle of wine in the fridge? What's your guess?) With the exception of airline pilots, candidates for national political office, and traveling salesmen, ballplayers probably do more traveling than any other group of Americans.

When I first arrived in the big leagues there was a typical yarn they liked to tell about Babe Ruth. Of course, in his time the Babe lived like nobody else in baseball. He once shared hotel quarters in the early 1920s with Ping Bodie (whose real name of Francesco Pezzolo probably wouldn't have been either remembered or correctly pronounced by Ruth). Ping had hit as many homers in his career—forty-four—as the Babe did in one modestly productive season, but Ping was a guy with a rascally sense of humor.

One day a reporter asked Ping about his roommate, and Bodie replied somewhat forlornly, "I room with a suitcase."

That remark has turned out to be as imperishable in baseball lore as Yogi Berra's "It's never over until it's over."

After you do the traveling stint for almost three decades, you accumulate a lot of memories, not all of them good. The routine can make you old (if not wise) before your time, and you can get damned tired of it in a hurry. There's no telling how much irreparable damage constant flying does to your system. But you have to harden your mind against such feelings in order to do the job of being a big-league ballplayer. I'm glad I never developed a fear of flying. Others weren't so lucky. Air travel definitely drove the late Jackie Jensen out of baseball before his time was up. In fact, Jackie died at a young age—I don't think he was even fifty. I have to think his phobia about flying contributed to his early demise. Don Newcombe, the great Dodger pitcher, had to undergo hypnosis to get his feet on a plane. Rusty Staub much preferred eating chili in his New York restaurant to climbing aboard airplanes. They aren't the only ones, either. There are many guys like that in baseball; some prefer to keep their fears quiet and not publicize their anxieties.

I have fears, too, but they're mostly about the lousy, understaffed, overwhelmed hotels that ballplayers usually stay in. When you travel as much as players do, you're bound to become something of an authority on rooms, service, food, and whatnot at these places, especially the big chains where the traveling secretaries of the ballclubs generally arrange for you to rest your head.

Clubs have to get people where they're going on time and at a reasonable cost. But I think clubs are too concerned about the cost. More care should be taken to supply better facilities on the road. Your body—an athlete's body in particular—is a machine, and eating and sleeping fuel that machine. To skimp on that fuel is analogous to buying a $50,000 car and using regular gasoline. One of these days, I hope, front office people will think of some better, more efficient, more congenial way of traveling as a group. I'm surprised that Bill Veeck, while he lived, didn't develop a new way to hustle ballplayers from one destination to another. Maybe if we had all been midgets, like his famous "designated midget," Eddie Gaedel, it would have been easier.

Traveling as a group isn't ever easy. I think it's a tribute to the spirit of the men who play the game that conflicts— physical or mental—don't occur more often. Yet whenever a fight does break out it's a headline. That's crazy. The *infrequency* of infighting is what should be in the headlines.

Baseball management has always been ridiculous in their approach to treating grown men like children. Their theory is that in groups lies more control. They like to keep the players in a herd. And if they need a dog or two to watch the sheep, they'll do it. That's why they don't like having too many independent ballplayers on one team. If a team's sheep start to stray, they've got to hire more dogs. Up until 1969, it was considered almost ridiculous for someone to think of rooming alone. But ballplayers live in such close proximity to each other that they've just got to get away from each other sometimes —it's necessary for their mental health.

Whenever I got an opportunity to be away from the group I took it. As much as I happen to like being with other players and shooting the bull about baseball and lifting a few beers, it really uplifts the mind and spirit to get away from the herd for a few hours.

Another thing I always loved in my years of tramping around the big-league circuit—and something I still do as an announcer—is going out to a swimming pool by myself. I never liked the sun shining through my hotel window in the morning because that was a reminder that I was going to have to catch and squat and sweat that day. But the sun beating down on me at a pool or on a beach, now that's a totally different matter.

Sure, I've always understood the risks of too much exposure. I know that sunlight can cause skin cancer and premature wrinkling and that it can fry you if you're foolish enough to fall asleep as it beats down on your unprotected head.

But sunlight, as any doctor can inform you, can also have salutary effects. Some experts also stress that it can increase your endurance, lower your blood pressure, and set off the production of vitamin D in the skin. It can also make you feel good in your *mind.* What really counts with me is the general feeling of well-being that I get after a day in the sun. It makes me feel loose—and feeling loose is one of the keys to your preparation as a catcher.

One of the tattered myths in baseball that's been dragged around for years, just like those suitcases we lug from city to city, is that players can't perform well in night games after they've spent a day in the sun. Obviously, you don't spend the day in the sun and play that night every day, because there's bound to be a certain sapping of your strength from such an imprudent schedule. But I discovered as a player that when I spent an afternoon in the sun—no more than three hours, no fewer than an hour and a half—it seemed to do an amazing amount of good for my mental health. Then I'd have to follow up with a nap in my hotel room. The two went hand in hand.

I never wanted to spend too much time in my room or to sleep too late. That can get your system all messed up. But I always looked forward to the sun routine to revive my spirits. Even if it didn't noticeably improve my batting average, it was good for my soul.

This system of mine has, of course, been censured for years by managers and general managers. If these guys caught us lolling in the sun, snoozing, or reading a paper or a book, sometimes they actually struck us with a fine. Imagine that. Ludicrous. Crazy. They might still do it. All stemming from suspicion, myth, poor information, ignorance. On some issues, these guys are still in the Stone Age.

It's especially silly when you consider that a good part of baseball is the annual ritual of spring training, when it's pretty hard for anyone to escape the sun, even if he's in a suit of armor. It's funny to see all the guys in their short-sleeved shirts, with their arms real tan and their necks bronze as berries and the rest of their bodies white as sheets. You can really get that farmer's tan in the spring.

It also used to be taboo—maybe it still is—for a pitcher to swim or spend time in the sun on a day he's scheduled to pitch. I recall little Bobby Shantz, who spent a couple of years with the Cards in the sixties and was MVP in the American League in 1952 as a member of the Philadelphia A's, diving and swimming on the day before he was supposed to pitch. Bobby, who was about five-foot-six and weighed no more than 140 pounds soaking wet, swam like a fish and was almost as good off the board as some of those Olympic divers.

He knew his bosses frowned on the whole idea, but Bobby didn't understand the problem. "I always feel real loose when I swim and dive," he said. That's exactly how I felt about it.

So much for this soliloquy on the sun.

When you play ball for a lot of years, there's always a temptation to blame misfortunes and bad periods—and all ballplayers have them—on the press.

In my book, men who constantly react that way are just looking for convenient scapegoats, but that doesn't mean I'm totally accepting and passive about all the things—truth and nonsense, fair and unfair, bullshit and otherwise—writers say about players. My perspective on this (and I don't think it's hindsight, either, now that I'm part of the Fourth Estate as a broadcast journalist) is that in the long run what the newspapers, radio, TV, and magazines have to say about you generally adds up to a plus for most guys. Pete Rose once said that the only thing the media can do for you is to help you make more money. That might sound a bit mercenary, but I think after all the things that have been said about Pete—controversial and otherwise—he's certainly right, at least for Pete. On the negative side, the media's obsession with players' salaries does tend to breed a lot of jealousy and bad feeling on the part of the fans. A contractual obligation should be between a player and his organization. Of course, the media play up all that stuff because they think that's what people want to read or hear. That's human nature, they say. But what I want to know is how come people say it's human nature only when something bad occurs? A guy cheated on his wife—that's human nature. A guy wants more money—human nature. Why don't you ever hear that phrase when someone does something good? A guy is very charitable—*that's* human nature. A guy's a loyal friend—*that's* human nature. But you never hear that. Not in the media or anywhere else, for that matter.

"Just make sure they spell your name right" is my philoso-

phy about press coverage, adverse and favorable. Now that
doesn't mean you have to like unpleasant things printed about
you or that you can't get sore as a hungry warthog over some
disparaging description of your talents. The point is, if you
have a bitch with a guy—a member of the media—you ought
to go to that guy to straighten out the problem, not condemn
the whole industry. The press is an integral part of the whole
structure of professional baseball. What's more, as these writers and broadcasters keep reminding you, they have their jobs
to do, too.

Look back in baseball history a bit and you'll see that
plenty of big stars, from Ty Cobb to Billy Martin, have raved
and ranted at the guys—and these days the women, too—in
the press box. Some have openly fought with them. It's a pattern of behavior I don't recommend to any young players.
Don't go after the messenger, friends. Try instead to heed the
message.

Biographers of Ty Cobb have reported that he had a burning hatred for many writers, and that went double for those
who ever dared to deprive him of base hits in the course of
rendering their decisions as official scorers. Cobb supposedly
walked around with a "son of a bitch" list in his pocket that
included practically all New York sportswriters and plenty
from other cities as well. Although Cobb had fistfights with
teammates, opponents, and spectators—especially black people (he was a virulent racist)—I don't remember hearing that
he ever took a punch at a writer.

On the other hand, Dizzy Dean, a much more congenial
guy than Cobb, actually came to blows with Jack Miley, a
columnist for the New York *Daily News*. The dispute had to
do with some reputed remark that Miley made about Diz's
being "a big man now, especially between the ears." Dean told
Jack that he didn't have to put up with such shit from a guy
who got paid little more than a tie salesman. For good mea-
sure, Dean gave Jack a bash over the head with a pair of spiked
shoes.

Around that same time, Bill Terry, the manager of the
New York Giants, accused all writers of being a bunch of rats
and entirely deserving of the pitiful wages they received for

their pitiful efforts. Funny, wasn't it, that Dizzy and Bill both seemed to lean on money as the barometer of someone's worth to society, or at least to baseball?

In more recent times, Billy Martin has managed on occasion to confuse sportswriters with marshmallow salesmen in his own combative way. My pal Steve Carlton simply chooses to regard writers as invisible men. But at least in Lefty's case there's never any laying on of hands.

Bo Belinsky, who threw a no-hitter and some mean haymakers in his time, once slugged a West Coast writer named Braven Dyer. Vada Pinson, the fine outfielder for the Reds, threw a punch at Earl Lawson. The late Thurman Munson spat at a wire service reporter (he missed him), and his manager, Ralph Houk, once tried to choke a New York baseball columnist. The normally restrained Card left-hander John Tudor seemed to come unstrung during the 1985 World Series. He threatened to punch a Los Angeles reporter in the mouth (he didn't), but reserved his best left hook for the metal fan in the Cards' dugout.

I'm sure there are plenty of other examples of such behavior, but I think you probably get the point—i.e., that ballplayers often feel they have enemies in the press box.

One of these days they may even give college courses on how ballplayers should relate to the press and vice versa. I'm not kidding about that, either. In January 1986, I jumped into a car and drove up to Vassar College—yes, Vassar College in Poughkeepsie, New York—as part of a group of baseball people putting on a seminar on the subject of baseball and the press.

Bob Fishel, vice-president of the American League; Lee MacPhail, former president of the Players Relations Committee; Roy White, a Yankee coach; and Mike Lupica, a New York *Daily News* columnist, were also on the program, which turned out to be a lively discussion with questions from the floor.

All I could think of as I sat there trying to field questions about George Steinbrenner and the press's treatment of players and the drug problem was, What was an ex-jock out of Memphis doing at Vassar on a wintry night? Only in America.

I've suffered a few maulings by the press in my time. By and large, I accepted them if they didn't get too personal. When they did, I went to the writer and argued my side of the story. I've got to admit, though, the only satisfaction that came of it was getting to say what I had to say. Certainly, no retraction of any of my infractions was ever printed.

But none of this stuff ever bothered me as much as the persistent questioning I was subjected to every year during spring training. Every year I'd get the same damn questions and I'd give the same damn answers. Mind you, the questions didn't always come from reporters. They often came from fans or spectators—and especially other players. Regardless of the source, it was all one large pain in the butt to me.

Spring training questions invariably went like this: How's the family? Is your weight down or up? Did you drive down? Where are you staying? Did you have a good winter? (Think about it: In what other business will people ever tell you to have a nice winter? A nice day, a nice weekend, sure—but an entire *winter*?)

These queries are never well-intentioned or sincere, and they do get to be a damn bore, especially when you hear them from the first second you arrive in camp. They're asked because people don't know what else to say. They're not signs of true interrelating. If they were, they'd sound more like, "How does Kelly like school?" or "Did Anne drive down in the VW?" This is one of the reasons the art of conversation is dying in this country. Evasive eyes are the norm in personal conversation. People just aren't interested in what you're saying. They're more interested in getting you to hear what *they* say.

Once I was on a call-in show on WCAU in Philadelphia. One of the callers started ranting and raving about how she didn't like the way I talked all through my broadcast. "You talk during the pitch," she said. "You break the flow. You just talk too much," she went on. And on. And on. In fact, she talked so much I couldn't get one damn word in. After repeated attempts to interject, I finally got to ask, "Are you through?" When she said she was, I said, "I hope you realize that in criticizing me for talking too much, you just talked too much." She didn't care for that at all.

But for spring training one year, in an act of self-preservation, I had over five hundred cards printed up just on a lark. This is what was written on them: *I had a good winter. I drove down. I'm staying on the beach. My family is fine. My weight's fine. Signed: Tim McCarver.* If anyone approached me, writer or fan, and then went into the usual song and dance, I immediately gave him a card. It was considerably more original than anything I could think up to say day after day.

I tried the same ploy one time with the Cards when I injured my thumb while trying to escape an errant pitch. I taped one sign on my locker and carried another on my neck. The sign had four responses written on it: *1. No, it's not broken. 2. Yes, it hurts. 3. I don't know how long it will be. 4. Yes.*

The first three answers were clear—clear enough to satisfy even someone such as that terrier of a reporter Sam Donaldson of ABC. But the fourth turned out to be a bit mystifying to some. In number three I was saying that I wasn't sure how long it would be before I'd be playing again. In number four I was trying to impart the information that yes, I was available for pinch-running duty.

A couple of years before, when Bob Gibson had a broken leg, he rigged up a similar sign, including the same number-four answer as mine. Gibby was joking, but you couldn't ever be sure.

In the care and feeding of reporters, I never thought funny signs and snappy ripostes to obnoxious questions were particularly offensive. In fact, since these writers were constantly on the prowl for angles or quotes of the day, they should have been a help to them. Besides, there's no law that says there can't be a little levity in the clubhouse.

When I discovered that many of my Philly teammates were hiding out in the lounge or the exercise room in order to duck reporters' questions—naturally, we were doing our share of losing at this time—I got the writers together and suggested a handy solution to the problem.

"Hey, you know what you guys should do?" I said. "When you're at spring training you ought to round up all your quotes and then save them up for the regular season."

"We'll consult our bosses about it," one of the writers

responded with a straight face. You'll have to admit, it wasn't a bad idea.

In the years I've been behind the mike, many fans have also gotten into the habit of asking me the same questions. Usually they corner me on the way into the park. It's almost an automatic reflex or a nervous tic. They know I'm a broadcaster for the club, so they come up to me and ask, "Are you going to win tonight?"

First of all they make a mistake by saying "you." *You* doesn't happen to be *me*, because I'm not out there playing.

My response usually is, "I don't know. If I knew, I'd phone it in." That may sound sort of fresh, but I try to be gracious when I say it.

In the course of a long career, any player is bound to run into a few snags and setbacks. Everyone's image is going to be tarnished a smidgen. I'm no exception. I'll tip you off about some of these embarrassing moments right here—before sending them on to *Reader's Digest*.

For instance, on July 4, 1976, when our country was celebrating its two hundredth birthday, I hit a bases-loaded home run for the Phillies against the Pirates. End of story? Not on your life. I was called out for passing Garry Maddox at first base. Let me fill you in on the gruesome details.

Larry Demery, a slight right-hander, was pitching for the Pirates, and we were ahead 1–0. In the second inning Maddox was intentionally walked ahead of me, filling the bases. This is the kind of situation that a vengeful hitter relishes. I hit the pitch over Dave Parker's head in right field for a home run. But Garry Maddox, apparently thinking that Dave would catch up with my drive, came back to first to tag up. I arrived at first base, intently watching the ball. When I saw it clear the fence, I clapped. Then I turned back to the base path and realized, much to my surprise, that Garry was standing right next to me.

Maybe I'd fallen asleep. Maybe I was too impressed with my sudden power. Or maybe I just wanted to do something memorable on the Bicentennial. Whatever it was, I stood there, red-faced. I ended up in the record book with a three-run single.

"I didn't pass Garry; he just lapped me," was my escape valve quote on that one. But perhaps the best excuse I could manufacture for my baseline malfeasance was that it wasn't very original.

My old hero Hank Aaron was involved in something similar on May 26, 1959, when Harvey Haddix pitched twelve perfect innings against Hank's Milwaukee club only to lose the masterpiece in the bottom of the thirteenth. What Hank did in the thirteenth had no bearing on the outcome of the game. Haddix had already had his heart torn out when Felix Mantilla scored the winning run from second base on Joe Adcock's right-field homer, the first and only hit all day for the Braves.

But Hank, who had been on first base, thought Joe's belt had fallen at the base of the fence instead of going over it. After touching second, Hank headed for the Braves' dugout while Adcock, running out his "homer," ran past Hank and toward third base. The result: Adcock got credit for a double, with the Braves winning 1–0.

Lyn Lary, a Yankee shortstop, pulled another similar bonehead play in 1931, costing Lou Gehrig the home run title that year. Lou had just hit a homer with Lary on first base. However, thinking the ball had been caught, Lary trotted past third base and right into the dugout. Gehrig, with his head down, kept right on running around the bases. Gehrig's homer didn't count.

Gehrig and Ruth both ended up with forty-six homers that year, so Lary's boo-boo had more sinister repercussions than did my own absentmindedness. In my case, all it really meant was that I finished with three instead of four homers for the year. My screwup didn't win quite the notoriety that came Babe Herman's way in 1926 when he doubled into a double play, but it is enough to make me cringe even in the retelling.

Even more distressing for my image was my fight with my old pal and teammate Lou Brock. It was September 1971, when I was a Philly. To this day I have to confess a certain embarrassment about that event.

You have to understand, since you've probably seen a few of them at the ballpark and on TV, that baseball brawls are generally as animated as the reception room at the morgue.

Baseball players seem to be incapable of landing harmful punches. With the possible exception of Ray Knight of the Mets, I can't think of one player who's had true boxing experience.

My moment in the pugilistic arena with Brock probably all started with a pop-up that I dropped with two Cards on base and nobody out. I committed the dastardly deed right in front of the Card dugout. Six runs followed as a result.

When Joe Torre of the Cards reached first base the next inning, I was still burning from my error. I really snapped when I heard Brock yell from the Card dugout at Torre, "Go ahead and run, Joe! He'll never throw you out!" By "he" Brock meant me. And don't forget that Joe Torre, even in his prime, was about as fleet-footed as Schnozzola Lombardi or Rusty Staub.

Those were fighting words, since I took my catching and throwing seriously. I encouraged my pitcher, Manny Muñiz, to "intimidate" Lou his next time up. Muñiz never hit him, just knocked him down once or twice. Actually, he didn't knock him down; he knocked him up—by throwing at his legs and making him jump over the ball.

Naturally, Brock wasn't buying this treatment, and he decided to walk out to the mound and talk it over with Muñiz. I followed him out. Before he got halfway there, I said, "Lou, you're not going out there!"

And he said, "Yes, I am!"

And I said, "Oh, no, you're not!"

And then he said, "Okay, I'll stay here and fight you."

The next thing I knew I was hitting Lou Brock with a right hand. A *Philadelphia Daily News* sportswriter said it was "the best punch thrown in an outdoor fight in Philadelphia since Jersey Joe Walcott was nailed by Rocky Marciano back in 1951," just twenty years earlier. I can't say I'm proud of what I did, but I do have to say that put in the same situation I'm sure I would react the same way.

A few other blows were landed before the two of us wrestled to the ground like a pair of knickered tarantulas. Then the benches of both clubs emptied. You'd have thought they were all traveling to a fire. Soon the whole contretemps (there's one of those Montreal words again) was over. Almost forty guys were piled on top of me, and Lou was still trying to get in a blow here and there. The only thing that stopped him was all that weight on top of him and me.

I'm sure that Lou has never held anything against me because of it. He was, and is, a good friend. He also was an extremely competitive ballplayer. And in moments like that, however irrationally, your competitive instincts simply take over. I didn't cry about it then and I won't cry about it now.

In the minor leagues in 1962, when I was spending the season with the Atlanta Crackers, I landed a right hand again, this time on the jaw of Bill Lajoie, an outfielder distantly related to the great second baseman Napoleon Lajoie. Of course, when I threw the punch at Lajoie, I wasn't thinking much about his relatives. (Bill is now the general manager of Detroit.)

The Toronto Maple Leafs had been whomping the day-lights out of the Crackers, racking up something like twenty-one homers in a four-game series. That wasn't very pleasant to the Atlanta pitchers or to me, the catcher calling for those pitchers.

So when Lou Jackson stole third for Toronto, with his team ahead 18–0 in the third game, he got plunked with a pitch his next time at bat. That's totally proper in my opinion. If a guy runs when his team's *that* far ahead, he's going down. But the bad blood got badder. Later, when Lajoie tagged up from third and slid into me with a stiff elbow in my eye, I'd had enough. So I let *him* have it.

Again, I wound up on the bottom of a pile of battling players—including Sparky Anderson, then the Toronto second baseman but in more recent years renowned as a pennant-winning manager in both leagues. When the umps finally broke it up, I was ejected from the premises and fined twenty-five bucks—which was a lot of money to me—out of my $8,000 salary. Sparky, to this day, says it's the best fight he's ever seen or been in. And he's been in a ton of them.

Baseball fights are often ignited when players feel that the other team is rubbing it in, maybe trying to run up a score in a game that appears beyond recall. (Of course, it's any man's opinion whether a game can be rescued from the loss column. And you *know* that home run hitters don't stop trying to hit homers, even if their team is ahead by a football score.)

When I was with Montreal, I almost came to blows with Joe Morgan, that bundle of hustle and energy, when he objected to my trying to steal second base on a three-two pitch.

"What are you trying to do out here?" Joe yelled at me. "Are you trying to show us up?"

"I get the sign, I steal," I answered. I might have even thrown a "fuck you" into the bargain. It's funny. Joe and I are very cordial now, but almost intuitively when we see each other, we think of that incident.

Nothing much really comes out of baseball fights—except some temporarily hurt feelings, a few chipped teeth, and maybe a fine or two. Sometimes, however, a good line comes out of one of them.

I'm thinking of what Reggie Jackson said when he was playing for the Oakland Athletics, in those days quite a menagerie of characters. A fight had developed on a plane trip—Blue Moon Odom, the pitcher, was one of the two participants—and Manager Dick Williams sought to move into the dispute as peacemaker. He was really going to earn his pay that week.

Casually eyeing the proceedings, Reggie leaned back in his seat. As Williams shot by him, he offered a few words of advice.

"Leave 'em alone, Dick," he said. "Neither one of 'em is going to help us, anyway."

If most players aren't very good at fighting, they aren't very good at eating, either—eating *good* food, that is. The best way to avoid ballplayers is to go to a good restaurant.

Let me tell you a few things about food and ballplayers in what is obviously an era of enormous preoccupation with food and nutrition in this country.

In my thirty years in the game, I've rarely run into a ballplayer in a really elegant eatery—unless I've gone with them.

When I see kids these days who make $300,000 or $400,000 constantly running into fast-food restaurants or roadside hash houses, it puts me in a state of shock. It's not that I have anything against the almighty cheeseburger (I happen to love cheeseburgers) or French fries. It's just that it would be a nice departure to see some of these guys do a little better as far as their stomachs are concerned. With the kind of cash these young men make you'd think they'd try to develop more sensitive palates and begin to discover other culinary worlds out there.

It isn't just the money, though. Kids today (and not all of 'em are kids) just don't know how to eat. They might cook a good steak at home, but they don't know anything about restaurants. The reason may be that most nights they're playing baseball, not scouting four-star restaurants. But really, that's no excuse.

When I was twenty years old and making about $9,000 a year, I thought nothing about ordering great wine—1959 Latours and Lafite-Rothschilds. Maybe I couldn't afford it, but, pal, I was doing it. I'll guarantee one thing. When I had a night to enjoy it, I had a good evening meal.

I've rarely run into ballplayers in good restaurants. Even in some of the towns—like Pittsburgh, which is relatively small and has maybe two or three good eating places—you don't find major leaguers. It goes back to that herding concept again. They're weaned on hotel food and they don't want to take the time or trouble to find a good place.

To me there's nothing like a wonderful evening out, nothing better than enjoying a really well prepared meal. I'm not talking about sopping up wine or lapping up booze or making a pig of yourself. I'm talking about a couple of glasses of wine and a good steak or a piece of fresh fish.

I've always been a restaurant buff. Even in the days when I should have been doing the fast-food bit, I used to search out restaurants that promised something more: an unusual dish, a good wine, offbeat decor. (Maybe I was a premature Yuppie.) Yes, I know you can't eat decor, but I was always looking for something to break the monotony of life on the road. A ballplayer ought to try for something extra—just like making the extra effort in the field or at bat.

What follows is the McCarver Restaurant Register—those

places I've liked that seemed out of the ordinary to me. No-body paid me for being on the list. It's just based on interesting eating, as I experienced it. (The highest rating is four catcher's mitts; the lowest is one.)

NEW YORK

Le Cirque—my all-around favorite (⚾⚾⚾⚾)

P. J. Clarke's—best cheeseburger I've ever eaten, anywhere (⚾⚾⚾)

Grotta Azzura—in Little Italy, wonderful

Pariola Romanissimo—good for veal chops (⚾⚾⚾)

ST. LOUIS

Tony's—great Northern Italian food, started as hamburger and chili joint; I love their moist cappellini (⚾⚾⚾⚾)

Miss Hullings—you haven't lived until you've tasted their braised oxtail joints (available only on Wednesdays); just a cafeteria, but, oh, my! (⚾⚾⚾⚾)

PHILADELPHIA

La Truffe—expensive but first-rate (⚾⚾⚾⚾)

Bookbinder's—usually lives up to its fine reputation (⚾⚾⚾)

Downey's—popular Irish pub (⚾⚾⚾)

Le Bec Fin—Georges Perrier, friend of Craig Claiborne, is the chef and owner (⚾⚾⚾⚾)

La Familia—family-owned, Italian food, but too expensive (⚾⚾⚾)

BALTIMORE

Phillips Seafood—second or third largest volume of any restaurant in the country (⚾⚾)

MONTREAL

Chez la Mere Michel—much frequented by writers; succulent lobster soufflé; great red house wine (for $11) (⚾⚾⚾⚾)

PITTSBURGH

Klein's—seafood, garlic rolls, homemade chocolate pecan bar; best-kept secret in the National League (☺☺☺☺)

SAN FRANCISCO

Tadich Grill—It was originally the Gold Rush Restaurant, founded in 1849. It's owned by the Buich brothers. Seafood, grilled Petrale sole par excellence (☺☺☺)

L'Etoile—elegant decor; can't beat the smell of the place, located in the Huntington Hotel (☺☺☺☺)

Phil Lehr's Steakery—yes, this is a ballplayer favorite, sort of an extension of the clubhouse (☺☺☺)

CHICAGO

Cape Cod Room, Drake Hotel—comfortable, warm, and friendly; world's best baseball fans as waiters; seafood (☺☺☺☺)

Eli's—National League hangout; Eli is a big baseball fan; steak (☺☺)

Runyon's in the Alley—good atmosphere (☺☺)

SAN DIEGO

Anthony's Star of the Sea Room—best swordfish I've ever tasted—it's coated in honey and two inches thick (☺☺☺☺)

HOUSTON

Maxim's—run by Ron and Michel. It has its own crawfish farm—and I just love those things. (☺☺☺☺)

CINCINNATI

The Maisonette—A real sleeper, but the food won't put you to sleep. Great fresh Kentucky bibb lettuce. (☺☺☺☺)

Mozart's—Near the University of Cincy and run by pony-tailed owners. There's a huge cappuccino machine on the premises that gives you the feeling you're eating inside one of them. (☺☺☺)

Pigalle's—interesting and nice; was better when Maurice, an old French chef, ran it (☺☺☺)

ATLANTA

Nicolai's Roof—on top of the Hilton—maybe the best Hilton restaurant of them all; top staff (☺☺☺☺)

LOS ANGELES

Bistro Gardens—features good food and Beverly Hills ambience, with wonderful paintings by Leroy Niemann (☺☺☺)

La Famiglia—For the Hollywood crowd. An Italian restaurant that appeals to Tommy Lasorda and his pals. (☺☺)

BOSTON

Antony's Pier Four—Great lobsters that they sell all over the world. Owner Tony Athenas is a dear friend of Tony Conigliaro. (☺☺☺☺)

Joseph's—If you're a ballplayer they'll cut your bill in half. And if you're a Red Socker they'll treat you even better than that! (☺☺)

Lockober—best-smelling place I've ever been in, probably due to the rich, dark wood of the furniture (☺☺☺)

I'm sure I've missed a few restaurants that have also been favorites over the years. But on the whole list, with the possible exception of Phil Lehr's and Eli's, there's not a place where you'll ever find players. Most guys in baseball grow up to be competitors, not gourmets, and the minor-league days of apprenticeship on five bucks a day of meal money don't help matters. At those rates some guys could be tempted to pick at garbage pails.

Which brings me to that celebrated institution of our national pastime—the clubhouse spread, which replaced cheese and dried-out crackers about twenty-five years ago. Next to their base hits, hitters probably can recall more about the spread than anything else in their lives. Nowadays most spreads feature hot dogs, potato salad, red beans, fried chicken, and assorted cold cuts or ribs.

For me, one of the great moments in feeding was on October 9, 1967, in the sixth game of the World Series between the Cards and the Red Sox at Fenway. The Sox were way ahead, and Cardinals manager Red Schoendienst thought he ought to try to stir things up in the top of the eighth inning. So he nominated a pinch hitter to bat for pitcher Ray Washburn.

"Get me Alex Johnson!" ordered Red, who had to think it was odd that Johnson wasn't in the dugout. After all, it was a tight, crucial Series game.

Alex Johnson, who grew up in Detroit, was a great athlete, but, in my judgment (and in the judgment of others), he had questionable desire. He was also a strange guy. How strange? He once pulled a gun on Chico Ruiz, one of his teammates. Anyway, when he finally answered Red's hurry-up call, he showed up not with a menacing bat in his hands but with food and mayonnaise trickling down from both sides of his mouth. One look at the guy and you knew he'd been having a little private feast in the clubhouse.

Red just took one look and sedately said, "Get me Gagliano."

So it was that Alex Johnson never pinch-hit in that game. What's more, he never made a single plate appearance in the whole seven-game Series. One of these days his grandchildren will ask him if he ever played in a World Series, and he'll have to say, "I had a shot but I was eating a sandwich." Elaborate on that, Grandpa, will you?

Further observations about the clubhouse spread are in order here.

First, I'd have to give the nod to a Pittsburgh guy named Tommy O'Toole for serving positively the worst postgame spreads in the history of modern baseball. O'Toole was always referred to as Mooch, which rhymes with Pooch, and that's whom he should have been feeding his spread to. As a matter of fact, you wouldn't feed your pet some of the things that Mooch put on the table for us.

Mooch plays a small part in my favorite Danny Ozark tale. Back in 1975 the Phillies and Pirates had wrestled most of the way for the leadership of the NL's Eastern Division, with the Pirates finally moving ahead to win by six and a half games.

When they clinched the division on a September night at Three Rivers Stadium, the Pirates let go with all that previously suppressed steam—and they deserved to. Willie Stargell, their leader and mentor, joined in with guys like big Dave Parker, Al Oliver, Manny Sanguillen, John Candelaria, and the other noisy Bucs. They hoisted each other on their shoulders and they carried their popular manager, Danny Murtaugh, off the field. And all this time the fans were running around shrieking and yelling stuff that made sense only in the context of what had just taken place.

The Pirates always had had a reputation for being loosey-goosey, and they were proving it. Champagne corks were popping down the hall from our locker room, and the clubhouse spread was being pitched around indiscriminately. Who wanted to eat Mooch's spread at such a moment?

Some of the Pittsburgh players even wandered good-naturedly into the Philly clubhouse. So did Bruce Keiden, a *Philadelphia Inquirer* sportswriter. Ozark sat there in his sweatshirt, his cap off, his spikes untied, exposed to all of the celebrating going on around him. For the moment he seemed lost in deep thought.

Doing his job, Keiden asked Ozark what pitching rotation he was going to use for the Phillies' remaining games. Danny, without letting Keiden finish, interjected: "Bruce, I'm going to use the same rotation that got us here. After all, we're not out of this yet!"

Imagine. Here's this crazy pennant victory scene going on in front of Danny, and the guy isn't even aware his team is out of it, gone with the wind. (Maybe Danny thought champagne was popped by Pirates players after every game they won.) Danny thought the magic number was still one; he truly believed the Pirates had only clinched a tie for the flag.

Tragedy and humor often run hand in hand in life, and this was the best example I know of. The press savaged Ozark after this incident, but I still find the whole episode hard to believe.

Can any player who was there ever forget the day in 1971 that Ron Stone, naked as the proverbial jaybird and hung like a proverbial mule, brought his genitalia perilously close to the onion dip in the Philly clubhouse? For most guys it was no problem—only Ron could *reach* the dip. He'd tug at his groin, then daintily go into the dip with his fingertips, then grope again, then dip again. Grope and dip, grope and dip. As a result, we established a fine system where guys had to wear their shorts around the clubhouse spread. If they didn't, it was a five-dollar fine. Cocks *in* the onion dip cost you a hundred dollars.

You'd be amazed at how few guys washed their hands after a game. They'd just head straight for the food. Ray Sadecki used to tell Butch Yatkeman, our clubhouse guy in St. Louis, "To make the guys feel at home, put the pine tar and the rosin at opposite ends of the table. That way they won't drop their chicken."

There aren't many gourmets in baseball, but I've run across plenty of *gourmands.* I'd nominate two to lead the crowd: Joe Schultz, who had a leading role in Jim Bouton's *Ball Four*, and Clyde King, who now works in the Yankee front office under George Steinbrenner and has also managed here and there.

Schultz was my manager in the minors with Memphis. (He often thought he was a reincarnation of John McGraw. When one of his players, like me, suffered a bloody strawberry from sliding, he'd more often than not rub ice-cold beer on it.) Later he was a coach with the Cards, where I was exposed to his singular gustatory habits. Joe sometimes appeared more concerned with his postgame meal than with the final outcome of the ball game. In Memphis he made it his business to oversee the daily clubhouse spread.

On the bus after a game we'd eat sandwiches. The trainer, Charley Foley, would go out and buy meat and white bread. Joe would make the sandwiches and pass them toward the

back of the bus. By the time one got to the poker players at the
back, there would have been ten sets of hands on it. And most
of those hands had on them the remains of the park in which
you'd played the night before. By the time I'd bite into my
sandwich, it would have half the batter's box on it. We used to
joke that bread would start out white and be pumpernickel by
the time it reached the back.

If a game went on too long for Joe's taste—and I do mean
taste—he would roam impatiently in the dugout, encouraging
us—no, demanding—that we put an end to the ball game and
quick.

"Come on, you guys," he'd bark, "the fuckin' ice is melting
on the beer. Let's pound that Budweiser! Get this damn thing
over with!" This is how we learned the fundamentals of baseball strategy in the minor leagues.

Later on, as a third base coach in the major leagues, he had
a habit of sneaking into the clubhouse and setting up a full
dinner plate for himself around the seventh inning of each
game. This way he could avoid the crowd in the clubhouse
after the game. While everyone ate, he'd shower, shave, and
then, while everyone else was showering and shaving, he'd
simply go get his stash, which he'd placed a towel over, from
a secret corner. At least he figured it was secret.

Bob Uecker, Mr. Baseball and the Cards' brilliant wit,
obliged Joe one day by devouring all of Joe's carefully con-
cealed food. Uke then put the chicken bones and the bare
corncobs back on the plate and covered them, of course, with
a towel.

After the game, everyone watched as Joe shaved and then
returned to his locker, sat down, and carefully lifted his towel.
When he discovered that his plate had been foodnapped, he
howled like a Shakespearean actor doing *Macbeth*.

"Who the fuck did that? Who the fuck did that?" he wailed
at no one in particular. No one answered. And I mean he was
pissed!

When Joe was in St. Louis he also swapped autographed
baseballs for anything he wanted. He was so tightfisted that, as
Dick Groat used to say, he wouldn't pay a nickel to watch
Niagara Falls run backward. So he'd trade baseballs for any-

thing he could. Anything! Joe once came up to me and said, under his breath, "Hey, Doggie, you need a new fan belt?" He'd gotten one for a bunch of baseballs (I don't even know how you're supposed to *know* if you need a new fan belt).

When Joe was in Detroit, Jim Campbell, the general manager, finally had to come up to him and tell him to stop taking so many balls. Joe used to swap them in Philadelphia for kielbasa. San Francisco was his sourdough town. He would never tell me what his fan belt town was.

And it wasn't just baseballs.

The Cardinals' groundskeepers kept sod stacked up in their maintenance room. Three-by-five pieces of sod. Well, one night after a game, when I was the only one left in the clubhouse, I saw Joe coming out of the maintenance room holding two plots of dirt, balancing them on his head.

"What *are* you doing?" I asked. I had to know.

"Sshhh!" Joe replied. "I just got a new house and I'm sodding my front yard."

It took two months' worth of home games, but he did get his lawn sodded.

Clyde King had been a pretty fair country pitcher in the National League. Every record book I've ever consulted puts his weight at around 175 pounds. Watching him eat, however, I had to suspect that the stat was wrong. The man had an *unbelievable* yen for food.

When Clyde managed the San Francisco Giants in 1969 they had one of the better clubhouse spreads in the business, thanks to Clyde's priorities.

The Giants featured a talented squad of players under King, too—guys like Willie Mays, Willie McCovey, Juan Marichal, Gaylord Perry, and others. But stories used to circulate around the league about how much and how frequently these guys ate. Rumor had it that they'd sometimes eat in the middle of ball games! Maybe that explains why the Giants never quite seemed to win in those days, even when they came razor-margin close.

There was a utility infielder named Bobby Heise on King's roster. Heise was one guy who practically never frequented the Giant clubhouse during a game. But he could not resist chili dogs, which every so often were part of the Giants' spread. When the Giants lost a nip-and-tuck game one day, Heise sneaked in there for a couple of dogs. When he returned to the dugout, all sorts of condiments were dripping from his mouth. King started walking toward him as a teammate tried to hand him a towel so he could wipe away the evidence.

"Where ya been?" asked King ominously.

"Nowhere," answered Bobby fearfully. He was on thin ice as it was since he was just a part-time player and hardly a star.

"Well, next time ya go in there, get me one of those chili dogs, will ya?" said King.

I've always considered food fights sophomoric stuff, not to mention wasteful and demeaning. But that doesn't mean I haven't been in them.

That's sort of a preamble to tell you about a food fight, or food bath, that took place in 1978, after the Phillies won the Eastern Division title in the NL. After a stirring 10–8 win to clinch it, the clubhouse exploded. I don't think I'd been around such an all-out celebration since the Cards beat the Yanks in 1964 for the world championship.

There were some "solid citizens" on that Philadelphia club, too, guys like Mike Schmidt, Bob Boone, Steve Carlton, Dick Ruthven, Tug McGraw, Larry Christenson, Garry Maddox, and Greg Luzinski. But no matter how "solid" they were usually, every one of them joined in the wildest food scene you could imagine.

This one wasn't staged for TV, either; it was spontaneous, with real emotions cascading all over the premises. You've got to understand, this is a different world we're talking about. I don't think that one should be apologetic about his antics as a player just because one wishes to be perceived as more sophisticated when his career is over. I was caught up in the moment, joyously celebrating, and it was the most natural thing in the world.

When the guys came rushing into the clubhouse after the final out, someone upended a big box of Tide, and the troops sloshed around in it. (I grandly announced to all, "Gentlemen, the tide has turned.") Then came the milk, Cokes, shaving cream, cold cuts, and champagne—Mooch's entire spread all mixed together into one grand solution. For the first time in my life I knew what it was like to skid on hunks of ham, liverwurst, bologna, and corned beef.

If that was the right way to celebrate, the wrong way is the stuff of newspaper headlines over the past ten years or so: drugs. Getting involved with drugs is wrong, all wrong. In baseball, maybe it's not comparable to the Black Sox scandal of 1919. But it's disgusting, embarrassing, and harmful to all concerned. Purely and simply, drugs erode your will. But nobody, including the commissioner, seems to know quite how to get the problem under control.

From a personal point of view, I am opposed to any mass testing. Testing the innocent to discover who's guilty isn't the right way to go about it. I'm against singling out *any* group in our society for tests, whether it's plumbers, airline pilots, doctors, landlords, or journalists. Drug abuse is not a ballplayer problem or a cop problem or a movie actor problem. It's a societal problem. What's gone on in baseball is a manifestation of that. Should ballplayers be held to a higher standard of behavior than the rest of us?

I'm not a constitutional lawyer, or even a Philadelphia lawyer (although some guys might once have called me a clubhouse lawyer), but I believe players have a right not to be tested. There's something in the Fourth Amendment that prohibits unreasonable searches and seizures.

The drug problem continues to boggle my mind; but so does the idea of invasion of privacy and the fact that the tests themselves are not always surefire in detecting users; they're far from perfect.

I don't think I'm blind to what goes on around me. On the contrary, I think I've often seen things I shouldn't. But in my entire professional baseball life I've never actually seen anyone use cocaine. This, despite the fact that most of the evidence seems to point to the conclusion that drug use runs rampant throughout America.

I've been to all sorts of places in this country: sports arenas, hotels, airports, museums, theaters, bars, restaurants, parks, clubs, you name it. I don't even know exactly what the damn stuff looks like. Maybe it's a generational thing.

But after doing a lot of thinking about the drug subject, I'd say that I probably would have accepted Ueberroth's drug test suggestion. Sometimes common sense has to take precedence over principle. At this stage of the game baseball probably should try to clear up its reputation once and for all. That doesn't mean I like the whole idea very much. I'm still an avid supporter of personal rights.

I know Keith Hernandez's procrastination spring of '86 bothered some people. But the guy has his rights and his feelings, and he was being penalized for something he admitted doing some five or six years ago, before any specific penalties were waiting for him from the commissioner.

There are no valid excuses to be made by me or anybody else on behalf of players who have been lost to the drug habit. Ballplayers shouldn't think they're privileged characters or a breed apart simply because they play a game well.

I'd like to make one final observation about this mess: The hell of being alone and bored is an enormous personal problem for some guys. I'm sure it has contributed to the spread of this habit. A lot of people will sneer at this observation. What kind of hell is it to make a half million a year, to travel first-class, and to live first-class all the way, with all the appurtenances of celebrity and the constant fawning attention of the media? Some hell, they say.

I'm saying that loneliness can be a disaster area for some people. When guys without substantial emotional and intellectual resources are alone they brood and worry. They can also get into trouble. Many of them become obsessed with how they're batting or fielding or pitching or running. They dwell on yesterday's results, how their bodies are feeling, what's going to happen in the future. Some of these fears are real; others aren't. Those things happen to everybody in baseball, I don't care if you're Ruth, Brett, Gooden, or Ozzie Smith.

This may seem idealistic, but players have got to learn to live with anxieties and insecurities without giving in to them. You cope with it and go on from there. But some guys can't, then they get into trouble. And some go for drugs. Excuses? No. Just a statement about what makes some guys tick. It's interesting. A lot of "normal" people couldn't cope with playing baseball in front of fifty thousand people. Well, a lot of ballplayers can't cope with being alone.

It took an old prizefight manager, the late Cus D'Amato, who steered José Torres and Floyd Patterson to world titles, to provide the best definition of fear I've ever heard. It's worth repeating here, even if you're surprised to see a boxing guy in a baseball book.

Cus said, "The hero and the coward both feel exactly the same fear, only the hero confronts his fear and converts it into fire."

When the Mets opened the 1985 season with two extra-inning games on the first two days (a new record, as Jay Horwitz of the Mets' PR department dutifully informed us), a young man named Roger McDowell, somewhat on the frail side, was sent in to pitch in the eleventh inning of the second game. Roger worked over his bubble gum with a jaw motion that could be seen in the last seat in left field at Shea; he pitched well, too.

The next day, in a candid newspaper interview, Roger revealed his inner feelings. He had been as jittery as a cat on a hot tin roof.

"Boy, I was really nervous out there," he said.

Roger's acknowledgment of his nervousness in his season debut was unusual, for players usually aren't inclined to admit such feelings. It made me think of *The Eiger Sanction*, a popular novel in which the hero, Jonathan Hemlock, was asked if he was afraid to climb an imposing two-thousand-foot ice wall known as the Eiger.

"Yes," said Hemlock. "If you admit your fear, you take your first step to overcoming it."

Roger McDowell did just that, and he was a gutsy kid to do it. I think it helped him in other relief efforts during the season. Relief pitching is one occupation in which you can't afford to have any incapacitating fears. The job calls for ice water in the veins, single-minded devotion to the task, and total concentration.

Three Pitchers:
Carlton, Gibson, Gooden

All pitchers are liars and crybabies.
—YOGI BERRA

You never really know a woman until you've wintered with her—and you never really know a ballclub until you've summered with it. To make the maxim complete, try this: You never really know a pitcher until you've squatted down behind home plate and caught him.

A couple of winters ago I happened to visit the Metropolitan Museum of Art in New York City to catch (no pun intended) the Van Gogh at Arles exhibition. This Dutch artist created, in something of a frenzy, some two hundred paintings and a hundred sketches in a period of about eighteen months.

When asked by his brother Theo why he painted so rapidly and how in the world he could conceive what he was doing, Van Gogh simply said, "I see things that I have conjured in my imagination and in my memory and mind over a long period of time. Then it all just pours out."

Maybe that story is a pretty fancy way to make a point about baseball, but I think it helps to describe the flow that a pitcher and catcher should have when they work together in a game.

There's a lot of thinking going on in the minds of pitchers and catchers before every ball game. But there shouldn't be that much thought taking place between the white lines, because all the thought should have already taken place. What you have left operating out there are instinct, activity, and animation, and it should all just pour out.

If a catcher thinks too long before putting down those signs, he's indecisive. If a pitcher takes too long to digest what a catcher has flashed to him, that's indecision, too. Ideally, pitcher and catcher should establish a true rhythm—that's art.

Three pitchers have dominated my big-league playing and broadcasting career. Two are guys I caught in hundreds of games, including World Series games, and with them I had that rhythmic relationship that I've just talked about. These two men were friends I advised, took advice from, cussed out, was cussed out by, joked with, cajoled, fought for, fought with, and learned to appreciate and admire as a couple of the finest pitchers of this or any era.

They are Bob Gibson—known as Hoot or Hoop—and Steve Carlton—or Lefty—the guy whose misanthropic treatment of the press has baffled more folks than his famous slider. Gibson made the Hall of Fame in 1981. Lefty is sure to join him one of these days.

The third pitcher whom I have not had the good fortune to catch is a young guy named Dwight Gooden, who seems irreversibly headed for the Hall of Fame. I guess what qualifies me to talk about and judge Gooden is that, as a Mets announcer, I've gotten to see him up close from the start of his big-league career.

Until I got into the announcing business some six years ago in Philadelphia, one of my claims to fame seemed to be that I was an appendage to Steven Norman Carlton (nice name— *Norman*), especially in Philly. When you thought of Carlton, you automatically thought of McCarver. It was like ham and eggs, or grass and dirt. I even told a newspaper guy once that when Steve and I die we're going to be buried sixty feet six inches apart, the distance between pitcher and catcher. Other journalists hinted in their yarns that I was the Svengali who talked and badgered Lefty into becoming the sixteenth pitcher in big-league history to win three hundred games.

When the Phillies signed me in 1975 I had good hands but a poor arm. I *could* swing the bat, but the big reason they wanted me was that I could communicate with Lefty from behind the plate. (The Phillies had gotten him away from the Cards before the 1972 season, but he'd had three rather pallid seasons after winning twenty-seven times in 1972.) Communication is the key.

In truth, I did help Lefty a little bit along the way—I know I did—but I really didn't structure him for victory. He structured himself. Nobody else could or did. But when I arrived, he really needed help. He was confused by his three subpar years. Also, his relationship with the press was starting to really wear on him and torment him.

Let me fill you in on how the Carlton-McCarver friendship started.

It was back in the Cardinals' spring training of 1965. I'd won the first-string Cardinal catching job in 1963 and was really feeling good about myself after a seven-game World Series win over the Yankees in 1964. I batted .478 in that Series and cracked a three-run, game-winning home run in the tenth inning of the fifth game. So I guess you could say that I had sort of arrived as a bona fide big leaguer.

Then along came Steve Carlton, a six-foot-five character from Miami with an independent streak wider than the Grand Canyon. I went back of the plate for Carlton, catching him for four innings in his first effort as a rookie in spring training. As I recall, he permitted something like two runs and five hits— not bad, but not sensational. When I went into the locker room for a postgame shave, there's this guy staring at me as if I'd just stolen his meal money.

"Hey," Lefty began, without bothering to use my first name (or my second, for that matter), "you've gotta call for more breaking pitches when we're behind these hitters."

Well, here I am, a recently canonized Series hero—fresh as hell at twenty-three, and doing my shaving alongside guys like first baseman Bill White, shortstop Dick Groat, and third baseman Kenny Boyer—and this rookie is trying to tell me my business. "You son of a bitch," I started out, delicately. "Who the hell do you think you are, telling me that? You've got a lotta guts. What credentials do *you* have?"

Lefty turned as crimson as the birds on the front of his Cardinals' shirt, but he didn't say a word. He just shrugged and walked away from me. The next day I apologized. He just shrugged again.

It wasn't the last time I let Lefty have it. A couple of years later I got into a shouting match with him on the mound—screaming, yelling, jumping up and down. Of course, all of that was done only by me. He just folded his arms and stared down at me the way a big dog might look down at a smaller dog who was infringing on his territory. The next afternoon I humbly apologized, but Lefty looked me in the eye and said, "I wasn't listening anyway."

You've got to understand that when Steve Carlton is pitching, he might as well have cotton in his ears. In fact, he usually *did* have cotton in his ears. He used it to keep out the crowd noise. Sometimes he left it in after the game so he wouldn't have to listen to the reporters. When Lefty pitches, he's in a trance, concentrating like nobody I've ever seen, as he works rapidly in a cadence that's the mark of a truly outstanding pitcher. Lefty, Gibby, and Gooden are all quick workers. Lefty learned that from Gibson, as a matter of fact. None of them are bothered by catchers' pleas or managerial intrusions.

(*If you think long, you think wrong.* That's a maxim for pitchers my friend Jim "Kitty" Kaat articulated many years ago. Jim had twenty-five years as a major-league pitcher. At the age of forty-four, in 1982, he pitched in four World Series games against Milwaukee. A lot of Jim's fellow pitchers have chosen to take his one-line epigram to heart.)

The press thinks of Carlton as a rather paradoxical fellow. He doesn't care to sign autographs, he's a devotee of the martial arts, he reads a lot about Eastern philosophy—stuff like Buddhism and Taoism—and he shares my interest in fine wines. Some years ago he told the Philly press department that the people he'd most like to meet are Socrates, Thomas Jefferson, Einstein, Jesus Christ, and Gandhi. No rock stars in that collection, please note.

In his top years Lefty liked to plunge his pitching arm into huge tubs of white rice, which should have made him popular with every Cantonese restaurateur in captivity. He also liked to walk around squeezing steel balls for friction to strengthen his wrist and forearm. These balls actually got tarnished and discolored from all that friction. And, as a result, Steve Carlton has the strongest forearms of any man I've ever met. That's what allowed him to get such a tight spin on his slider.

A funny story about those steel balls. We were eating at the Maisonette in Cincinnati once, and Steve left them on the table. The maître d' came running out. With a fake French accent, he presented them and said, "Monsieur Carlton, you left your balls on ze table."

Steve may not be a complete recluse, but he comes close. If he hadn't wound up in the majors, he probably would have been a hunting guide in a desolate cabin back in the mountains fifty miles or so from any paved roads. Or he could have opened a kung fu training center. But that doesn't sound right —Lefty's Kung Fu Center. Sounds like his right arm was ripped off. He's always insisted that he doesn't read newspapers or magazines and doesn't care what's printed about him. It seems to me, though, that I've caught him on more than one occasion sneaking a look at the sports page.

I'm just the opposite of Lefty. I'm a newspaper compulsive. Maybe the only guy I've ever heard of who "consumed" more newspapers than I was the late Moe Berg, a catcher in the American League in the 1930s and 1940s. They used to joke that Moe could read and speak twelve languages flawlessly but couldn't hit in any of them.

Did you ever hear this one? Who are the two best pitchers in the National League who don't speak English? Answer: Fernando Valenzuela and Steve Carlton. That joke went out of style in 1986 when Fernando's English greatly improved and Steve went to the American League.

Lefty sometimes went an entire season without speaking a word to a writer.

What caused Lefty's ostracism of newsmen?

As late as 1972 Steve was cooperative with the press. But when I got back with the Phils midway through the 1975 season he seemed to be on edge. He wasn't himself. He didn't appear happy. He said he felt maligned by "the subjectivity with which the press can work."

There had been some comments and cracks in print that drinking was affecting his physical condition. Lefty reasoned that when he had a good year the press didn't write or speculate about such things. Why did they do it now?

In 1978, when Lefty won his two hundredth game, he finally consented to a mass interview. Someone present asked Lefty a question that started with a quote from Danny Ozark, the Phils' manager, a very decent man but one whose baseball knowledge Lefty didn't respect.

"Danny has a theory," the reporter began. It was Stan Hochman of the *Philadelphia Daily News.*

"This oughtta be good," Lefty said with a chuckle, sort of *sotto voce*.

The next day the Lefty chuckle made the *News* and was picked up elsewhere. That was the end of Lefty's openness. He shut down, from that time on, like an aggrieved clam. That was his last official interview until he met the press to announce his retirement in July 1986.

"There's no mystique about it," Lefty's teammate, Mike Schmidt, said a few years ago. "He just doesn't think it's anyone's business what he does or doesn't do, or what he thinks when he's off the mound."

Lefty isn't the only well-known athlete to shut off his flow of information to the press. Rocky Marciano, heavyweight champ in the fifties and unbeaten in all forty-nine of his fights, was normally an affable and agreeable man. But his manager, Al Weill, decided that Rocky would be better off if he didn't have to fence with reporters before or after fights. Instead, Weill assigned himself to field all questions, and Rocky remained mute in the background.

Weill even went so far as to pronounce what round "we" would end the fight. "We'll finish it in the fifth," he would grumble. Another time he'd promise, "We'll end it in the third." Still another time, "We'll take it in three."

Before another title fight, an annoyed reporter directly confronted Rocky, going against Weill's ground rules.

"Don't you get tired of hearing Weill answer questions

that only you can really answer? How the hell can you put up with all this 'we' stuff from him?" jabbed the writer. "Who's doing the fighting, you or him?"

Emerging from the shadows, Rocky finally spoke up in his pronounced Massachusetts accent.

"In my last fight, when the bell rang for the first round," Rocky said quietly, "I moved out to the center of the ring. When I took a quick look back into my corner, I saw Mr. Weill's ass climbing out of the ring. That answer your question?"

Some years ago Lefty and I decided to spend an off-season vacation elk-hunting. We drove close to six thousand miles together, arguing for at least half that distance. Of course, he'd never think of arguing with an umpire, but he didn't hesitate when he was with me.

On another hunting trip Lefty and I went to Canada. We flew first to Montana, drove from there to Alberta, then hopped a seaplane to Loch L'Orange in northern Canada, where we picked up an Indian guide.

We had our usual agreements to disagree, and then we were getting off the plane to greet our guide. As the self-anointed front man for our group, I approached the guide, confidently assuming his English was nonexistent.

"Me great white hunter come down from sky in big bird," I said, in rather tortured language. "Me boss man."

Then, pointing my finger at Lefty, I added, "Big guy here know nothing. Can't hunt a lick."

Whereupon the guide responded, with perfect diction right out of Boston's Back Bay, "Hi, fellows. I'm Ray Mackenzie, Harvard, class of sixty-six. I'm also from the land of the white eyes."

Lefty had been in a bad mood up to that point, but he broke up with laughter. So did I.

During the years I acted as Lefty's link with the outside world, his less-than-a-dollar-a-year liaison with the press, and his designated catcher, Bob Boone caught everybody else on the team. It would have been natural if some acrimony developed between Boonie and me. After all, I was getting most of the ink and he was getting most of the work.

Lefty never really had anything against Bob Boone—"The

only animosity I feel in baseball is against hitters on other clubs," he'd always say—but he and Boonie did have their differences when it came to baseball philosophy.

"I don't like to have to keep shaking a catcher off. It bothers my concentration. I like to get it over with," Lefty explained. "I only have three pitches and we're always four pitches apart."

But Boonie, one of the finest gentlemen ever to suit up on a ball field, never, but never, made a disparaging remark about me to the press or TV.

In his own wry way, Boonie, a psychology major at Stanford, summed up our *ménage à trois* this way: "If I had challenged your role with Lefty, maybe all three of us would have been released by the Phillies!"

The guy is a class act, a pro without peers, and he's still catching over 130 games a year with the California Angels. If I had a son, I wouldn't mind having him be a carbon copy of Bob Boone.

True to his own tradition, Lefty never uttered a single syllable about the whole well-publicized situation. Sure, there continued to be occasional friction between Lefty and me, but that's natural in any friendship. We're still very close friends.

The 1985 season wasn't a very happy one for Steve. He was 1–8, not too good for a guy with 317 lifetime wins. He was out of action almost half the time with rotator cuff miseries. By the winter of 1986, anticipating spring training after this first major injury of his career, Lefty invited me to go down to Tarpon Springs, Florida, with him.

"I'd like to play a little golf," said Lefty.

Then he put *the* question to me: "Would you like to catch me, Timmy?"

I didn't want to hear that question, and my response was a bob and weave.

"Yes to your first invitation, Lefty," I said. "No to the second. I just don't play catch with anybody anymore."

Lefty looked like a sad little boy in a Norman Rockwell drawing. Of course, we were both acting and sounding like little boys—two grown men talking about playing catch.

"You don't have to squat, Timmy," he said. "I'm just asking you to warm up the old cannon. A bit of soft-toss."

"If I just stand up, is it okay?" I asked, not quite believing that I was being cajoled into doing something again that I'd done almost as religious faith for two decades.

We *did* go to Florida. I *did* catch Lefty, for a half hour. I *didn't* squat. It *was* fun. Memories came flooding back. And while I didn't miss the work, since I'd hung up my mitt in 1980, I realized I had missed the fun.

Lefty now faces 1987 with an uncertain future after being released by the Phillies, then playing for the Giants and the White Sox. I've talked to him and I know he hates the American League. They don't let him hit over there, and he loves to hit. There's also no place for him to work out. Most of the American League stadiums are old and don't have the proper facilities.

Southpaws like Carlton don't come down the yellow brick road that often. As a matter of fact, aside from Lefty, Warren Spahn, Lefty Grove, Koufax, and a few others, most lefties I've known and have heard of seem to be able to get by with a lot less of the ball than righties. Why?

For one thing, there aren't as many of them in the majors; 36 percent of 1986 National League pitchers were southpaws (up from 21 percent in 1981). That means hitters don't see them as often, so they don't know as much about them or hit them as well.

Another thing is that every left-hander I've ever seen just can't throw a ball straight. They've got a natural tail on balls that they throw. On the other hand, right-handers have to *do* something with the ball to make it move.

One theory says that the earth turns on its axis one way, and lefties throw the other way. If you turned John Tudor around to the right side, do you think he'd be as effective as he was in 1985? Remember a guy named Randy Jones? Pete Rose insists that Randy once won twenty games with absolutely nothing. All I know is that no right-handed batter hits a left-hander as well as left-handed batters hit right-handers.

Believe me, I'm not talking myth here. Lefties invariably get by with less. But just leave Steve Carlton out of that generalization!

•   •   •

For my money, the most intimidating, arrogant pitcher ever to kick up dirt on a mound is Bob Gibson. Some people called him Hoot, after the one-time cowboy star of the silent movies, and others called him Hoop, because he played a year or two for the Harlem Globetrotters during the off-season. (As a matter of fact, one year the Cardinals paid him $1,000 a month *not* to play for the Globetrotters because they were terrified he'd get hurt.)

In the first game of the 1968 World Series he struck out seventeen Detroit Tigers for a record that still stands. I squatted to catch every pitch he threw on that unforgettable day. In 1981 Gibson was elected to the Hall of Fame. Nobody deserved it more than he did. In each of two recent books, one by Lawrence Ritter and Donald Honig, another by Maury Allen, there's a list of baseball's hundred greatest players. Gibson appears on both lists. (Carlton was also nominated in the Ritter book, but for some reason didn't make the Allen selection.)

If you ever saw Gibson work, you'd never forget his style: his cap pulled down low over his eyes, the ball gripped—almost mashed—behind his right hip, the eyes smoldering at each batter almost accusingly. That was how Hoot looked out there before the right arm went to work. Restless as an imprisoned cougar, Hoot would then unwind, and the ball would accelerate faster than a runaway locomotive. He didn't like to lose to anyone in anything. When you watched him, you had to know that.

Gibby was a difficult friend and a tough guy to get to know well, mainly because he had such demanding standards for friendship. But most of my arguments with him happened before games. As the years went by, I got closer to him and understood him better. And he understood me better, too.

He came out of the black ghetto in Omaha, Nebraska. His father died just before he was born. Gibby had pneumonia, rickets, and a rheumatic heart condition as an infant. He once told me that his mother was afraid to carry him out of the house when he was just a little kid. I guess that once Gibby did get out, he didn't like too much of what he saw out there.

But he never took out his frustrations on his teammates.

When Curt Flood lost Jim Northrup's fly ball against the background of the Busch Stadium crowd in the seventh and decisive game of the 1968 World Series, opening the gates to Detroit's game-winning three-run inning, Gibby refused to blame Flood for anything.

"It's all my fault," said Curt in the dugout afterward.

"It's nobody's fault," said Gibson.

Bob was a man of mulish competitive instinct. He could throw a ball into a Campbell's soup can. Choose whatever simile you want, the guy never stopped throwing hard, even at the risk of hurting his arm.

"Sure it hurts," he would growl. "It's supposed to hurt when you throw hard."

Gibby firmly believed, and so do I, that ballplayers could and should play hurt. He always did. But he always emphasized the difference between pain and injury.

"They aren't the same thing," he'd maintain. "You can play with pain, even if some guys refuse to. But you don't play when you're injured."

Solly Hemus, Gibson's first pilot with the Cards, continually miscalculated the pitcher's talents. He said Gibby'd never make it as a big-league pitcher. "Hell," he'd mumble, "the guy throws everything the same speed." Maybe he did, but that speed was about a thousand miles an hour, and it nearly tore up my hand every time I caught him. He had to be the hardest pitcher I ever caught, with that fastball moving and sailing away like a belligerent butterfly.

One day in July 1967, the incomparable Pittsburgh star Roberto Clemente broke Bob's leg with a fierce one-hopper that went for a base hit. Gibby got up, threw five more pitches, then collapsed again, and was carried off the premises on a stretcher. But he came back to pitch the clincher in Philadelphia (about five minutes after Joe Schultz exchanged two autographed baseballs for some kielbasa). In the World Series that year he won three games. In 1968 Gibby compiled an ERA of 1.12 in 305 innings. Only Dutch Leonard, with a mark of 1.01 in 1914, Three-Finger Brown, 1.04 in 1906, and Walter Johnson, who had a 1.09 ERA in 1913, ever did any better.

When Gibson pitched he was an angry, scowling man who put to rest all of those ugly stereotypes that for decades had plagued American blacks. He possessed more guts and determination than most pitchers of his generation, and his career is a dramatic case history that sociologists can use to disprove those vicious tales implying that blacks always fail in the clutch or can't cut it when the chips are down.

In the 1964 World Series against the Yankees, Gibson pitched a ten-inning victory on October 12, striking out thirteen. Then, just two days later, looking for a pitcher to beat the Yanks in the seventh game, Johnny Keane, the Cards' manager, wanted to give the ball to Hoot again.

"Feel like pitching, Hoot?" asked Keane.

"Why not?" Gibby responded.

Keane's decision was made in the face of a grueling end of the year for Bob. From August 24 to October 15, he had started a dozen games, completing nine and going eight innings in two others. He'd been the down-the-stretch key to the Cards' astounding National League pennant victory, as the Phillies dropped ten in a row and we took nine out of ten. On the last weekend of the season, Gibson lost a 1–0 Friday night game, pitching eight innings, and came back Sunday afternoon to pitch and win the clincher against the Mets.

Ahead 7–3 in the ninth inning of the seventh game of that 1964 Series, Gibby was laboring, breathing deeply, sighing, wiping his glistening forehead. He seemed wasted. Yet he fought back. He was not throwing batting practice tosses; he was throwing hard. On this Indian summer day at Busch Stadium, the hometown fans must have wondered why Keane didn't visit the mound and inform his pitcher that his chores were finished for the year. But Keane, a patient and understanding man who had managed Gibby in Omaha, where the pitcher broke into baseball, made no such journey. He was sticking with the man who had brought our club this far.

By 1964 I had become an unqualified admirer of Bob Gibson, despite the roots of my Memphis upbringing. As I watched the struggling, fatigued Gibson, my thoughts went back a few years to the time I'd first met the man.

The schools I had attended had been strictly segregated. I'd hardly known anyone who was black. In my first year with

the Cards I went to spring training in St. Petersburg, Florida
—just a raw kid in my late teens. Up to that point I hadn't even
had many conversations with black people.

I approached Gibby warily, for he was some six years older
than I and already a promising major-league pitcher. The
scowl on that handsome black face was forbidding at first for
a Memphis youngster. But when I got to know him and talk to
him, I found out he was much more than a thrower of baseballs.

I believe Bob taught me a good deal about relationships
with other human beings. If I came to that first spring training
with many of the preconceptions of my birthplace, it was probably Gibby more than any other black man who helped me to
overcome whatever latent prejudices I may have had.

That first spring training, before I'd gotten to know Bob
well, I sat across from him on the team bus after a spring
exhibition game. It was one of those scaldingly hot days that
makes the sweat drip from your forehead and the seat of your
pants stick to your backside.

"Hey," Gibby said, pointing to a bottle of cold orange pop
that I had in my hand. "Can I have a swallow of that stuff?"

Maybe he saw me cringe, ever so little, as I gazed first at
his mouth and then at the lip of the bottle. After a moment's
pause I volunteered timidly that I'd "save him some." He
broke up because he knew he'd gotten me.

That was how I started to know the pitcher who was trying
so gallantly to hang in there in the ninth inning of a World
Series game five years later.

And it looked as if my friend was in trouble, which meant
our team was in deep trouble, too. Scrappy Phil Linz was at
bat. Bob reared back, his left leg kicking in the direction of
Phil's bespectacled face, and the ball danced in, high and delicious. The harmonica-playing Yankee shortstop swung around
on it. Not a power hitter in anyone's book, he stroked the ball
hard enough to reach the left field stands.

The score was now 7–4, two out. Clete Boyer, up next, also
connected off Gibson. With that home run, he and Ken Boyer
became the only brothers to hit home runs in the same World
Series.

It was too close for comfort for the Cardinal fans, who

were waiting on the edges of their seats for the first St. Louis Series triumph since 1946, when Country Slaughter ran all the way from first base on a double by Harry Walker in the seventh game.

Bobby Richardson, who already owned a Series record with thirteen hits in this one, was up next. (Marty Barrett, by the way, tied this record in the 1986 Series.) If he got on, that would bring up Roger Maris, the home run hitter, and, after him, Mickey Mantle. And then maybe the Series would be down the drain.

Now we met, at last, on the mound—Gibson, Keane, and me. I stood there like a friend of the court, but I didn't say a thing; I wasn't asked. Gibby absently brushed his forehead with the back of his pitching hand. A moment's silence. Then Keane said hoarsely, looking into Gibby's eyes, "Well, pal, it's yours to win or lose."

Then the two of us, Keane and I, turned around and walked, me to the catching slot, Johnny to the dugout. As I settled into my crouch, I told myself I was glad Keane had left Bob in there to win it or lose it. He was the best that we had and if you're going to lose, lose with your best.

Richardson watched the first pitch go by for a ball. Then Gibby threw a strike, but the pitch had little more than his hopes on it. On the third pitch, Bobby swung. It was a pop-up close to second base, and Dal Maxvill gulped it down for the third out. That was it. We had won. So had Gibson. The fans went wild. Keane's judgment had been on target.

Later, when the press engaged in its postmortems, Keane was asked why he'd gone with Gibby, an exhausted pitcher, in that desperate ninth inning.

"I had a commitment to his heart," said Johnny Keane, moving his hand over his chest. That succinct statement said it all.

Being Hoot's catcher did not necessarily make me invulnerable to his hot head or his explosiveness. He could throw a temper tantrum when he saw me coming out to the mound to pay him a visit. He often acted as if the pitcher's mound were his private office, and when he was working, he didn't want to be interrupted by anyone, even his catcher.

However, there were occasions when Keane would ask me to go out and talk to Gibby, and I don't mind telling you, I dreaded it. "Go out there, goddammit. Slow him down!" Keane would order me.

"Hell, he doesn't want me talking to him," I'd plead with Keane.

"Well, I'm running this damn club, and I don't give a damn what he wants," Keane would respond, his neck getting redder by the second. I often thought that if I could only go halfway, I could manage to appease both parties. But, of course, that wasn't practical. So, following managerial orders, I'd drag myself out, or maybe halfway out, to this fuming figure and stand there like a supplicant, catcher's mitt in my hand and my heart in my mouth.

"Now whatinhell are you doing here?" Gibby would bark at me. "Keep your ass away from me while I'm working. I like to work fast, and I don't need any help from you. Just put those goddamn fingers down as fast as you can. If I don't like it, I'll just shake you off."

On another one of those delightful occasions when Gibby and I had a Kaffeeklatsch at the summit, he waved me away with a disdainful motion of his glove. "Get back there where you belong," he snapped. "The only thing you know about pitching is that it's hard to hit!"

Such benign exchanges are called communicating with your pitcher. With Bob and me it was pretty much a one-way street. Which was okay, because a catcher's responsibility, regardless of what you may have heard or read about a catcher's need to take charge, is to find out how his pitcher wants to operate and then operate accordingly.

While Bob and I may have had some problems initially, imagine how he communicated with the enemy if he treated *me* as a spy. There was a game, for example, when Pete Rose, then only in the incubating years of his Ty Cobb pursuit, came to bat against Gibby with me catching. Bob greeted him with a knockdown pitch. After it scarily whizzed by Pete's helmet, Pete scrambled up and spit toward the mound. The second pitch was behind him, and those are the most dangerous. Pete got up more slowly and grunted. A Pete Rose grunt does not mean he's giving in. But this one was an acknowledgment that Gibson was serious.

In the first game of the 1968 World Series with the Detroit Tigers, Bob faced Denny McLain, the flamboyant winner of thirty-one games. With Gibby on his way to a new strikeout record (beating the fifteen Ks Sandy Koufax recorded against the Yanks in 1963), I made a move toward the mound several times. The crowd was totally involved in what was happening. As they kept roaring for Hoot, my own nervousness and excitement reached new levels. But each time I took a few tentative steps toward Gibby, he signaled me to go back where I came from.

When he tied the record, I held on to the ball and walked a couple of steps out in front of the plate. Bob couldn't see the scoreboard, which was flashing the news that he had tied Koufax.

"Let's go, godammit! Let's go," he shouted.

Finally, I pointed to the scoreboard and he turned around. His only acknowledgment was to turn back to me, without changing the expressive scowl on his face, and in a much more subdued manner say, "Okay, give me the ball."

Bob was always a man in total control of his own destiny —and he wanted me to know it, without any reservations. He was uncompromising, a guy who flat out refused to settle for the back of any man's bus.

He didn't only challenge enemy batters and friendly catchers on the diamond; he could challenge you off the field, too, where life could be a bit more complicated.

One day I carried a message to him from a man who was outside the locker room.

"There's a colored guy waiting for you," I told Gibby. "He says he's got a date to see you."

Gibby was taking off his shoes and didn't even bother to look up at me.

"Oh, yeah?" he shot back without expression. "What color is he?"

That was Gibby, a man with a knack for putting things in their proper perspective.

Some years ago Bob's first wife, Charlene, wrote a book

called *A Wife's Guide to Baseball*. In it she revealed how she used to plan intimate after-game dinners for her husband. She soon learned that if Bob lost or got knocked out of the box, he wouldn't eat; and if he won, he would be so charged up he couldn't eat.

Maybe that's a good way to lose weight.

It's also a pertinent way to tell you how much the game meant to Bob Gibson.

By this time the whole world, or at least that part of the world that pays attention to baseball, knows about Dwight Gooden, so I won't bother throwing statistics at you. I'll just say that after three years he's ahead of every other pitcher in history at a comparable age. If Dwight remains healthy and lucky enough to last into his forties, as Tom Seaver and Carlton have done, he's certainly got a shot at three hundred wins.

Funny thing about Dwight. People don't seem to regard him as a competitive guy. People rarely connect competitiveness with great talent. They think players are either talented or competitive, seldom both. They expect their competitive pitchers to look rough, tough, and angry—maybe like Gibson or Goose Gossage or even like Sal Maglie, who used to show up for work with a three-day growth of beard and a look on his face that would frighten everybody out of town.

Well, Sandy Koufax was one of the most competitive athletes I've ever seen, played against, or batted against, but he had the most subdued, docile manner—nothing offensive or abrasive about the guy. Even when he quit the game in 1966 at the age of thirty, he was low-key and mild-mannered.

Gooden sort of reminds me of Sandy. He doesn't appear competitive, and he has the most matter-of-fact approach to his job—at least on the surface. It's only when you look at Dwight's eyes that you learn what he's all about. There are fire, intensity, determination, and total concentration in those Gooden eyes—and don't let anyone ever kid you about that! Just watch Dwight's eyes when he's trying to pitch out of a bases-loaded jam.

Dwight rarely gets excited. There aren't a lot of highs and lows with him. He always keeps things on an even keel, both within himself and with others. Sometimes, as you watch him, he appears to be pitching in a room all by himself. The crowd can be screeching and imploring Doctor K for more and more strikeouts, but he seems absolutely oblivious to it all.

This is essentially a very happy kid we're talking about. I've never seen him in a bad mood. Even in the 1986 play-offs against the Houston Astros, when he lost 1–0 and got a ten-inning 1–1 no-decision against Nolan Ryan, he was imperturbable.

On the night of September 6, 1985, in Los Angeles, Dwight hooked up in a classic pitchers' duel with Fernando Valenzuela of the Dodgers. For nine innings these two pitchers yielded next to nothing. Then, true to Davey Johnson's program of protecting his great "natural resource," Gooden came out of the game. The score was 0–0.

Now, it's sad to say, but I have to tell you that some professional baseball pitchers would, at that point, disappear from the premises, skip the scene, just like that. But that's not Dwight's way of doing things. He knew he couldn't get credit for the victory, even if the Mets emerged as winners, and he knew his own involvement in the game was at an end. But after he got into his street clothes, he promptly returned to the Met bench to root and give moral support. The win in his own win column meant a lot, sure, but so did the outcome of the game. When the Mets scored a couple to take the game in extra innings on a Darryl Strawberry hit, Gooden was as delighted with the outcome as Darryl was.

The fact is that even though Dwight is just out of his teens, he handles himself like an old pro. He roots for the other guys as well as for himself. Aware that he's one of the most highly publicized young men in the country, Dwight takes it in stride. *Dignity* may be an overused word, especially in regard to athletes, but Dwight's got it.

However, 1986 was a tough year for Dwight's dignity. Not only did he get roughed up a bit on the ball field (although a lot of pitchers would like to be roughed up to the tune of 17–6), but he had a few problems off the field. In January he missed the New York baseball writers' annual dinner. Then he had a car accident in spring training and Davey Johnson had to fine

him for not calling in. Then there was the incident at La-
Guardia Airport in New York with the rent-a-car clerk, his
sister, and his fiancée. And he missed the ticker tape parade
celebrating the Mets' World Series victory.

Dwight had excuses for all of these incidents. Taken indi-
vidually, none of them are particularly serious. However, in
December 1986 Dwight had a rather sobering altercation with
the police down in Tampa. Dwight was accused of assaulting
a police officer, and he in turn accused the police of excessive
brutality. The whole thing was more or less dropped and settled via plea bargaining. Gooden was placed on probation. But
everyone—including Dwight—must recognize the pattern.
Gooden is living his life in a fishbowl, and thus there is real
potential for trouble.

When you're extraordinary you can do anything you want
to do—for the most part. But if you slip off that extraordinary
high, even just a little bit, all your detractors are waiting for
you like a pack of hyenas waiting for a wounded wildebeest.

We're all human, but our perception of our heroes is that
they're superhuman and that they don't fall prey to normal
problems. The year 1987 will be an interesting one for Dwight.
It will be interesting to see how he handles the public's perception of him now that he has shown he is at least mortal. Bob
Gibson told Phil Pepe of the New York *Daily News* at the
beginning of the 1986 season that Gooden would never be any
better than he was in 1985. What a flattering remark to make
about a twenty-one-year-old pitcher. On the other hand, what
a remarkable burden to carry around for someone so young.

My guess is that Gooden's roots down in Tampa, Florida,
will help him in this transition period. He has a pretty close
family, with three older brothers and two older sisters, and
although the brothers were away most of the time, he's always
seen his sisters a good deal. His dad, Dan, who retired from a
job in a chemical company because of arthritis, provided the
inspiration for Dwight to take up baseball, since he had played
some semipro ball and also coached in the semipros. His
mother, Ella, a nurse's aide, encouraged Dwight in sports and
has been credited by Dwight with helping him with his "attitude" problem.

What was the problem? Dwight had something of a temper, if you can imagine that!

But it's his attitude and mental approach to baseball that have contributed as much to Dwight's progress as his obvious physical assets (he's six-foot-four and 198 pounds, and maybe still growing).

Just think of this, for example. In 1984, at the tender age of nineteen, after pitching 218 innings, striking out 276 batters (a big-league mark for rookies), and then being named the National League's Rookie of the Year, did Dwight run off to the Caribbean or sit on his backside waiting for the next baseball season to begin?

Not on your life! He went almost immediately to the Mets' Instructional League in St. Petersburg, Florida, where he worked hard on his move to first base and on pitching from the stretch position. He had been a fairly easy pitcher to steal on during his freshman year; if batters were lucky enough to get on against him, they could move pretty quickly to second base. The reason was that Dwight didn't have a facile, effective move, either to first base or home plate.

But after working with Lynchburg's pitching coach, John Cumberland, he successfully cut down on the time it took him to kick out that left leg and throw home. When Cumberland decided that Dwight had shown enough improvement, Dwight felt he had finally earned his off-season rest.

Cumberland's judgment turned out to be accurate, too, for Dwight has had considerable success since then in holding runners on first and picking them off occasionally. Runners can no longer take advantage of Dwight's previously vulnerable pickoff throw.

It's often said that in order for pitchers to succeed in the majors they've got to be mean and fierce; they can't be afraid to throw at the batter when the situation warrants it.

It isn't necessary to hit a guy. But a pitcher must show that he has absolutely no reservations about throwing knockdown pitches or throwing inside. That means a pitcher must have a fearless approach to pitching as he plays on the innate fear that batters have about being hit. In 1986 Dwight clearly came inside more than he had in either of the previous two years.

When Jim Lonborg, one of everybody's all-time favorite people, went over to Milwaukee after being a Red Sox ace for several years, the first time he faced the Red Sox he threw knockdown pitches at several batters. First time up, first pitch —knockdown. Jim wanted to show that his past friendships couldn't override his professionalism.

Back in the old days, Ty Cobb was said to have "owned" the blaze-balling Walter Johnson, simply because Cobb was aware that Johnson flat out refused to intimidate batters with his deadly fastball. So, following his hunch, Cobb would crowd quite close to the plate, knowing that he'd always get a good pitch to hit. He had no fear that Johnson would breeze one at his head or drive him away from the plate.

You wouldn't think that a guy like Ty Cobb would need an edge. But he got it against Johnson. In sixty-seven games over twenty-one years, Cobb amassed a robust .335 batting average facing Johnson. All a hitter needs is an edge. If you know a guy won't throw at you, you've got that edge.

The first time I ever saw Gooden pitch, I made a mental note, as did everybody else on the premises, that yes, indeed, he threw hard and had a nasty curveball. But almost as important, I observed at that time that he appeared to have enough "mean" in him to do well in the majors.

It was on May 19, 1983, when Dwight came to Shea Stadium for his initial appearance on a major-league diamond. He was pitching in an exhibition game for the Lynchburg Mets, a Carolina League farm team, against the Salem Redbirds, the Texas Rangers' Class A ballclub.

In a late inning of a tight, low-scoring game, a Salem batter hit a dinger off Dwight, a long home run. As the guy made his tour of the bases, he aimed some unflattering gestures in Gooden's direction. Picking up the message, Dwight plunked the next Salem batter with a pitch in the back.

Assessing what Gooden did that day, I had to figure that he possessed enough toughness of body—and mind—to win in the big leagues with the Mets. What Dwight did may be one helluva strange yardstick to go by, but it's a very practical one. And it's the way good, hard baseball has always been played.

There was one other time I can recall when Dwight put

his brand of "chin music" on display. It was in a game with the Montreal Expos in 1985. Bill Gullickson, the big right-hander of the Expos and a pitcher noted for excellent control (thirty-seven walks in 226 innings in 1984), unleashed a pitch in the direction of his ex-teammate Gary Carter. When Gary went scrambling for his sanity, a few voices of protest were raised in the Met dugout—and Dwight's hearing and eyesight are pretty sharp.

When he took the mound, who should be facing him but the same Gullickson. Without wasting a moment, Dwight proceeded to square accounts for his catcher. Gullickson went plummeting to the earth to escape a Gooden breezeball, the umps issued a warning, and the whole incident became a chapter in the dawning Age of Gooden.

What came through to me loud and clear was that Dwight could be counted on to be a reliable protector of his hitters. He wouldn't back away from throwing warning pitches, especially when the opposition chose to play rough.

My learned sidekick in the broadcasting booth, Ralph Kiner, who once hit home runs on a rather frequent basis, says Dwight is "the most exciting guy in baseball today." You'll get no argument from me on that one.

And, oh, baby, do the fans love him at Shea! During all three seasons he has played, the home fans have posted K cards, mostly out in the left field seats, every time Dwight cuts down another batter on a strikeout. The anticipatory clapping that greets every two-strike count on an enemy hitter is a phenomenon that I've rarely seen in big-league parks. At the very least it shows a sophisticated fan involvement. And it sure as hell is better to listen to and watch than the Wave!

In 1986 Dwight's strikeouts were down, considerably down. My antenna went up in spring training when Dwight started talking about economizing on his pitches by keeping the ball down to try to lure hitters into hitting ground balls early in the count, thereby throwing fewer pitches. That's fine, well and good—if the hitters cooperate. But hitters are not concerned with saving Dwight Gooden's arm.

Was this approach a mistake? It certainly has been one of the theories as to why his 1986 season was not as good as his 1985 season.

I asked Dwight one day how he reacted to the constant noisy barrage that comes on the two-strike count. Did it get his adrenaline going? Did it spur him on to greater deeds? Did it make him nervous? Was it proper to be concerned about it as a distraction and bothersome goad?

"It really gets me pumped up," answered Dwight. "It helps me."

If he does get pumped up—and there's no reason to think he's being disingenuous—he doesn't show it. Gooden remains, at all times, the coolest man in the ballpark when he's pitching. Only his adjusting and readjusting of the medal around his neck and the long sleeves of his shirt are signs that maybe, just maybe, he doesn't have as much sangfroid as he's cracked up to have. That long-sleeved shirt, by the way, is always standard equipment when Dwight takes his turn—even in the most stifling weather. "I'd feel naked without it," he says.

Dwight Gooden is "street smart." The expression is badly overused, but again it seems appropriate, if only because people seem to know what you're talking about when you use it. In Dwight's case it refers to his innate ability to cope with things on the ball field. It has to do with the young man's incredible poise and presence on the mound.

He also knows how to listen to people, whether it's his manager, Davey Johnson, his pitching coach, Mel Stottlemyre, or his catcher, Gary Carter. That means he manages to get along with all kinds of people, a substantial achievement for a kid just out of a working-class black neighborhood in East Tampa.

It's been amusing to see how Dwight has become an instant legend, even before reaching the ripe old age of twenty-one. In August 1985, Dwight was scheduled to face the Phillies at Shea. Their broadcaster, Richie Ashburn, and I talked before the game. (I had once worked with Richie behind the mike in Philly, where I learned that he's as quick with a quip as he was as a base runner in the National League.)

Richie assured me before the game that the Philly players were positively "dying to get at Gooden." As unlikely as that seemed to me, Richie went on to say that *he* could have hit Gooden when he was an active player.

"You have no idea," he continued, "how all of our guys

can't wait to beat this kid's brains out. They all say he's got only one pitch and he throws that all the time. Yes, sir, our Phillies are fearless today!"

He went on and on until I responded, thoughtfully, "Bullshit."

With that the two of us roared with laughter. Richie was whistling in the dark on behalf of his Phillies. I knew it, and he knew it. Such is the legend that has already sprouted all over baseball about a guy named Gooden.

Richie knows how to whittle a guy down to size. He would never cease reminding me how I had devoted over twenty years of my life to the dubious pastime of coddling and cosseting pitchers. Then one day he brought umpires into my act.

"Do you realize," he began, as we worked a Phillies game together, "that you've spent more time with that umpire down there at home plate than you have with your wife?"

Going for the bait, I said yes, I realized that.

"And do you also realize," continued Richie, making certain he was speaking away from the mike—he is nothing if not a prudent man—"that you've probably been screwed more by that umpire than you have by your own wife?"

My response has not been chronicled by any historian.

Another facet of Gooden's personality that has gone largely unnoticed, because he isn't the most verbal of people, is his sense of humor. Maybe he's not Johnny Carson, or a twenty-year-old version of George Burns, but he's got a good sense of humor and he likes a good joke, even if it's at his own expense.

In August 1985, when the pennant race between the Mets and Cards really heated up and things got sort of tight in the locker room, one of the clubhouse boys for the Mets walked over to Dwight. He shook his head sadly. At the time Dwight's won-lost mark was 19–3. The Cards' margin over the Mets was two games.

"Ya know," the boy began, with a straight face, "if you hadn't blown those three games, the Mets would be in first place right now."

Dwight laughed out loud. The kid knows a good crack when he hears it, even if he turns out to be the butt of it.

Another time Ed Lynch, the six-foot-five Brooklyn-born right-hander, then with the Mets, watched as Dwight started to down his lunch—a peanut butter and jelly sandwich. After Dwight took a small bite, Lynch asked if he could have some.

"Sure," said Dwight. "Here."

When Dwight handed the sandwich to Lynch, the big pitcher stuffed the entire remains of Dwight's lunch into his mouth with one mammoth bite.

Dwight's eyes followed the feat in utter amazement, and then he laughed. Dwight thought the whole thing was very funny. It helps to keep things light around a pennant-contending locker room.

It's interesting to think about the links among Carlton, Gibson, and Gooden. They're linked by talent and by a few other things: concentration, competitiveness, and their fierce desire to be the best at what they do.

Gibson's done, Carlton's doing but clearly is not able to do what he's done in the past, and Gooden, off to a better start than either of them, has to prove that his future will equal or be better than their past.

Catchers and Pitchers

If a pitcher and a catcher can combine to keep the ball off the fat part of the bat, the sweet part, then they're doing their job.
—GENE MAUCH

There's many a claustrophobic catcher lurking under those fifteen pounds or so of oversized mitt, mask, chest protector, and shin guards. Bearing up behind all that burdensome crap—dubbed "the tools of ignorance" by Herold "Muddy" Ruel, a catcher with a law degree who played for the Washington Senators in the 1920s—there's a guy charged with grabbing everything thrown in his direction while performing 130 to 150 deep knee bends per game.

Much is expected of a major-league catcher. He is expected to throw, hit, run, think, flash crafty signs to his pitcher from his vast mental repository, back up first base with alacrity, be reasonably diplomatic with umpires, and spit his tobacco juice only where his manager won't sit on it. He must also accept criticism and dole it out, keep the infielders in a constant state of vigilance, act as a cheery adviser to managers who think they know more about pitchers than catchers do, retain his sense of humor, and, above all, be a pitcher's friend in good times and bad.

But the job is never done. The catcher has got to avoid

injuries from onrushing base runners, wild swings of the bat, and finger-scorching foul tips. Even though his hands are sore most of the time, he's not supposed to complain. Just rub a little dirt on it, as Joe Schultz used to say.

Did you ever try to figure out why a catcher's batting average isn't usually as high as that of most other players? The answer: His hands are swollen and always in pain. Try swinging a bat when your hands hurt.

How many guys do you think would opt to become catchers if they knew that the palm of their receiving hand would hurt for the rest of their lives? Nevertheless, stalwart catchers don't grouse about their injuries. They just get on with it. That's the name of the game—the catcher's game.

Willie Sutton chose to become a bank robber because that's where the money is. I became a catcher because that's where the ball game is.

Catching is the most demanding, underrated job in sports. Don't tell me about the beleaguered quarterback or the besieged goalie. No athlete has it any tougher than a catcher.

Roger Angell, writing in *The New Yorker*, has testified that with all of his armature and despite his many onerous duties, the catcher still remains largely "invisible." It is apparent that even if catchers are "take-charge" guys they seldom present recognizable faces to the fans.

Without his handy bubble gum card, the average fan probably doesn't know what his home catcher looks like. It's only when a catcher whips off his mask and gazes heavenward for the vagrant flight of a foul fly or when he comes up to hit that fans can appreciate the man behind the mask.

Back in 1941, catcher Moe Berg, in a typically philosophical discourse about catchers that appeared in a national magazine, anointed the catcher as "the Cerberus of Baseball." Close students of Yogi Berra and Greek mythology will recognize that Berg thus implied that catchers are three-headed dogs guarding the entrance to Hades.

Another on-target description of the catcher's role was provided by the writer Robert Smith, who said, "The catcher must shout defiance into the face of an onrushing Sherman tank and snatch a baseball, if it happens to be in play, out of the mouth of a hungry tiger." Smith was referring to Mickey Cochrane, the Philadelphia Athletics' backstop who is often picked as everyone's all-time catcher, but I'd like to think that what he wrote is a generic statement about all catchers.

I've always maintained that catchers enjoy body contact, at least a certain amount of it. The late Thurman Munson liked it. Johnny Bench did, too, before he ran into troubles with his body. Tony Peña of the Pirates, Mike Scioscia of the Dodgers, Gary Carter of the Mets, Carlton Fisk of the White Sox, and Rick Dempsey of the Orioles won't ever walk away from a bruising confrontation at home plate. You can't tell me these guys don't like that banging around in the dirt, that tooth-rattling concussion. Catching takes a certain approach to life —tough-headed, combative, competitive, macho—call it what you choose. Some call it nuts. But this macho approach is not a negative thing in this instance. Just the opposite. It's part of the job; it's *necessary*. You can't catch without it, just the way an interior lineman in football can't play unless he can live with pain. Gene Mauch put it best in describing Bob Boone. "Billy Olsen couldn't pole vault over Boone's pain threshold," Gene said.

When Johnny Roseboro caught for the Los Angeles Dodgers he was as intransigent at home plate as a derrick. He inspired crazy rumors that in the off-season the Dodgers hired three or four guys a week to run into him, just for practice.

One time I foolishly tried to score against him from third base on a ground ball to the infield. John was there, his glasses askew, to block my way. He stood his ground, as always, his knee digging into me, and the whole right side of my face opened up like a can of tomatoes. I had a long burn along one side of my face and he knocked my neck into a stiff state. I felt like a sparring partner in a Rocky movie.

When I picked myself up off the turf, dizzy, dirty, and blood-smeared, my teammates gathered around me as if I were lying in state.

"Are you all right?" Kenny Boyer asked.

"I think I am," I responded woozily.

Gibson came by to take a look.

"Hey, Timmy, you never looked so good," he said.

My pal. I couldn't even feel my nose.

P.S. You should have seen the other guy! Roseboro was out for a month with a bad knee.

The next night we had a game against the Giants. Harvey Kuenn was on third and Jim Davenport was at bat. With the infield back, Davenport hit it to Julian Javier, our second baseman. Much to my surprise, Javier threw home. I scrambled to rip my mask off so I could make the tag. As I took the throw I looked to my left, and Kuenn's belt buckle was about two inches away from my face. There was another collision. Only this one snapped my neck back into place. I still suffer from nerve damage in my neck, though, over twenty years after that Roseboro collision. Leo Durocher, among others, said it was the worst collision he'd ever seen.

I've survived collisions at home plate with other guys, too, including my pal Hank Aaron, who was always much underrated as a base runner. Lou Brock, Frank Robinson, Joe Torre, and Cleon Jones also could come barging into home as if their lives depended on it. Tommy Agee, with thighs as wide around as his waist, always slid straight into me. He was the toughest. Twice he slid so hard his spikes stuck in my shin guards! But I defended my position as if my own life depended on it. Because often it did.

I believed in denying the runner the plate on bang-bang, very close plays. That was the way I was taught, and I continued to think that's what I was being paid to do. But if I had time, I'd get the ball in my bare hand and give the runner part of the plate to slide toward. When he started his slide, that's when I'd try to take the plate away from him.

That's what catcher Ray Fosse was trying to do in the 1970 All-Star Game when Pete Rose crashed his seemingly invulnerable body into Fosse to score the winning run for the National League. Poor Fosse probably still doesn't know what hit him. For sixteen years we've watched him get stomped in TV replays. Not only was he knocked off his feet, but also the shoulder injury that Pete laid on him impaired his abilities for several years. Did Pete do it purposely? No, he was just playing the game the way he has always played it. (I've often wondered what kind of a defensive catcher Pete would have made.

Would he have been as unyielding in that position as he was as a base runner?)

Catching is a rough, tough, physical occupation. The catcher is the infantryman of baseball. Maybe some guys can stand the heat a little better than others, but I've heard some people suggest that plenty of catchers are afraid of physical injury and leery of body contact. I can't believe it's true. I don't buy the notion that any catcher would have any real fears about the job. If you choose to spend your time as a catcher, you can't be preoccupied with getting hurt.

Yet Birdie Tebbetts, who caught for many years in the American League and then managed Cincinnati, spread such talk not too long ago. Tebbetts had a theory that catchers build up fears over the long winter layoff and that they have to take a sharp foul or two in spring training before they can lay aside their fears and terror of the job. Now I know that some psychologists insist that if you have a fear of flying you should get right on a plane and if you have a fear of cats you should try sharing the same room with one. But I can't agree with Birdie that catchers have to get themselves hurt in order to reorient themselves to their work. They're going to get hurt sooner or later, whether they seek to or not. I think Birdie is trying to implant fear when there is no fear. If a guy nurses latent (or active) fear, get him out from behind the plate, quick!

On the other hand, some people close to catchers nurse a fair amount of fear. I remember once talking to my wife, Anne, about this. There was a chance, I thought, that she might be preoccupied with my vulnerability behind that plate.

"In your first few years with the Cards," Anne told me, "I had so much confidence in your skills that I never thought very much about your getting hurt. If that was unrealistic, that's still the way I felt. As time went on, I did think more about it, but that was because I was a bit older and more sophisticated about the role the catcher plays."

Much more important than the body-threatening chores a catcher must perform is the psychological and emotional strain of working to be the "pitcher's friend." I put *friend* in quotation marks because I learned early that a catcher is a fool to spend his time hanging out with starting pitchers. After all, every four days with a pitcher is either a feast or a famine, a wake or New Year's Eve. Either way, after they pitch, they're off for at least three days. You've got to play those games. If the strain on your relationship doesn't kill the pitcher, it may kill you. The moral of the story: Never hang out with starting pitchers.

The notion that a catcher should become a pitcher's best friend was the brainchild of Bill Dickey, the stalwart old Yankee catcher who had wanted to sign me as a Yankee back in 1959. Even after Dickey failed to get my name on a Yankee contract, he was kind enough to pass along to me one of his most cherished theories about the pitcher-catcher relationship.

"You do everything for a pitcher that friendship implies," Bill told me when I was still a teenager with a mossy layer on my chin. "When he's down, you try to pick him up. When he's too high, you try to get him back on an even keel. You've got to be a confidant as well as a psychologist without extra pay. Anything you can do to build up his confidence and to relieve him of thinking too much is well worth it for both of you. You select the pitches because the pitcher's primary concern is with technique, not selection."

The idea that the catcher should always be the final authority for selection of pitches is logical, when you think about it for a moment. Who sees the immediate results of what the pitcher is doing better than anyone else? The catcher, of course. And a catcher is an expert on results. If there is to be a "quarterback" in the catcher-pitcher tandem, it's got to be the catcher.

Does a catcher actually remember all the weaknesses and strengths of batters? Or does he take copious notes in his little black book and pore over them every night before he goes to sleep?

Well, I don't qualify as any kind of genius, but I never took a note in my life about hitters' glitches. All I had to know was already safely stored away in my mind, and as soon as I got between those white lines, I was ready to use it. Most good catchers operate pretty much that way. To tell you the truth, it's just not that difficult. It's a catcher's *job*, that's all.

Some catchers hint to reporters that they've got a cache of secret notes on certain hitters hidden away, but they're probably saying that just to impress the reporters. It also adds to the mystique about catchers.

The key ingredient in getting a pitcher to communicate properly with you is trust. You can't meander out to the mound every few minutes and issue the standard incantations— "What you have to do is throw strikes" or "Don't give him anything good to hit" or "Don't walk this guy." Or the all-inclusive combination of the last two. Those instructions are about as useful as advising a prison guard "Don't unlock the door to that killer's cell!"

It's incredible how many pitchers are forced to listen to such silly comments and how many summit meetings are just pure rubbish as a result. When a catcher lumbers out there with that kind of advice on his mind, he might just as well hop a freight to Hoboken. Better yet, he ought to learn something about the fundamentals of his job.

If the true mission of a catcher is to work on a pitcher's confidence, handling the pitcher properly is the true essence of that mission. Most fans don't see this essence, nor do many broadcasters. It's the hidden game of the catcher, one of the nuances of baseball that isn't understood or talked about very much, even among well-informed followers of the game.

How do you establish this mutual trust with a pitcher? Well, it usually starts with a good open dialogue, but it doesn't happen overnight—it needs time to develop. I can't tell you how many times, even in my close relationships with guys like Bob Gibson and Steve Carlton, that I'd ask, over and over, stuff like this: "What do you wanna do in this situation? In that situation? You've done it before when I've caught you, and there's no reason you can't do it again." It's all got to narrow down to what your pitcher throws. You can't call pitches based on a hitter's weakness. Too many guys are concerned with pitching away from their own strengths. If you've got a good lowball hitter up and Kent Tekulve on the mound—and Kent is a sinkerball pitcher—you've still got to go with what the pitcher throws best. If, coincidentally, the hitter's weakness corresponds to the pitcher's strength, you're in luck. But that is often not the case.

Once you've established trust, you've cleared a big hurdle. You've taken the heat off your pitcher, and now he doesn't have to worry about making the decision on each pitch. He can simply concentrate on the mechanics of delivering the ball, without the preoccupation of having to make pitch selections.

This mutual trust, of course, is based on more than a simple dialogue with your pitcher or the fact that he thinks you're a regular guy or can tell funny jokes. It's based on the fact that he knows that you understand baseball, that you've absorbed, as a vegetable absorbs water, damned near everything that should be known about hitters' weaknesses and strong points, and that you sense what your pitcher is thinking and planning. All these factors must figure into your pitch selection.

Sure, there's bound to be plenty of anger, overt and otherwise, in the catcher-pitcher relationship. There was always plenty of screaming and yelling between Gibson and me, but that's the way it should be. A catcher's job is to cut through all that crap and get down to the issues: getting the ball pitched and winning the ball game.

A catcher must keep his pitcher honest and aware of his own limitations as well as his own capabilities. Don't forget, even the best of them have limitations. The more honest your pitcher is, the better chance there is for a positive outcome. Sometimes you even have to go eyeball to eyeball. Carlton thinks this statement of reality is absurd. His thinking is that he *is* superhuman. My response to that: Who am I to argue?

I did argue with Steve Carlton in spring training of 1965, when I practically backed him up against a wall in our first meeting. I don't know how many arguments I had with Bob Gibson. But all those brouhahas had to do with the substance of pitching, not personalities, politics, religion, or the latest movie we'd seen.

Once the pitcher trusts a catcher, then the two-way relationship can begin. "A real intimacy develops between pitcher and catcher," right-hander Carl Erskine told Roger Kahn in *The Boys of Summer*. "You work some hundred and twenty pitches together every few days, and after a while you think like one man."

When the relationship is a strong one, there are times when a catcher will find that his pitcher needs him. That's not when he's on top of the world with a five- or six-game winning streak. When a pitcher's going good, nobody needs to pat him on the back. But when things turn sour, that's when pitchers are walking nervous breakdowns, when they grope around for advice from everyone—mailman, elevator boy, florist, taxi driver, dentist, etc. "Hey," a frustrated pitcher once informed me, "my barber just told me I'm not coming over the top with my curveball. You think he's right?"

These are the times when a catcher has to soothe his pitcher, to comfort him, and to get him to forget the past and turn the page. Some pitchers are able to put home run balls out of their minds almost the moment they're hit—an invaluable trait. A catcher must work on a pitcher to help him forget.

During the 1973 season, when I was with the Cards, I realized I'd reached the point of complete trust with Carlton. Lefty, then with the Phillies, wasn't doing too well. One day, after he was belted out of the box early, he sent one of the clubhouse boys into the Cards' dugout to get me. Lefty wanted me under the stands, and since I wasn't playing that day, I said fine.

When we got together, Lefty told me he wasn't getting any pop on his fastball. "It's flat and gliding in," he complained.

"You're dropping your hand down and pushing the ball," I said. I remembered Ray Ripplemeyer, the pitching coach for the Phillies, explaining that where most pitchers drop their arms down and push the ball, Carlton would drop his hand down, causing him to push the ball. Carlton's arm was always in perfect position, but he'd get in trouble when he would incorrectly cock his hand. Even if we were then with different clubs, I knew Lefty trusted me and believed what I was telling him.

One of the toughest assignments a catcher faces is working with a pitcher who just doesn't have much on a particular day. When a pitcher is throwing like a five-year-old with the measles, the catcher shouldn't dwell on it. What he *should* do is try to keep his pitcher in the game with careful pitch selection. (It's sort of like leading someone through a mine field.) You work with what the pitcher's got, even if it isn't much, on a given day.

A catcher has to dwell on what a pitcher *can* do, not on what he can't do. When a pitcher can do a helluva lot of things the right way and a few things the wrong way, he should be encouraged to do what he does right. The so-called wise observers used to knock Gibson because he couldn't hold runners on first base, but what was the point? He couldn't hold runners on, so just let the guy pitch without distractions. A catcher has to pay attention to his pitcher's strengths.

There's a certain amount of morale building that goes on from behind the plate. Some catchers are more chirpy and talkative than others. I did a fair amount of that with my pitchers, but usually it didn't amount to much more than plain blather. When Roy Campanella worked behind the bat for the Dodgers, before his tragic auto accident, he liked to do a lot of talking, especially when he teamed up with big Don Newcombe. Campy would often waddle out to the mound, sometimes with Manager Chuck Dressen also in attendance, and urge his big pitcher on to greater deeds for the sake of the faithful citizens of Ebbets Field.

Some catchers also like to sustain a running dialogue with the hitters as they step up to bat; the prevalent theory is that it's distracting to hitters. Gary Carter of the Mets has been accused of talking while the ball is still on its way to the plate.

"I'll talk a blue streak to try to make them laugh," acknowledges Gary. "I'll do anything so their mind isn't a hundred percent on hitting or the pitch."

Distracting batters may be a way for a catcher to spend his time, but I'd rather spend it on pitch selection or trying to give a pitcher the right signals to work with. When I caught, I'd sometimes greet a batter with "Hello" or "How ya doin'?" But that would be about it. I never believed that the Power of Positive Annoyance worked very well.

Pitching coach Johnny Sain was one of the keenest students of pitching I've ever known. (Johnny had some great years as a pitcher for the Boston Braves.) In 1948 it was Johnny and Warren Spahn, the southpaw, who led the Braves to the National League pennant. Their two-man operation inspired that famous line of poetry: "Spahn and Sain and pray for rain."

It is Johnny's belief that pitching is simply the "art of fooling the hitter," and that the catcher must assist in this duplicity in any way he can. Sain always maintained that sooner or later most big-league hitters will catch up to a pitcher's fastball, and I agree. One way for a pitcher to avoid having to come in with that not-so-fastball is to get ahead in the count. The biggest pitch in baseball is that first strike. If a pitcher can get that oh-and-one count on a batter, he is truly ahead in his confrontation with the guy. You can talk about getting breaking balls over the plate when you're behind in the count, 0–2 fastballs, 0–2 breaking balls in the dirt. You can talk about a lot of things. But the biggest plus your pitcher has going for him is that first strike on the first pitch. Just get it in there, regardless of what kind of a pitch it is. If a guy happened to be a first ball hitter, we used to tell pitchers in pregame meetings to throw him the second pitch first. First ball fastball! Rubbish! Doesn't that mean you should always throw him a breaking ball on the first pitch? Don't you think he'll adjust?!

Even if I wasn't in a talkative mood before a ball game, the one thing I'd say to my pitcher was, "Get that first one in there." No psychiatrist, hypnotist, or veterinarian ever gave a pitcher better advice than that.

You get that first strike over, especially with a good hitter up at bat, and you don't have to worry about that 1–0 pitch, 2–0 pitch, or 3–0 pitch, then the chance of throwing that fat fastball that a lot of hitters are going to jack right out of the ballpark. Baseball is a game of firsts, if you think about it. First out, first run—that gives you an edge. But nothing gives you as big an edge as getting that first strike.

The reason some pitchers choose to "nibble" or get too fine with pitches is that they suspect their stuff isn't too good that day. This is a key point because it's dead wrong. You should do just the opposite of what your instincts tell you. Think about it: If you don't have good stuff and you fall behind in the count, it stands to reason that your fastball is going to be much more hittable. If you've got good stuff, it's not as necessary to stay ahead of the batters. But how many times does a pitcher go out there with overpowering stuff? When the count is even, there's an element of doubt in the hitter's mind. The further you fall behind, the less doubt there is about what you're going to throw. And if a big-league hitter knows what you're going to throw, the chances of his getting the fat part of the bat on the ball skyrocket.

When a pitcher minus his good stuff is nibbling, his catcher has to stand up and be counted. It's his job to tell his pitcher in no uncertain terms to get that ball over the plate—without just laying it in there. There *is* a time to nibble. There's also a time to challenge, but challenging should always come before nibbling because of the aforementioned element of doubt. All challenges do not have to be power pitches. You can challenge with finesse, too. It's the difference between the Thrilla in Manila and the Joffrey Ballet. They're both challenges, but one is power and one's finesse. You can start a guy out with a straight change-up. That can be a direct challenge—but you've got to get the ball over the plate.

In recent years I've noticed many pitchers falling into the habit—a bad habit—of throwing too many sliders. The slider is the easiest pitch in the world for the catcher to call for. It's comfortable to handle, and many catchers think it's a tough pitch to hit. But that defies logic. If a pitch is comfortable to handle, it stands to reason that it's also comfortable to hit. On the opposite side of the coin, if a pitch is tough to handle it's probably going to be tough to hit.

The difference between the major leagues and the minor leagues is not the velocity with which a pitcher throws. It's control. Major-league pitchers can pitch effectively to the corners. You've heard and read about pitchers whose control is supposed to be so razor-sharp that a catcher can loll back there in his rocking chair. Well, a pitcher who pitches effectively on the corners isn't setting up his catcher to sit in an old rocker. No way. When a catcher says he can sit in a rocking chair, he's talking about working with a pitcher who has the uncanny ability to hit the outside corners with precision. For most of 1985 John Tudor of the Cards was that kind of pitcher. Bobby Ojeda and Fernando Valenzuela were like that in 1986.

One of the most horrendous mistakes catchers make is to call for pitches that give *them* trouble when they bat. When he was with Montreal, Gary Carter often was guilty of that. Gary would fall behind with a breaking ball by calling for it too often. Then he'd be forced to signal for a fastball at 2–1 or 3–1. When you're behind the hitter, you do like to come in with more breaking balls if your pitcher can get the breaking ball over. But a lot of pitchers can't. So, as a result of Carter's tendency, lots of smart hitters just sat back and waited for the fast one.

Carter is with the Mets now and is no longer such an easy catcher to read. He's learned his lesson. Now he's in an active conspiracy with all of those talented Mets pitchers to keep the ball off the fat part of the plate.

In a manner of speaking, the top hitters in baseball don't hit off pitchers. They hit off catchers. It's the catcher who's in there, day after day, ordering up the pitches, and in most instances the pitchers don't shake off their catchers.

It seems to me that a catcher's worth shouldn't be predicated on his last errant throw to second base or on how many times he allows a pitch to get past him. Forget those imperfections. Obviously, a catcher has to throw well and certainly he has to catch balls in the dirt. But at least as important, probably more important, is a catcher's judgment in calling for certain pitches and in guiding his pitchers to throw to certain locations.

As far as pitchers are concerned, they are only as good as their movement, location, and speed. Notice that I prefer to place speed last. Sure, it's important, but it drives me up the bleacher wall when guys tell me constantly how well—or poorly—a pitcher is doing on the radar gun. Sure, the gun is a help in telling you how well a pitcher is maintaining his strength. And it may help the few pitchers who depend on power alone. But it doesn't tell you *everything* you need to know about a pitcher.

When things go wrong for pitchers there are always some who will second-guess and harass their catchers. Second-guessing can make even the most devoted husband insecure. Imagine what it can do to the confidence of a catcher, even a levelheaded one!

How do you tell if a catcher is a victim of insecurity as he squats down there, his features blessedly hidden from everyone? Generally, the tip-off to a catcher's insecurity is his deliberateness and slowness in giving signs. A catcher must work with conviction and speed. I've been personally criticized for having a quick trigger and being very opinionated and too cocksure. I believe that all of those things are true—but those traits, I am convinced, come from the fact that I was a catcher for all of my adult life. You *have* to be like that if you want to catch. Being a catcher is not so dissimilar from being a politician. Politicians say things with such conviction they make you believe them. That's basically what a catcher does. There *are* catchers, such as Carlton Fisk of the White Sox, who prefer to work slowly. That system seems to be part of Pudge's style and strategy—or maybe he gets paid by the hour!

But if you see a catcher getting down into his crouch, then getting up and going down again, then getting up like a jack-in-the-box, he's showing that he's not sure what he should signal to his pitcher. That's when a manager, not to mention a pitcher, has trouble.

If a catcher is doubt-ridden, he'll communicate that attitude to his pitcher; he'll get a tentative fastball or a doubt-ridden curve in return. Sometimes the way in which a pitcher goes about throwing a pitch is more important than the pitch itself. If a catcher calls for an inside pitch and the pitcher shakes him off, preferring to throw outside, but then finally acquiesces, you know where that pitch is going to be? Right down the middle of the plate. Because it was thrown with doubt.

Is it easier for a catcher and pitcher to confront or think along with a bad hitter than a good one? Strangely, no. The poor hitter generally doesn't have the slightest notion what a pitcher is about to throw at him, so why should a catcher try to outthink him? You don't need a careful pitch selection when you face the inept batter. Just go with *stuff*.

But with a good hitter, catchers can have their minds challenged, and that's part of the fun, isn't it? That's where a catcher can make like a squatting Picasso as he works with his instincts and guile.

Many real students of hitting are more apt to study catchers than pitchers. Some years ago, when third baseman Ron Santo was with the Chicago Cubs, Santo said he made it his business to try to figure out what catchers were up to on each pitch rather than to try to analyze pitchers.

"I did it with you, Timmy," Santo said late in his career, "because I always thought it was much more important to know a catcher's habits and how he selected pitches than to read a pitcher's mind." Keith Hernandez operates in much the same way as Santo did.

With each ball a pitcher throws when he's ahead in the count, the batter fills up the hole a bit. He's not in trouble as deep as he was; he's not forced to protect the outside of the plate. He's looking for a pitch on the inside part of the plate —always the most fertile area for a power hitter. The plate is immobile, but it really *isn't* because of the flexibility of the hitter. If, for instance, you threw three straight change-ups over the outside corner, doesn't it stand to reason that the third one is going to be much less effective than the first one? Why? Because the batter will be leaning that way, thus having a better chance to get the fat part of his bat on the pitch. Conversely, if you just knocked a guy on his ass and *then* throw an outside change-up, the odds are you're going to get him. The bigger you make the plate, the more area you've got in which to get him out.

But a lot depends on where you come from, too. If you come from 2–0 to run the count to 2–2, the hitter's going to be thinking more defensively. If you come from 0–2 to 2–2, the hitter's on the offensive. Another consideration is a pitcher's strengths and weaknesses. When a pitcher gets even in the count, he should follow with a pitch that he has mastered. If you're Mario Soto, come in with a change-up. If you've got Bert Blyleven's curve, come in with an El Swervo.

You'd be surprised how little many hitters know these days; they're as unfamiliar with the strike zone as they are with the sovereign countries of Africa. For instance, a guy such as Steve Garvey, who is generally thought to be a good hitter and certainly is, hardly ever walks more than twenty-five or thirty times a year out of over six hundred at bats, which makes me think he victimizes himself with poor selection. And he's not the only one, either. Dave Parker and Mookie Wilson are two others—they're very aggressive. Ralph Kiner calls them Bible hitters—they live by the rule "Thou shalt not pass."

So what do pitchers and catchers do with guys such as Garvey, Parker, and Wilson, all of whom appear to be allergic to the base on balls? Naturally, hitters like this should be thrown an awful lot of pitches out of the strike zone.

The strikeout pitches thrown by the best pitchers are rarely balls in the strike zone. These pitches only give the illusion of being strikes. By the time the hitter realizes that, he's already made his commitment to swing. I'd bet that more than 70 percent of the swinging strikeouts thrown by pitchers like Carlton and Valenzuela and Scott come on pitches clearly out of the strike zone. So if you're talking about the art of pitch location, the big thing to remember is that the illusion of a strike can often do as much, if not more, damage as a strike that comes straight over the middle of the plate. Think of the split-finger fastball. The reason it's so effective is that it gives the illusion of a strike. Bruce Sutter, who popularized the pitch in 1977, almost never threw it for a strike. Since that time, pitchers have realized they don't have to throw strikes with that pitch. Batters can combat that by taking early in the count. Pitchers will then, in return, start throwing strikes again. That's the constant cat-and-mouse-and-cat battle between a pitcher, a hitter, and a catcher. Notice the first three letters in the word *catcher*.

I can recall Lefty Carlton sitting in the training room before a game, concentrating, with both eyes closed, on the lanes of the plate. In his mind he divided the plate into three sections: the outside lane, the inside lane, and the fat part of the plate.

Gibson used to say to Lefty, "The plate's seventeen inches. The middle twelve belong to the hitter. The inside and outside two and a half are mine. If I pitch to spots properly, there's no way the batter is going to hit the ball hard consistently."

While the pitcher concentrates on those lanes, the catcher gets ready to work the hitter inside out. Literally. How many times have you heard someone say that a pitcher just has to keep the ball down to be successful? Red Alert! Red Alert!

Another baseball myth! Carlton never mentioned the lane from the knee to the letters. There's no lane there, and it's precariously close to the middle part of the plate, where the fat part of the bat lies in wait. The gut lanes, where pitches get guys out, are those few inches inside and outside.

Once the decision is made to pitch inside and outside, there are no stringent rules about where you can be most effective. Remember, it's not the pitch itself that's most important; it's how you got there. And the way you get there is by staying ahead in the count.

Catchers, knowing that their pitchers are set to work the batters inside and outside, move their targets accordingly. Pittsburgh's gymnastic catcher, Tony Peña, who has an uncanny ability to snatch balls out of the dirt, makes a fascinating picture on TV as he gets into his crouch with one leg sticking way out. But technically his position is not correct, because he *should* be working both sides of the plate.

However, catchers have to be careful not to set up that target too early, because many guys peek. What a catcher should do is give a signal, then watch the pitcher go into his windup. While the hitter's waiting for the pitch and too intent to notice, the catcher should move to either the inside or outside of the plate. Watch Bob Boone do this—it's how he frames the pitcher.

If a catcher sets up outside, the ump may be inclined to give him the outside pitch. While the catcher is off the plate, the umpire has probably moved with him. So, when the pitcher hits the mitt perfectly—even though the pitch may not be a strike, it'll be too close to take—the ump will thrust his arm in the air for a strike.

Once a hitter figures that you're setting up outside, you should occasionally decoy. Hitters with good hearing and instinct may be attuned to where the catcher is squatting by hearing the pounding of the mitt. So a lot of times the catcher will go *boom, boom, boom* inside. Then, surprise, the pitch is delivered, and the catcher is sitting on the outside with the ball safely in his clutches.

By and large, it's the catcher's job to ignore the batter. He's got to imagine that he's involved in a nice, elevated game of catch with his pitcher, just like a couple of kids in a sandlot. (Are there any sandlots left these days?) Any pitcher who hopes to make it has to learn to throw through the batter and to the catcher. Too many pitchers, intimidated by a batter's reputation, throw *to* him, not *through* him.

Earning the respect of pitchers is always a formidable challenge for a catcher. When I caught for Curt Simmons, Ray Sadecki, Gibby, and others in my early years, they were all more experienced and knowledgeable than I was, even if some of them were only slightly older. I learned quickly that a young catcher has to do plenty of listening and learning. Let other guys talk and explain things. Listen. But always keep in mind what Del Rice once told me: "In meetings, make sure you listen." Then, smiling, he added, "Then go out and follow your instincts."

I think I got started on the right foot. I tried to care more about the pitchers than about my own individual performance. Was I being selfless? No. But I made a sincere effort in that direction, and that's all any catcher can do.

Today most catchers don't have the luxury of not worrying about an oh-for-four day. Even when the front office and the peerless leader in the dugout tell you they want you to concentrate only on handling pitchers, you're still going to be thinking of home runs and RBIs. It's only natural. Because long-term contracts come with offensive production.

But in the future, if management expects its catchers to handle pitchers with care and shrewdness, they won't be able to depend solely on a catcher's pride in a job well done. They're going to have to think about incentive bonuses for catchers, possibly based on how well the pitching staff performs and on what the catcher's role has been in that performance.

You can't totally forget your offense, but too many catchers don't appreciate the defensive elements as a positive bargaining factor. At present such reward bonuses don't exist to any great degree, to my knowledge. As of now, owners and managers don't seem to be prepared to reward such talent, so I can anticipate overtime for the arbitrators.

So what's a young catcher going to do? Does he concentrate on his development as an all-around catcher and a nurturer of pitchers, or does he just go out and try to get base hits?

I'd still prefer that catchers try to be unselfish and devote themselves to pitchers. I really cared about my hitting, but I was trained to think about the pitchers I caught. Don't get me wrong. I'm not living in a fool's paradise. Under current conditions, it's unlikely that that kind of selflessness will develop for most catchers. Nor was I a totally selfless catcher.

I've been going on here about pitchers—how to work with this strange breed, friendship with pitchers, all that cerebral stuff that comes under the heading of a symbiotic relationship. But I haven't gotten into what happens when there's an obvious failure to communicate. When that happens, you've got a real problem.

First let me tell you about a pitcher I *could* communicate with. Then I'll chronicle the details about Mike Marshall and me.

In the 1964 World Series, with the Yankees and Cards tied at one game each, we came into the bottom of the ninth inning of the third game with the score locked at 1–1. Despite the fact that over sixty-seven thousand people were screaming for their hometown heroes—Mantle, Maris, Elston Howard, and Joe Pepitone—our southpaw Curt Simmons had done a fine job for us for eight innings.

Manager Johnny Keane decided to come in with a fresh pitcher, so he nominated our ace relief pitcher, Barney Schultz, who led the Card staff with fourteen saves and a 1.64 ERA.

Bob Gibson always enjoyed getting on Barney, who came out of Beverly, New Jersey, as one of the nicest men you would ever want to meet. By 1973 Barney had become the Card pitching coach.

Every time he would come to the mound, Bob would say: "What can you tell anyone about pitching? You never threw anything but a knuckler."

One day Gibson, in a most unusual turn of events, was getting his tough ass kicked by the Phils. After less than three innings they had scored eight earned runs off him.

Manager Schoendienst reluctantly decided it was time to send out an emissary to inform Gibby he'd had better days.

The man he chose for this unenviable mission was Barney. So, fully expecting an explosion, Barney literally tiptoed out to the mound with his head bowed.

When Gibby glared at Barney, you could almost see Barney wilt.

"Whereinhell have you been?" growled Gibby. "I've been getting my ass knocked off out there and nobody's come to get me!"

Anyway, to return to that Series game, Keane brought in Barney to face none other than Mickey Mantle, first guy up. Nice work, if you can avoid it.

The crowd roared with anticipation. Barney leaned forward to get my sign. I squatted and gave it to him. Knuckler. What else? Barney's best pitch.

Barney wound up. In came the knuckler. Out went the ball—and the ball game was over.

I couldn't believe it. That homer was high as the sky, a typical Mickey shot. To get where that ball was going you'd have to change planes twice.

If you're a catcher in that situation, and the guy's hit a game-winning homer in the last of the ninth, all you can do is stand there looking sheepish and make damn sure Mantle touches home plate. Big deal!

So I cocked my head and tried to follow that ball. As I did, my line of vision hit Mike Shannon in right field. That ball wasn't going to come down in the same country, and there was Mike, bracing himself, with his left leg over the cyclone fence, getting ready to make a leap! I couldn't believe it. He actually had one foot in the stands.

Afterward, in the clubhouse, I sidled up to Mike and said, "What were you doing out there?"

He looked at me, really seriously, and said, "Timmy, you never know."

And what was poor Barney Schultz doing all this time? Was he screaming at my bad call? Was he bitching about what a lousy catcher I was? Was he blaming me for calling for his knuckler? Nope. Not Barney.

"That's the way it goes," said Barney, shrugging his shoulders. "We'll get 'em the next time."

Both of us knew that Mantle, who had just hit his sixteenth

Series homer, to break Babe Ruth's record, could have hit anybody's knuckleball—or anybody's fastball, for that matter. There was no sense in complaining. You come back and play another day. That's baseball.

Now we come to 1972, a year during which I caught seventy-seven games for Montreal. We were playing the Pirates at Montreal's Jarry Park. Pitching for us in relief was Mike Marshall, who specialized in kinesiology and being an asshole. His usual catcher, John Boccabella, wasn't in there that day. I was.

In the top of the eleventh inning Vic Davalillo led off with a single and moved to second. Roberto Clemente was up next. Manager Gene Mauch joined me at the mound with Marshall. No, Marshall didn't want to intentionally walk Roberto, even if Bob Robertson, up after Clemente, was batting a white sale ($1.89), but Mauch did. So did I. So what happens? We walked Roberto, then Robertson gets a double, the strategy backfires, and we lose.

Enraged at the sequence of events, Marshall, a student of the science of motion, was all motion himself. He belligerently tossed the rosin bag up and down maybe a half dozen times, with his back turned to me. He was giving me a shorthand message: It was my fault.

He got the next guy out, ending the Pirates' half of the inning. In the dugout, he turned to face me. "McCarver," he bellowed, "don't ever come out to the fucking mound again unless I call for you!"

I snapped. Had the dugout been a little larger, I would have charged him right there, but I waited until we were in the clubhouse.

Marshall was in the shower when the game ended, since they pinch-hit for him in our half of the inning. I ran in after him with my uniform and spikes still on. Not a helluva lot of traction—spikes on wet tile. It had to be a funny sight. Meanwhile, I'm trying to nail him, but I can't keep my feet.

"What the hell's going on here?" asked Mauch. "You going crazy?"

If Mauch didn't know what was going on, Ron Hunt, an ornery little infielder who made a living for years by being hit by pitched balls, sure did.

"You gotta stand in line if you want to get Marshall," Hunt said. "Calm down."

I did calm down. When Marshall went to retrieve his valuable box, he gave me a smirk, and I went for him again. He went for me, too. I went down, tumbling in an embarrassing heap near Kenny Singleton's open locker. Then some kind souls pulled us apart.

With Barney Schultz, in that numbing ninth inning, I was dealing with a guy with whom I had a respectful catcher-pitcher relationship. With Marshall, I was dealing with a totally self-centered man, a guy who never thought of his team first and himself second.

There's no perfect formula for compatibility between a pitcher and a catcher, primarily because each relationship is different. But a catcher's job is to strive to make his relationship with each different personality he encounters as utopic as possible. Maximizing productivity is the goal here.

That Old Devil Pressure

> Higher stakes tighten the strings of
> the nervous system.
>
> —HEYWOOD HALE BROUN

One guy's heart pumps twice as fast as usual. Another guy is as calm as three in the morning. One guy's hands are clammy. Another guy's grip is firm. One guy doesn't want to pitch. Another guy wants to pitch more than ever. One guy doesn't want to come to bat. Another guy can't wait. One guy can't eat a thing. Another guy has one helluva big appetite. One guy is convinced he's a coward. Another guy knows he's going to be a hero. One guy prays that the ball won't be hit to him. Another guy prays it will. One guy can't wait to get to the ballpark. Another guy can't get out of bed. One guy's stride is long and steady. Another has a bad case of jellylegs.

What's going on here?

You've just been supplied with quickie profiles of how ballplayers of all shapes, sizes, and abilities react to that old devil pressure.

Some guys thrive on it; others can't cope with it. Some make it work for them; others let it get in their way.

I'll never forget how Sparky Anderson, a pilot of four pennant winners, in Detroit and Cincinnati, described his own reaction to pennant pressure.

"It can eat you alive," said Sparky, whose white hair and corrugated face give clues to his own inner tensions.

In 1947, after the Yankees beat the Dodgers in the World Series, Dick Young wrote a lead for his column that read, "A tree grows in Brooklyn . . . and it's an olive tree." Meaning the Dodgers choked.

I went through some tough, demanding, tense pennant races with the Cards, Phils, and Red Sox. I can assure you that the word *pressure* isn't hyperbole or an invention of the media. In some respects, it's a euphemism for *pain*. The pressure of a down-the-stretch drive can get you in the belly, the mind, the legs, and the heart, and when you're involved with it there's no escaping it. It's with you day and night.

After the Phils pulled one of the great el foldos in National League history in 1964—they lost ten straight games beginning on September 20, and the Cards won eight straight to cop the pennant—Manager Gene Mauch of the Phils was almost speechless. But he did describe the "fear in the eyes" of his pitchers when he walked to the mound in those final days.

What Gene Mauch saw out there was not in his imagination. I've seen it, too. Sometimes I'd walk out there to a pitcher, and I'd swear to you he didn't want to unleash that ball. Other pitchers I knew used to throw up before a big game. I used to go to the bathroom in the second inning of every game. And I could feel it coming during the National Anthem. It was a running joke. Someone once asked me what I did in the winter. "My wife plays the National Anthem," I said, "and fifteen minutes later I go to the bathroom." I used to tell Red Schoendienst, our manager, that I could hit in the top third or the bottom third of the lineup, but I couldn't hit in the middle— because I'd be in the bathroom.

Ironically, everyone concerned with baseball—the players, the front offices, the fans, the press, the announcers—love the game's incomparable old September Song, when the games dwindle down to a precious few. The Mets' general manager, Frank Cashen, has even gotten poetic about it, calling it the "agonizing ecstasy of a pennant race."

What's not to love about a pennant race? It's the essence of the game. But, man, what it can do to you! It can take your emotions and bounce them around like you're in a stagecoach in a Western movie.

Sure, I know baseball's only a game, a pastime, an athletic contest, even a frolic. It's full of hype and self-promotion, and, sure, it's not open-heart surgery, as Steve Blass, the Pittsburgh pitcher, once remarked after winning two World Series games against Baltimore in 1971. Yet despite his comment, Blass himself may have had his promising career terminated because of uncontrollable tensions. (He couldn't get the ball over the plate anymore, for some inexplicable reason, and the Pirates couldn't keep him. Steve tried everything, including mantras and psychiatry—but all to no avail.)

Okay, maybe the pennant race isn't open-heart surgery or even World War II, but I'll tell you what it is. It's a time when there are deep circles under your eyes and a big lump in your throat as you walk out on the field. It's a time when even water goes down in lumps.

Watch those players breathe when they step up to the plate. Watch those pitchers trying to act normal. These men are being asked to control their emotions, and, believe me, it's a tall order.

A pennant race is a time, also, when there are no last-place teams or mediocre ballclubs. The anemic clubs get their biggest charge out of swatting down the league leaders. Look at what the Pirates did to the flag-seeking, frustrated Mets in the last days of the 1985 season—it could have caused mass suicide at Shea Stadium. Then go back to prehistoric 1934. In the last two games of the season, the sixth-place Brooklyn Dodgers, under that voluble dugout philosopher Casey Stengel, knocked off the New York Giants, who were in a dead heat for first place with the Cards.

On the eve of those two games, Manager Bill Terry of the Giants, normally a prudent man, was asked how he thought his club would do against the Dodgers.

"Is Brooklyn still in the league?" asked Terry. You know the rest. The Dodgers, with the help of their big pitcher, Van Lingle Mungo (whose name has been celebrated in a song bearing his own name and written by David Frishberg), bashed the Giants two in a row in the Giants' home territory, the Polo Grounds. Meanwhile, the Cards took two in Cincy to win it all.

September can be the month not only of great collapses but also of brilliant surges. The Cubs of 1935 won twenty-one games in a row in September, and in 1938 they edged out the Pirates in the last few days of the season with the help of a famous "homer in the gloamin' " by catcher Gabby Hartnett. (Everyone thought it was too dark to see the ball, since it was six o'clock in the evening at Wrigley Field, but Gabby connected off Mace Brown. The blow finished the Pirates.) Another catcher, Cincy's Willard Hershberger, who subbed for Ernie Lombardi, cut his throat and died in a hotel room when he thought his bad calls in a late-season game with the Giants cost his team heavily in the pennant chase. Talk about second guessing!

In 1951 the Giants, under Leo Durocher and in Willie Mays's freshman year, won sixteen in a row in August, overtaking the Dodgers, who had been thirteen in front on August 12.

"If we lose this thing, we can only blame ourselves," snapped Carl Furillo, the Dodgers' right fielder. But he was not entirely correct. The Dodgers only partially let it get away. The Giants won it—by winning twenty-nine of their last thirty-four games.

Gene Oliver said he'd jump off the John Hancock Building if the Cubs lost in 1969.

So it goes.

You hear a lot today about guys in a pennant tangle who don't keep their minds on the task at hand. After Hartnett blasted the Pirates out of that 1938 pennant, Paul Waner of the Pirates, a Hall of Famer and one of the best pure hitters who ever lived, moaned, "The trouble with us is that we were trying to win the flag by just watching the scoreboard."

Anyone who tells you baseball is mostly a game of muscles, brawn, and physical prowess doesn't know what he's talking about. In the stretch drive or in crucial World Series games, it's also a game of tremendous mental strength.

The mental strain that a team experiences is often more pronounced for a team that's being pursued than for the one in pursuit. As unlikely as it may seem, many managers claim they'd rather be two games behind in the final week than two games in front. Do I buy that? Hell, no.

There's always pressure to hold on to what you have—whether it's a two-game advantage or two million bucks in the bank. But try being two games back or being two million dollars in arrears: I think I'd opt for being ahead.

Vin Scully, the veteran announcer of thousands of games, has said about the playoffs: "I've seen guys go half crazy from the constant phone calls from well-wishers and ill-wishers. On the field, I've seen a player sitting in the dugout, his head in his hands, for fifteen minutes, totally crushed in spirit, after making a final out in a crucial game. During the regular season that's a scene you'll rarely ever see."

Since 1969, when baseball changed to divisional play, an entire new element of pressure was introduced—the playoffs. The pressure of the regular season, or even the World Series, just isn't comparable. The playoffs are the wedge between the season and the World Series. If you lose, it means you won't be going to the greatest sports event in this country. It's the quagmire before the promised land. It's the Red Sea that has to be crossed. If you don't cross it into the World Series, you're a loser. You're forgotten by Thanksgiving. It might not be just, but it's true. What is pressure, really, but fear of failure? And some players in baseball are more concerned with their fear of failure than they are with the potential rewards of success. When you're out there in the public arena, playing and competing in front of screaming, imploring crowds of forty and fifty thousand people, that fear of failure can be magnified. For some guys it can be crippling. This game can do strange things to men. I've seen it happen.

With the Cards ahead of the Tigers three games to one in the 1968 World Series, and with left-handed pitcher Mickey Lolich going for Detroit, Red Schoendienst nominated Ron Davis, a right-handed hitting outfielder from North Carolina, to play right field in place of the left-handed Roger Maris. Ron had played in one other game in the Series, going hitless.

Looking over at Ron before the fifth game, I could see that he was wired so tight you could have strummed a tune on his chest. When you're wired that tight, there's no way you can perform up to the limit of your skills. There he sat, entranced, not able to even look away from his locker, his eyes as big as saucers, his suffering so obvious that some guys had to turn away because, believe it or not, they were tempted to laugh. Ron's nerves were so exposed you could almost see them. And the fact that he was playing in Detroit in front of fifty-four thousand home fans didn't ease his anxieties, either.

With one out in the bottom of the seventh and the Cards ahead 3–2, incredibly, Detroit manager Mayo Smith let Lolich bat. It turned out to be an inspired move. Lolich hit a looper to right field, where Davis failed to get a jump on the ball and let it drop in front of him. Playing too deep, Ron may have been deceived by the fact that Lolich had connected for a home run off Nelson Briles in the second game—the only home run of Lolich's entire career!

Mickey's single seemed to open the floodgates. The Tigers went on to score three times in the inning and win the game 5–3. They also took the next two games, providing all the Cards, including me, with a haunting memory of a World Series that got away.

I'm not suggesting that Ron Davis's tensions did us in. That would be a cruel postmortem to make on the guy, but the difficulty he had in handling pressure was so overt that I've got to mention it here. Ron, wherever you are, I hope you're enjoying life more than you did that day in Detroit nineteen years ago.

While I can't personally relate to what Ron went through that day, it's interesting to look back and compare my 1964 World Series with my 1967 Series. In 1964 I didn't realize the magnitude of a World Series and the far-reaching effects such naked exposure could bring. For me, that Series was simply an extension of the 1964 season. As far as I was concerned, it just gave me a chance to play ball for a few more games. As a result, I didn't succumb to the pressure and wound up hitting .478 as well as getting the game-winning home run in the tenth inning of the fifth game.

Now, in 1967 Orlando Cepeda and I finished one-two in the Most Valuable Player voting for the regular season. Consequently, we were *expected* to carry the Cards in that year's

Series. True to form, we were co-MVPs in the Series—Most *Vulnerable* Players. We hit .250 *together*, a buck and a quarter apiece. It wasn't the pressure of the Series itself that was my downfall, it was the pressure of the *expectations* that got to me. Expectations don't necessarily match performance.

Even in broadcasting that kind of pressure can stymie you. When I did the 1985 Series in the ABC booth, I put extraordinary pressure on myself because I felt that people's expectations were so high. But I don't feel like I did a good job in the first game. I was just too damn nervous. I felt that people wanted more—and what they got was less. Al Michaels's total professionalism eventually helped bridle my nervousness. With his help I did calm down and did a good job the rest of the way.

Is there anything players can do to defuse all the anxiety and tension that build up, sometimes to an awful climax? Is there any antidote that'll work on the nervous system?

Some teams these days even hire psychologists to try to work things out for the guys. In 1973 we had a team psychologist. By the end of the season, we had him running for cover. It's *tough* to analyze a bunch of ballplayers in the middle of a hard season. How do you analyze a guy like Ray Busse, who, in 1973, made four errors in one game and then refused to come out for the ninth inning? He just wouldn't leave the tunnel. In fact, he never left the tunnel again, because he was sent back down to the minors the next day.

It was a little weird having a guy with a pipe sticking out of his mouth hang around watching our behavior. Imagine someone doing it in your office—every time you go to a water cooler, there's someone staring at you, taking notes. I don't think it worked particularly well that year with the Cards, but I do think it's a good idea if it can be better executed. It's hard for a player to be positive all the time, especially after he screws up in front of fifty thousand people. What's wrong with getting some help, especially if it can make you feel better and play better?

I'm no psychiatrist, but it's always been pretty clear to me that what most guys need to allay the demons of the pennant frenzy is some distraction, something to take their minds off themselves, something to lighten the mental load.

Hypnotists have been put on the payroll, too, although I've never quite figured out how one of these guys could help you swallow better or sweat less in a tough situation.

Athletes are often in excruciatingly stressful situations. They are exposed to great extremes—the highs and the lows. To get away from the lows, they sometimes resort to extreme measures. I'm talking about ballplayer humor now. It's a hard thing to communicate because out of context it can seem goofy, dumb, sometimes even cruel. But I'm telling you that *in* context not only is this stuff funny, it can be a lifesaver.

I used to love to clown around when I was with teams that were chasing after pennants. It helped ease the strain for me, and I think it might have helped some of my teammates, too. Comedy can definitely help to relieve anxiety.

I didn't do it all alone, though. I had Tom, a Neanderthal-faced mask I used to drag around with me. Tom did everything but draw weekly pay from the Cards. He went wherever I went. When you've got a bunch of guys spending all their time preoccupied with scoreboards and shuffling from one airport to the next, checking in and out of hotels, peering through dirty bus windows, and having a tough time holding down their fast food, you need something to laugh about.

I've got to give proper credit here for the use and co-creation of Tom to Ray Sadecki. Ray, who roomed with me, had the quickest wit I'd ever seen or heard. The key to Tom's success—and Ray's genius, there's no other word for it—was timing and detail. With a simple tie, a coat, or some other important prop, Ray could bring Tom to life in the most hilarious of circumstances. He used to love to bring Tom out on airplanes, and the lengths he'd go to get the gag right were extraordinary. Once he propped up Tom on the toilet in the rest room of a plane. He put the tie on Tom, wrapped a sport jacket around a white pillow—he went for the formal look that time—and even took a few puffs of a cigarette before sticking it into Tom's mouth so the smoke would curl just so. Then he told the stewardess that there was a foul odor in the rest room and he suspected someone was sick in there. "You'd better take a look," he told her. When she rushed in, she saw this strange character sitting on the pot with a cigarette in his mouth. We broke up.

We also would go to any lengths to surprise a teammate with Tom's appearance. We loved to make Bob Uecker laugh, especially, and we'd plot and scheme for hours if necessary to get that laugh.

Once we were supposed to be in our room—it was after bed check—but we were antsy. We needed some activity. We knew the elevators were well patrolled by Vern Benson, who was checking rooms that night, so, using the hotel stairway, we snuck Tom down to Uecker's floor. We also snuck a huge, stuffed easy chair—one of those chairs that seem to weigh a ton —out of the room. We carried this chair down eight flights of stairs, set it in front of Uecker's room, and set Tom up, making him as comfortable as we could, a stogy stuck in his mouth. Then we knocked on Uecker's door, got the hell out of there, and waited around the corner until we heard Uecker's laugh. That's all we cared about. As soon as we heard it, we were happy to go back to bed.

Critics can dismiss such behavior as child's play or as a product of a sophomoric mentality, but it definitely serves a purpose. You've got to understand that this type of humor serves as a diversion from the extraordinary pressure. Keeping things light and loose around the clubhouse doesn't count in the saves column for a relief pitcher or register as a run batted in, but you never know just how much good it does for the spirit—and the stomach.

Some guys are better than others around the locker room. Bob Uecker was a master at it. For instance, in the last days of the 1964 season the Cards had a meeting to divide up our shares, not knowing if we'd be receiving first-place or fourth-place money. If you remember, the Giants were eliminated that year on the next to the last day of the season and finished fourth. Bing Devine, our general manager, had been fired in early August, and Roger Craig, one of our pitchers, got up to make a plea for Bing. "Guys," he said, "if we do go on to win this thing, I think voting Bing money would be an insult. But if we win, I do think we should at least give him a ring." Without a second's hesitation, Uecker said, "I'll call him." The place fell on the floor.

I've heard there were a few Yankees in the late 1970s—

Lou Piniella, Catfish Hunter, Graig Nettles—who could all keep things light and loose.

Sweet Lou, who's now the Yankee manager—at least for the moment—knows how to give and take a needle, a talent that's helpful when the passions of a pennant race are on high boil.

In 1978, in that famed Red Sox playoff game, Lou made one of the truly amazing and most memorable defensive plays I've ever seen when he stabbed, on one bounce, Jerry Remy's fly ball to right field. That play prevented Rick Burleson from coming home with the tying run from second base.

Well, a couple of years after that, Reggie Jackson—a bit more renowned for his hitting than his fielding—was really on Lou's case, taunting Lou about his defensive abilities. Lou just turned to Reggie and came back with: "Reggie, if you'd have been in right field on that one, we'd have been watching the World Series on television then, instead of playing in it."

One thing about Reggie, even though he has a big ego, he has a sense of humor and can be surprisingly self-deprecating in his humor.

Catfish Hunter and Piniella used to go at each other pretty good. Catfish would say, incredulously, to Piniella, "You were traded for Jim Wohlford. What is a *Wohlford*?" And Piniella would come back with, "If a guy robs from a 7-11 store, they'll send him up for ten years. But some guys can steal over a half million from Steinbrenner and still walk around a free man. You're a thief." Oscar Gamble, who'd just come back to the Yankees via San Diego, and who had a tremendous contract even though he was a platoon player, jumped up and said, "Please don't talk about anybody stealin'!"

You've got to try to laugh off pressure and tension. As Joe Torre, who once managed the Mets and Atlanta, used to say, "There's a big difference between being tense, which is bad for you, and being intense, which can be good for you."

Sure, the game has to be taken seriously, but humor helps you cope. In baseball circles, guys who laugh are perceived as guys who don't take their jobs as seriously as they should. In fact, I think a case could be made to show that ballplayers who have a sense of humor are probably the ones who take the game of baseball *most* seriously. It may sound strange, but my experience with comedians shows that, beneath their joking veneer, they are usually extremely serious people. The same applies to athletes. Life should always be approached from the lighter side, especially in the stomach-gurgling days of a fading pennant race.

It angers me that the baseball establishment doesn't realize this. One of the things that promotes failure is fear. And humor is one of the best devices for corralling fear.

Where Have All the Pep Talks Gone?

> Just hold them for a few minutes,
> fellas. I'll think of something.
>
> —CHARLIE DRESSEN,
> BROOKLYN DODGERS MANAGER

Managerial rhetoric, more familiarly known as the pep talk, boasts a long and honorable history. Baseball managers pursued such free-form group psychology long before college football's Knute Rockne delivered his "win one for the Gipper" speech to a locker room full of highly suggestible Notre Dame players in 1928. Thus inspired, the underdog Irish proceeded to deliver a swift kick in the pants to a favored Army team.

According to historians, Rockne was beaten to the verbal punch by the gentlemanly Connie Mack, among other orators. Mr. Mack—or Mr. Cornelius McGillicudy, as he was named at birth—addressed his troops and pointed his bony fingers in the faces of his Philadelphia Athletics in the early 1900s. It is said that Mr. Mack was quite masterful at delivering what amounted to temperance lectures.

A contemporary of Mr. Mack was John J. McGraw, one of the most accomplished bench jockeys in baseball history. McGraw was also reputed to be as joltingly foul-mouthed as a longshoreman when trying to rouse his New York Giants.

So when the Mets' Davey Johnson resorts to a well-turned phrase or the Dodgers' Tommy Lasorda beseeches his athletes in his almost daily revival meetings, they're not up to anything new. What is new, perhaps, is the attitude that some of today's managers have toward meetings. In short, they're not all believers in it.

Take Pete Rose, for example. Pete has turned out to be a very effective manager. In between base hits, Pete pays close attention to such managerial matters as his pitching rotation, his Cincinnati starting lineup, and the strategic use of pinch hitters. He even put beer and TV back in the Reds' clubhouse after some previous killjoys had banned them (Pete isn't entirely opposed to various forms of psychological manipulation of his personnel).

But one day, when a reporter asked him if he held many team meetings, Rose, a guy who usually likes to stretch his vocal chords, squinched up his nose.

"Meetings? Hell, players don't like to hear all that bullshit. If they're playing hard and still losing," he said, "what can anybody tell them or say to them that'll make things any different?"

Rose then pointed out that Dave Bristol, who had been one of Pete's managers with the Reds in the late sixties, used to call team meetings almost every time the team lost a game.

"The guy would come into the clubhouse after a defeat," recalled Pete, "and he'd say, 'Get that damn food outta here!' Then he'd throw the food around pretty good. Now what good does that do anyone? If you're gonna lose, why do you have to starve, too?"

Pete Rose is some kind of philosopher, even if he might have a hard time explaining the current Cincinnati club policy that prohibits facial hair. Where would that leave bushy-faced gents like Abe Lincoln, Albert Einstein, or Tom Selleck if they wanted desperately to play for Pete? (One owner, Charlie Finley of the Oakland Athletics, actually paid his players $300 back in 1972 to sprout mustaches. That bunch of hirsute characters went on to win three straight world titles!)

Dick Howser is now battling a courageous fight against brain cancer. In 1985, he steered his underdog Kansas City

team to a world championship after the clairvoyants gave the
Royals as much chance as Mondale had against Reagan in 1984.
Dick was quick to admit that his oratory hadn't played much
part in the whole process.

"When things looked bad for you in the playoffs with
Toronto," a reporter inquired, "did you decide it would be a
good time to talk to your players?"

"We didn't talk our way to the American League West
championship," he said. So much for Dick Howser and pep
talks.

Where do I stand—or sit—on meetings?

Well, for one thing I can tell you I've been to enough of
them, led by guys like Johnny Keane, Solly Hemus, Red Schoendienst, Gene Mauch, and Danny Ozark. Some of these ora-
tions have been funny, dry, and commonsensical. Others have
been witless, ungrammatical, and nonsensical.

I'd have to peg these gatherings, on a day-to-day basis, as
being overrated. It seems to me that inspiration comes more
from the gritty example set on the field—by a Pete Rose or a
Dale Murphy—than it does from a sermon. Inspiration, too,
can come from a single word, rather than from a thousand
words. The gamy exhortation of a well-meaning Danny Ozark
—"Come on, you guys. I can hit this guy with my cock!"—
might be every bit as effective as the religiosity of someone like
Alvin Dark.

Our society in general is much more critically oriented
than it is geared to be supportive. Negative comments are
much easier to dole out than are compliments. With that in
mind, pep talks can serve some useful purpose—when a team
is all revved up. In my eyes, you don't deliver tongue-lashings
when a team is down. It doesn't make any sense to harangue
a locker room full of down-in-the-mouth guys. They're already
down; they don't need a manager to make them feel any
lousier.

Get 'em when they're up—and try to keep 'em up!

Leo Durocher, apparently, was the easiest manager in the
world to play for on a bad team, but the toughest on a good
team. Understanding was his modus operandi if you were
going poorly. But if you were going well, he never let a day go

by without reminding you what a responsibility you had *be-cause* you were good. That kind of faith makes most ballplayers play harder. And better. Mike Schmidt once said that the reason he was such a big Dick Allen fan is that Dick "was the first guy who told me how good I was."

Not everyone agrees with me—or Leo or Mike—of course.

For instance, after the Mets were practically bombed out of Philadelphia's Veterans Stadium in June 1985, with the Phils scoring twenty-six runs on a mere twenty-seven hits, Manager Davey Johnson didn't hesitate for a moment to close the door to his clubhouse and paint a word picture for the boys. His philippic lasted about ten minutes, and when it was over some of the players emerged from the lathering agreeing with what Davey had said. They agreed, too, that he should have said it when he did.

In particular, I remember pitcher Ron Darling, the Yalie, insisting that Johnson's words were necessary. "It was like a wakeup call," said Ron. "If they don't respond to what he said, then we're in trouble."

It should be pointed out here, in fairness to Johnson's policy, that the Mets went on from that low point to play good ball. Cause and effect? Who knows? But the essence of what Davey had to say is worth repeating here.

"What happened here tonight was like being in a fistfight," I imagine Johnson suggesting. "It's like you're lying on the ground and they keep beating on you. If you ever recover, it's something you don't forget. They kicked our butts completely. As far as I'm concerned, this better be a rallying cry. I know we're better than this, gentlemen. When you play tomorrow, carry this game on the field with you. Do not forget what happened out there tonight."

Davey, it should be pointed out, is also one of the biggest advocates of telling a guy how good he is. The game is changing in that regard. Johnson, Lasorda, Tanner, Herzog, Roger Craig—they're all sensitive to a ballplayer's need for positive reinforcement. But, as Davey's story reminds us, sometimes shock tactics can certainly be effective.

Keith Hernandez, the Mets' brilliant first baseman, thought that night's session was the "best meeting" he could remember. And don't forget, Keith had once listened to Whitey Herzog, a guy who could deliver some pretty good lines, when Keith played for the Cardinals.

The Cards, dating back to Frankie "Oh, those bases on balls!" Frisch's tempestuous years with the Gashouse Gang, have been pumped up with more than their share of fiery words. Frisch always had his troubles keeping his boisterous, rambunctious crew working for the common cause in the 1930s.

Before the 1934 World Series between the Cards and the Tigers, Frisch thought it might be worthwhile to remind his colorful athletes—among them Leo Durocher, Pepper Martin, Joe Medwick, and the Dean brothers—that they were in for a tough scrap. So Frankie drummed up a meeting.

I would like to have been there, first to have heard Frankie talk, then to have listened to what guys like Dizzy, Leo, and Ducky had to say about their leader's words—and not under their breath, either.

Dizzy responded publicly to the widespread rumor that the Tigers had scheduled a pre-Series pep session by their manager, Mickey Cochrane, an aggressive Hall of Fame catcher whom I tried to emulate in my own career.

"If them guys are thinkin'," Dizzy said, laughing, "they're as good as licked right now." Dizzy always believed in the theory of positive pitching, rather than the power of positive thinking.

In my years with the Cards, after Frisch's generation had become history, Red Schoendienst took over as an occasional locker room orator. There was one time in 1966, Red's second year as manager, when the team wasn't doing very well. So Red, in his rather diffident manner and with a bit less preparation time than Abe Lincoln put in on his Gettysburg Address, delivered one of the most unforgettable talks I've ever heard in a locker room.

"I've got something I want to say to you guys," began Red. We waited eagerly for the precious words that might propel us to new heights of emotional fervor and a better position in the flag race.

"This is it," he continued. Pause.

"Run everything out." Pause.

"And get in before midnight." Pause.

That was it—nothing more, nothing less.

Needless to say, all of us, in deference to the seat of power, obeyed Red to the letter. Unfortunately, although we kept running, we kept losing.

Another Schoendienst pep-'em-up I recall with fondness occurred when the Cards journeyed to Japan in the off-season of 1968. Having just lost the World Series to Detroit after leading three games to one, most of the guys cared as much about being in Japan as about being in the Arctic Circle. (In fact, we were close to the Arctic Circle; we were in Sapporo.) We lost three of our first five in Japan, and Red must have felt obliged to do something about this messy state of affairs. With an unexpected knack for history, Red expressed the feeling that all eyes were on us as we invaded the land of our bitter enemy of World War II.

"I want you men to know that this is like a war between countries," Red said, grim-faced, as the players regarded him with amazement. Schoendienst was never invited to join the United States diplomatic corps in Japan.

Sometimes a ballplayer who has a way with words and phrases will preempt a manager's role. During one of the last years in which I played with the Phillies, Mike Schmidt, who normally is not anxious to assume the role of clubhouse leader, decided that five straight Philly losses were enough. Also in a desperate slump of his own, Mike, who likes to analyze and talk over problems—as opposed to being talked to—felt the pep talk therapy might work on himself as well as on his teammates.

"Some of you guys might take this seriously, and some may not," Mike began. He then proceeded to deliver about a five-minute soliloquy. I don't remember what he said—and I don't know how motivationally effective it really was—but he did vent his anger and frustrations, and most of the guys seemed to pay attention.

A few moments later, batting in the unaccustomed spot of leadoff man, Mike went out and hit a first-inning home run. So clearly his speech worked—at least for him.

As a rule, ballplayers are not the best public speakers or debaters. Why should they be? They haven't been trained in the forensic arts. So sometimes, when they choose to deliver talks with a message to their teammates, their efforts can backfire miserably.

Tug McGraw, a verbal guy who always says what's on his mind, opted to deliver a clear-the-air speech after the Phils clinched the National League East in 1976.

What was he clearing the air about? Well, it appeared that after the clinching in the first game of a doubleheader at Montreal, some of the black players, including Richie Allen, weren't very visible on the bench during the second game. As a matter of fact, Allen went home to Philadelphia after the first game. Tug and a few other players wondered what the hell was going on, and there were a lot of unhappy murmurs in the clubhouse.

Tug was more pissed off a day or so later when Richie, with Manager Danny Ozark's permission, didn't bother to return for the next game.

"Some of us white guys looked around," said Tug in his oration, "and wondered where the black players were." He kept saying things such as "Don't get me wrong" and, to Dave Cash, "Dave, you're black and I like you," and, of course, it all came out wrong. There was no harm intended, but the more he searched for the right words, the more muddled the speech became. Tug was trying to say that all the Phils, black and white, had worked to produce the victory. But it just didn't come out quite that way. What started out as National Brotherhood Week ended up as bad diplomacy.

Following the sixth game of the 1985 World Series between the Cards and Kansas City, Manager Whitey Herzog of the Cards sorely felt that his men needed more than lame excuses and umpire baiting as they confronted a seventh game. The Cards' mood was dark and seemingly self-defeating. It was a losers' mood, and Whitey must have perceived it.

So, prior to the final game at Kansas City, Whitey collected his best verbs and adjectives and met with his dejected constituency.

"You won more games than anybody else this year," Herzog reminded his players, "and if you win one more, you win the Series. Win and there's a parade for you at noon in St. Louis. Either way, there's a dinner for you tomorrow night in St. Louis. But whatever happens, happens."

What happened, of course, was that Whitey's words didn't do a damn bit of good. His restraint and soft sell didn't do the job. His less-than-cocky Cards were blown right out of the premises. Did the pep talk fail? No, it's more likely that the Royals succeeded.

In 1984 Sparky Anderson's Detroit team mopped up the world, dynasties were predicted, and Sparky was more euphoric than usual. In 1985 they found themselves floundering, and Sparky didn't like it one bit.

As I told you, I believe that at a time like this managers should avoid the grouchy put-down, but Sparky wasn't buying that approach. He assembled his declawed Tigers one evening before a game with Oakland and laid out just how he felt. Which wasn't very good.

After his grievances had been aired, Sparky told the media —and thus the world—what he'd had to say to a team that only a year before had been the pride of Detroit and the American League.

"Don't tell me it's lack of concentration," growled Sparky. "Don't tell me you're struggling at the plate. Don't tell me it's lack of preparation. Just tell me you're terrible."

The long faces got longer. The downbeat oration simply didn't spark (pun intended) any renewal of winning habits, if that's what Anderson had anticipated. What must be made clear here is that, most likely, Sparky was frustrated and just wanted to get a load off his chest. It's sort of like a parent-child relationship. In this instance, Sparky was reacting to his "child's" bad behavior. He wasn't necessarily disciplining the team for its own good. He was just ticked off and needed to express that. The Tigers finished third, by the way, behind Toronto and New York.

If I had to make a guess, I'd say that Los Angeles's Tommy Lasorda remains the leading advocate of the inspirational pep talk. He thinks it helps get his players' heads together. He's a back-slapper, a praiser, and a cajoler—rarely a scold, but always quotable.

Perhaps Tommy reached his quotable peak when he welcomed his Dodgers to Florida for 1985 spring training and immediately launched into his "patriotic" theme.

"If the president of the United States informed me I had to take twenty-five guys to Nicaragua to fight for the United States," said Tommy, according to the story in *The New York Times*, "I'd take you twenty-five guys who are going to play for me."

There was dead silence in the locker room.

Then Orel L. Hershiser 4th, a tall, singularly mild-looking right-hander, spoke up.

"You better make that twenty-four, skipper," Hershiser said, "and one conscientious objector."

Another great Lasorda meeting came in June of 1985, when Tommy wanted to calm the Dodger waters. After he had had his say, Tommy turned to Pedro Guerrero, who he announced was moving from third base, where Guerrero hated playing, back to the outfield, where he was more comfortable. "I do want to ask you one thing, Pete. You know that you have to anticipate every ball being hit to you when you're playing in the infield. What did *you* think about?"

Pete promptly replied, "Two things. Number one, I was hoping the ball wasn't hit to me. Number two, I was hoping the ball wasn't hit to Steve Sax." Sax, of course, is the Dodger second baseman who's had plenty of fielding problems.

There are some guys these days who would prefer a prayer meeting in the clubhouse to a managerial harangue. That's their privilege, of course, but I've never been quite able to understand what being born again or expressing Christian fellowship among athletes has to do with playing baseball.

In my opinion, baseball "chapel" doesn't belong in a baseball locker room any more than a pepper game belongs in the aisles of a church. ("Chapel" consists of organized prayer meetings among the players. Bible verses are often recited in these sessions, which invariably take place on Sunday, but occur on other days as well.) There are some players around who agree with me on this, but when you get into peer intimidation (which baseball chapel is, in a way), guys have a hard time backing away from it or saying out loud what they might think.

Too often, players will use God as a cop-out. Occasionally, around the league you'll actually hear wins or losses attributed to "God's will." Jimmy Frey, when he was a coach with the Mets, once set Pete Falcone, a devoted member of baseball chapel, down with the question "Do you think God would mind if you threw your breaking ball over for a strike every so often?" It really is up to the individual to perform or not to perform. I seriously doubt that God is interested in the outcome of a ball game.

Everyone in this complex, troubled world seems to be reaching out and searching for something, but I don't think prayer meetings are going to help with base hits, good pitching, stolen bases, home runs, or even a good sacrifice bunt. George Will, the conservative columnist with a lifetime addiction to the Cubs, wrote recently that the "decline of Baltimore pitching has coincided with some of the Birds' pitchers becoming born again. . . . Religion is fine in its place, but whatever became of the red-white-and-blue principle of a wall of separation between church and dugout?"

I think there should be one.

The Not-So-Gentle
Art of Managing

I pitched for Casey Stengel before
and after he was a genius.
—WARREN SPAHN

Soon after I joined the Mets' broadcasting team, I was invited to engage in "preliminary" talks about the manager's job in Montreal. The Expos probably figured I had managed from the booth long enough. (This, by the way, is a common but mostly unfounded criticism of some broadcasters by managers.)

However, Montreal never did hire me, or even offer me the job although I did become an expert in preliminary talks. I realize now that I'm a very lucky guy. Managing is too insecure, especially compared to the security of a broadcasting career. In the booth you're responsible for yourself; as a manager your fate is destined by a roster of other people.

Everybody knows that managing a big-league club is supposed to make your hair turn white before its time. The past strains and challenges leave their everlasting scars. Look at Sparky Anderson's silvery dome. Take a look at Gene Mauch. Managers get that way by having to wet-nurse ballplayers and trying to be all things to all men.

They've got to be strategists, disciplinarians, psychiatrists,

policemen, magicians, father figures, public relations special-
ists, after-dinner speakers, you name it. And, of course, all of
the aforementioned are secondary to the job of winning pennants.

There have been managers who were paid for not managing. There have been managers who have quit even before the
season got under way. There have been managers who have
upped and quit after one game. Eddie Stanky, the manager of
the Cards for several years before I got there, did that in 1970
with the Texas Rangers.

"When the game ends," Stanky, known as the Brat, said,
"you go back to your hotel room and stare at four walls. I don't
want to die in some hotel room on the road."

Eddie Sawyer resigned as manager of the Phillies after his
team suffered an opening day defeat in 1960. "I'm forty-nine
years old and want to live to be fifty," he said as he stepped
down.

Chick Stahl, an outfielder with a lifetime batting average
of over .300, is on record as the only big-league manager ever
to commit suicide—a most surprising stat. He swallowed car-
bolic acid at the Red Sox spring training camp in March 1907
at the age of thirty-four. Stahl may be the only documented
suicide among all of baseball's managers, but who knows how
many have worried themselves into disease, early dismissal,
migraines, quick retirement, or premature death?

There's a typical little story about a former big-league
manager who attended the seventh game of the 1956 World
Series between the Brooklyn Dodgers (managed by Walter
Alston) and the Yankees (managed by Casey Stengel). The guy
had nursed an ulcer for years, so even before claiming his seat
he visited a refreshment stand and ordered a container of milk.

"How come the cow juice?" a friend asked him. "You
haven't got a team in the game today."

"Yeah, I know," the ex-manager replied. "I'm just drinking up for both managers."

(Stengel always proclaimed that he never got ulcers—he
gave them to other people.)

Don't get me wrong, though. Managing a big-league team
has always intrigued me. The thing that most intrigues me is

that the job, in terms of how important it is to winning and losing ball games, has almost always been overrated—and in some cases underrated.

Traditionally, for instance, baseball has lived and died with the sacrifice bunt. But these days—as long eschewed by Earl Weaver and now promoted by Davey Johnson—a three-run homer tops a sacrifice anytime.

I played for lots of managers. Some were very smart men with agile minds. Gene Mauch fits into that category. He's got a reputation not for being a risk taker, but for being conservative in the early innings, for playing for one run too often. He's also still pining for a championship after over two decades of managing.

Gene is the best defensive manager I've ever seen. One common criticism, however, with which I agree, is that he manages his offense defensively. Another is that he has a tough time communicating with his players. I don't think this is true. Gene's a good communicator. He may be a bit too impatient, which could be what he communicates so well.

When Gene managed the Expos, he had a six-foot-three, two-hundred-pound left-hander named Balor Moore, out of Smithville, Texas, on his roster. If he was known for anything, Balor was known as the guy who gave up Mike Schmidt's first major-league home run, in 1972. I know. I called for the pitch.

Mauch was becoming increasingly dejected about Balor's ineffectiveness. In total exasperation one day, Mauch, never really a profane man, went up to his pitcher and hissed, "Moore, you're nothing but a big cunt!"

Trying to absorb the shock of his manager's colorful remark and choosing his words carefully, Moore responded in an equally colorful way.

"You might say," he began, in his laconic, Southwestern manner, "that you don't necessarily like the way I pitch, or you might say you don't care much for my curve or my fastball, or you might say I'm nuthin' but a fuckup. But I gotta tell you one thing, Gene, that I just absolutely am not and never will be a big cunt!"

I'll say this for Balor: He refused to be intimidated, even by an intimidating guy like Mauch.

Managers are in a cruel occupation, so it shouldn't come as a surprise to anybody that managers can get pretty cruel at times. When players and teams don't live up to their expectations, they can get frustrated—and mean as hell.

One manager I know of had a player on his roster he never liked. He didn't have much use for the player's wife, either. The fact that the player always brought his wife to spring training didn't help to endear him to his manager.

"Why do you think this guy always brings his wife down here to spring training?" the manager snarled at a reporter one day. The reporter said he hadn't the slightest idea.

"So he doesn't have to kiss her good-bye," answered the manager.

Like the catcher with his pitcher, the manager should be a "friend" to every player on his club. That doesn't mean he has to go out and drink with his players or attend lousy movies with them or write them sweet little notes about what charming guys they are. It means he should be around and available to his players. It means he should listen to them. It's not a question of closeness. It's a question of being on hand to respond to complaints, grievances (real or imaginary), and problems. A lot of managers take the old party line that they're not there to win popularity contests. Why not? While respect is obviously a prime ingredient of success, doesn't it make sense that you can communicate better with a friend? And isn't lack of communication the most common reason cited for a manager's dismissal? You'd better believe this is true.

A manager can be like Tommy Lasorda. That's one way to go about it. Or he can be like Chuck Tanner or Whitey Herzog, wise and pleasant but firm in their relationships with players.

The guy on the club who's always the toughest for a manager to deal with is the pitcher. Pitchers are highly individual people, often not very communicative. But if a manager can't relate to his pitchers, he might as well go into another business.

Good managers never panic. If you ever watched Bobby Cox, the former Toronto manager, in the dugout during a losing streak, you saw that he never blinked an eye. He had himself under control. The same goes for Tanner, now at Atlanta. There's no panic or hysteria with men like these, and the players can relate well to that kind of even-tempered display.

Sympathy isn't what players are looking for. It's intelligent handling. Friendship is not synonymous with sympathy. Sympathy alone would cause managers to blow their jobs even more quickly than they do now. Sympathy, as once was properly stated, is in the dictionary between shit and syphilis.

When I played for Frank Lucchesi in Philadelphia, I asked him for more time in batting practice, since I had been out most of the season with a broken hand and was trying to catch up with my timing and rhythm. Lucchesi wouldn't agree to my request. It was September, we were only seven games out of first (even though in last place), but Lucchesi wouldn't let me get some extra hitting in. The reason was—are you sitting down?—he had given the coaches the entire month off from having to oversee extra hitting. Lucchesi's peculiar logic was that if a guy couldn't hit by September, he wasn't going to learn at that late date.

One day, after taking the horse collar in five at bats, I stormed around the clubhouse, complaining about Lucchesi's policy.

We had a meeting the next day, and he called me a clubhouse lawyer. He said, "Nobody's going to tell me how to run my ballclub." What a shame.

I didn't expect Lucchesi to demonstrate sympathy for my situation. I just wanted him to use his brains, to be empathetic —not sympathetic. Had Lucchesi done that, it would have been better for the ballclub and for me.

A manager has to get twenty-five guys (or twenty-four now) to play all the right notes from the same sheet of music. Baseball may be a game of individuals, but the manager must deal with them as a unit *and* as individuals. The process of managing successfully is a good deal more than platooning players properly—as Davey Johnson does so well with the Mets —or writing out a lineup card without misspelling or sticking the right pinch hitter in at a critical situation or pulling a pitcher out of there at the proper moment.

Handling men and getting the most out of them, whether they're youngsters or guys playing out the string, is the chief challenge of any manager.

There's an old maxim in baseball that the best manager is the one who doesn't manage. The guy who tries to overmanage invariably gets into deep trouble. Like a father might with his Little League son, the manager tries to put too much of himself into the player. (While we're on the subject, I do not like Little League baseball. Too often it's a battle between parents rather than kids having fun on a ball field.)

If a manager can exercise sufficient influence to break down barriers between players—if he can get players to say what they honestly feel about each other and what they're doing—those barriers are bound to come down. You often hear about teams that have become "close units." Close units often win pennants. The question remains: Did they become close as a result of winning, or did the closeness produce the winning environment? I'm not a philosopher, but I think it works both ways.

Some think that managers should not show favoritism. But let's face it: Agnew got fined $10,000 for income tax evasion, Nixon got pardoned. And Ron Darling and Tim Teufel were indicted for getting into a minor scuffle in a bar in Houston. It's too idealistic to pretend that favoritism won't exist. Every manager needs a punching bag, a whipping boy. Chuck Tanner said it best: He only keeps one eye and one ear open. He has twenty-four sets of rules—one for each player.

Discipline is necessary on a club, but the punishment should fit the crime, so to speak.

Sometimes the most unlikely guys turn out to be the most effective disciplinarians. When Johnny Keane took over the managerial reins of the Cardinals at midseason in 1961, after Solly Hemus had gotten us off to a lackluster 33–41 start, he was not expected to be a tough dispenser of punishment. It had often been written that Solly went too far toward being one of the boys. So Keane felt he had to be a bit tougher when he stepped in.

At the age of nineteen, I was not about to test Keane, even if he was generally known as a docile man. But there was a guy on the club who did test him. That was pitcher Mickey McDermott, a southpaw who had had some success previously with the Red Sox and Senators, where his press clips suggested he was slightly addled. A garrulous thirty-three-year-old, Mickey was a night club crooner in the off-season and one season had hit .301 for the Red Sox (remember, he was a pitcher!). Such credentials enabled him to walk around saying "I can pitch, hit, and sing."

After his first few days as Cards manager, Keane called us together for a team meeting. We had no idea what was up. What took place was a painful scene that none of us anticipated.

Pointing to McDermott, Keane said, "We checked your room four nights in a row, and you weren't there." They also checked his room during the day—he was *never* there. As a matter of fact, no one had any idea where he stayed. "We gave you cab fare and we gave you a job. You came to spring training and you were broke. I will not have guys like you tear down the tradition of this organization."

Nobody uttered a word. You could hear a pin drop. The clubhouse was as quiet as an ancient church. In a hoarse voice, McDermott finally spoke up. "John, if you feel that way, maybe I oughtta take my uniform off," he half whispered.

"That's exactly what you'll do. Here's your pink slip," answered Keane, and he pulled the paper out of his pocket. Most players, almost to a man, are released quietly, normally in the manager's office. But Keane wanted this made public. He was making a statement. Mickey never pitched another game in the majors.

Johnny Keane's decisive action had quite an impact. At least it did on me. The general reaction was that he'd been fair and just. Interestingly enough, the team finished out the year playing 47–33 ball under Keane. Could be that Keane knew what he was doing.

The great southpaw Warren Spahn, now sixty-five years old, doesn't think it takes too much to be a manager. In a recent interview he suggested that most managers these days seem to be guys who were once "utility infielders or catchers." He was convinced that a prejudice existed in baseball against making pitchers managers.

"Who gets a manager's job when there's an opening?" Spahn, who pitched no-hitters at thirty-nine and forty, asked a reporter for *The Wall Street Journal.* "It's usually not a pitcher, who knows more about the steal, and the hit-and-run, and about hitters, because it was his job to get them out."

Spahn went on to say that 90 percent of the moves a manager is called upon to make come from the book.

"What really wins games," Spahn said, "is talent and fundamentals that can be taught. Too many managers look over their players' shoulders. Nobody can do a good job with that going on."

Okay, but if Spahn insists catchers don't make very good managers, I'll have to disagree. Al Lopez, Mickey Cochrane, Ralph Houk, Gabby Street, Yogi Berra, and, yes, a guy named Connie Mack all made pretty good managers in their day. And don't forget that Gil Hodges, a wonderful manager with the Mets before he died so tragically young, started out as a catcher.

Some managers are plucked out of the ranks of coaches, but the transition can be difficult. As Don Shula, great football coach of the Miami Dolphins, said about Buddy Ryan, when Ryan took over the Philadelphia Eagles, "Now he's got to answer for the losses."

A third base coach attracts attention because he's out there on the field making moves that are animated and highly visible. A third base coach is technically the manager offensively once the game begins, so it's natural that third base coaches rate high when it comes to managerial consideration.

I don't want to give the impression that managers don't occasionally introduce a bit of strategy into the proceedings. Of course, they do, and some obviously are more alert and enterprising than others. Some prefer to reject hoary tradition by pulling their outfielders in instead of always keeping them deep. Others don't ask their first and third basemen to protect the lines in late innings of games. Others refuse to have a first baseman stay close to a runner at first base when the runner has as much chance of stealing a base as a three-legged hound. (But how many times do you see a first baseman holding a runner on, probably at the insistence of a manager who's hogtied to tradition?)

There's a lot of talk, too, about managers who are particularly adept at signal stealing. I don't know of too many solid examples of this—but I do recall that Gene Mauch used to be able to pick up the interaction between the enemy shortstop and second baseman that would determine which man would cover second base on an attempted steal.

One fielder, according to Mauch's sharp-eyed diagnosis, would shield his face with his glove and open his mouth. This meant the other guy would cover. If the same guy kept his lips closed, that meant he'd do the covering. Mauch couldn't actually see the open or closed mouth—he'd watch the vein in the infielder's neck. If the vein contracted, his mouth was open, and that meant he was saying "You!"—so Mauch knew the other guy would cover. He was *never* wrong.

When I played for Montreal, Gene was so perceptive about these gestures that I added a half dozen hits one year by guiding ground balls through the area vacated by the second baseman.

After I talked about this delectable bit of Mauchian espionage on the air in 1985, Stan Isaacs, the *Newsday* columnist, went to Davey Johnson and asked him why such signals never changed.

"If guys like Mauch can pick these things up, why do they insist on using the same old techniques?" Isaacs asked Johnson.

"A coach working at third base, or anybody else, probably can't pick up those signals," insisted Johnson. "I don't think they can see it or read the veins in somebody's neck."

When I heard what Davey's response was, I further explained how Mauch's signal swiping had been possible. The answer was that the Expos, at the time of such skulduggery, were playing in the intimate, 28,000-seat confines of Jarry Park, which they used when they first entered the National League in 1969. The dugout was quite close to the playing field, affording sharp-eyed characters such as Mauch an opportunity to decipher the exchange between the two infielders.

Looking over the current crop of managers, I'd still have to go with Whitey Herzog of the Cards as the best at what he does. (Whitey knows he's the best, too. Recently he told a reporter that if he were a general manager the first thing he'd do would be to hire himself as manager.) (Augie Busch recently offered Whitey a lifetime contract. Whitey looked at Augie and, realizing he was nearing ninety, said, "Whose life? Yours or mine?")

I'd choose Whitey as the best because he knows how to deal with his players. He knows when and how badly to kick their ass, when to give a pat on the back, and when and how much to flatter. He gets players to work *for* him, not *against* him. He gets across one significant message to his men: They won't be around long, and neither will he, if they don't put out on the field.

Davey Johnson is certainly one of the top managers, too. He proved it by being voted runner-up for Manager of the Year in 1986. For a guy so young, he's got his share of smarts. He's sensitive, understanding, and bright—with and without his Rolaids.

Never forget Chuck Tanner of Atlanta, who doesn't say he was hired to be fired but that he was "hired to be re-hired." Few players don't like to play for him. He's been called "the player's manager," and that's not a put-down. There have been some suggestions that he's too easygoing, but I've always felt he had brains to go along with his congenial manner and optimistic approach.

Sparky Anderson, whose track record really backs up what kind of manager he's been, also belongs on the list.

Speaking of track records, who can argue with the success of Dick Williams? Players say he has an irascible disposition, but they don't pay managers on disposition, just on their position in the standings.

I guess I have to come back to Gene Mauch, too, a man under whom I always enjoyed playing. It's worth repeating what Mauch used to say to us when we sat there marveling at how far Willie McCovey or Willie Stargell had just hit a ball.

"Don't just sit there *oohing* and *aahing*," he'd say somewhat crankily. "Go out there and put a stop to it!"

I don't know what the hell he expected us to do about mile-high, five-hundred-foot clouts, but Mauch was on the right track. Managers are paid to get you to "do something about it."

I Love—and Hate—It: Likes, Dislikes, Pet Peeves, and Gratuitous Opinions

> Ninety feet between the bases is
> the nearest to perfection that man
> has ever achieved.
> —RED SMITH

There's no way you could call me an unvarnished sentimentalist or a professional flag-waver, but sometimes I do get a little carried away by baseball. I don't know if the game is a metaphor for life, as is so commonly uttered, but I do know I've never gone to a ballpark where I felt worse after the game began. I've been in baseball a long time, and there are lots of things about the game I like and a few I dislike. My opinions obviously may not be the same as yours—but isn't that what makes baseball so great? Disagreement is part of the fun.

Opening Day. Most baseball fans regard opening day as a combination of Christmas, Thanksgiving, and a lottery victory all rolled into one. Only two breeds of people are ever treated unkindly on opening day: umpires and politicians. Most politicians don't hang around long enough to attract any fan flak. Take New York City's Mayor Ed Koch, for example. He's a three-out man—he's gone from Shea Stadium after three guys make out.

Opening day in baseball represents a new beginning,

which everybody needs at one time or another. It represents renewal and hope. It represents sunshine sometimes, good feelings, a day away from work, and reassurance that some of the good things in life are still around and flourishing. It's a reminder of many dusty afternoons in summers that are now only misty memories. It represents the first box score in a sea of box scores to come—now fans know exactly what they'll be doing the first thing every morning when they open their newspapers.

A lot of nice things have been said about opening day, but Joe DiMaggio said it best: "It's like a birthday party when you were a kid. You think something wonderful is about to happen."

The National Anthem. Perhaps the only part of opening day I take some minor exception to is the traditional playing of "The Star-Spangled Banner." I'm all for paying respect to our incomparable land with a pregame tribute. But why "The Star-Spangled Banner"? The tune is too tough to sing, even for the pros. Many people may be under the impression that "The Star-Spangled Banner" came with the Constitution. Not so. It's been the national anthem only since 1931. I love to sing, but I don't think I'd accept an invitation to sing the national anthem.

Why can't it be replaced by "America the Beautiful"? The lovely, idealistic words of "America the Beautiful" celebrate the best features of our country. Few patriotic songs in the world can compare with "America the Beautiful." Baseball is played from "sea to shining sea" and under "spacious skies" (at least until domes came in!).

Maybe Commissioner Peter Ueberroth, who likes surveys so much, can take a fans' survey on this issue. I'd like to hear something singable and more representative in our ballparks by the time the two hundredth anniversary of our Constitution rolls around in September 1987.

Hard-noses. I love all hard-nosed guys who play hard-nosed baseball, even when all hope seems to be gone. John Madden has his dirty, gritty interior linemen to revere. I have my players who love to get their uniforms dirty, who barrel into second to turn a sure double play into a force-out, and their defensive counterparts who can turn a tough take-out slide into a difficult double play.

The Battle Between Leagues. For overall speed, aggressive play, and power in pitching, the National League has the edge —in style. But with the crop of youngsters introduced to the American League in 1986 (i.e., Joyner, Canseco, Incaviglia, etc.), style may be overcome by talent.

Astroturf. It may be hard on the knees, but I like it. That's because I was a catcher and I was usually in the dirt part, the cutout around home plate. I loved hitting on the stuff! Also, in plays from the outfield, the ball got to me quicker, which meant I had time to confront the runner with the ball in hand. This is crucial because if you have the ball in your bare hand when making a tag, you never drop it. Never. You can die with it.

Relief Pitchers. Adamantly opposed to the Dave Righetti move to the bullpen initially, I now rate the move as astute, an indication of what I think about short relievers. I don't think a team can win without relief pitchers who can give you that late-inning closeout.

Designated Hitters. I am an antitraditionalist about many things relating to baseball, but I hate the DH, just *hate* it! It changes the nature of the sport.

Women Reporters in the Locker Rooms. Some players, such as Dave Kingman, are just ornery and nasty about it. Others, like Dale Murphy, who has a dignified sense of privacy, don't particularly like it. Personally, I've never had difficulty with the concept, even if one or two of these women journalists are "pecker checkers," with mixed motivations for being around clubhouses.

Club House Meetings. For the most part, they are so much hot air. Once at a clubhouse briefing session, Orlando Cepeda was asked to provide some insight about a certain player he had once played against. Orlando replied, "He's a nice guy!" You get my point?

Old-Timers' Day. Some years ago my garrulous friend Joe Garagiola wrote a best-selling book called *Baseball Is a Funny Game*. Today he'd probably retitle it *Baseball Is a Money Game*. But no matter whether it's dubbed a funny game or a money game, either title is superior to that dreadfully contrived event called the Old-Timers' Game.

To me, the Old-Timers' Games rate somewhere between poison ivy and a rattlesnake bite, with the exception of the Crackerjack Old-Timers' Game. That event's really for the players and is a classy operation. I'm sure many people will sharply disagree with me on this, but I don't like commercialized nostalgia, and that's what Old-Timers' Games are.

These games exploit some players at a time when many of them are atrociously out of shape and in a mental state of disrepair. Most fans who go to Old-Timers' Games usually don't even remember who the Al Weises or Hal Woodeshicks or Art Shamskys are. Sure, they know Mantle and DiMaggio, but that's about it. I can recall seeing one terribly overweight National League pitcher coming to an Old-Timers' Game and slinking around as he tried desperately to hide from public view.

No doubt some of the players who show up for these brief exhibitions can use the token fees they receive, but by and large it's an unnecessary, often humiliating hype and an ill-conceived promo.

The World Series. I love the fall of the year, when everything seems so sharply in focus; the skies are a clear, rich sapphire blue; and the pennant races are sizzling. I love the fall, too, because the World Series—baseball "abstracted to its finest crystal" (as Arnold Hano wrote)—is not far away.

Anticatcher Sentiments. I don't like to hear guys say that such-and-such a player "runs well for a catcher." I think I ran pretty well, better than plenty of other guys. I'm not limiting that claim to catchers. I'm convinced that catchers do as well on the bases as anybody else, often better. Dubbing catchers slow and lead-footed is a bad rap. Which brings me to the subject of stereotypes.

"Jockocracy." Although Howard Cosell has never savaged me personally, I presume I'm included in his "jockocracy," that elite boothful of ex-athletes he's carped about on frequent occasions. He has contended that these jocks have wrongfully invaded the broadcasting business, getting their jobs strictly because they played certain sports well and have marquee value. He concludes that they're a bunch of incompetents who use the language improperly and prepare poorly.

Now I'm sure there have been some jocks for whom Howard's assessment applies. But don't you think that goes for plenty of nonjocks, too?

I don't like stereotypes of any kind, and if Howard is supposed to be open-minded, why does he persist in generalizing?

I'm sure Howard doesn't believe that any racial or ethnic group—blacks, Italians, Jews, Catholics, Latins, Poles—should be stereotyped. He probably wouldn't be caught dead doing that. So why do it with ex-jocks?

Howard has also made disparaging comments about newspaper guys as a group. He rates them as a collective "ogre" called the "print media." Yet I also notice he's employed them to help him with his books. He also now writes for a New York newspaper!

Even if some of the negative things Howard has said about jocks might have been partially true at one time, that may not give them validity now.

Sure, I have my critics. Who doesn't? In this highly exposed line of work you're bound to attract all sorts of comment. But I worked hard—and continue to work hard—to make my transition from jock to broadcaster.

Things I Really Love. I love to bask in the sun. I love black maple walnut ice cream. I love Sondheim, Cole Porter, Berlin's oldies, and Gershwin. I love hotels with piano bars, where I can sing along with the piano player. I love everything about a ballpark, even when it's empty and, of course, also when it's full. I love newspapers and magazines. I love to swap stories with old friends and I love to hear people laugh.

I love broadcasting in New York, where you can buy anything from a toothpick to an elephant.

I love to play baseball name games—especially when the Expos are in town with Raines and Shines, or when the Cubs start a battery of Trout and Lake, or when the Mets once fielded Strawberry, Valentine, and Darling.

I love to play around with words, as in "Should Gooden throw a hook to Bass to see if he bites?"

Warm-Up Jackets. When I see Dwight Gooden wriggle into his warm-up jacket after reaching base on a day when it's hotter than your private sauna, I could throw a small fit. And I often do.

I know that a jacket is supposed to keep a pitcher's arm warm and protected. But who needs warmth on a 90-degree day? When I was with the Cardinals, I used to ride to the stadium on buses in those hot St. Louis summers. And the pitchers used to make me roll up the windows so no draft would hit their valuable arms. How many times have you seen a newspaper headline that read: 95-Degree Breeze Destroys Pitcher's Career!

The only time a pitcher should don a jacket is when the temperature gets to be menacingly cold. If snowflakes the size of white socks are floating down, then, okay, put on the jacket. But otherwise, Dwight (and all other pitchers), do me a favor. Please don't put it on.

Name Tags. Churlishly, I've got to tell you how much I hate hotels that hold conventions. It has nothing to do with the food or the rooms. It's all those people running around wearing name tags.

Why would anyone choose to wear a name tag? Especially when they walk in the street or go out in public? The disturbing part about this whole thing is that these people didn't just forget and leave them on by mistake; they intentionally meant to leave them on. This is sick!

Umpires. I never met an umpire who much cared for catchers turning around and griping about their calls. Umps don't like to be shown up, and players don't show them up if the umps show consistency. All players want from umpires is for their calls to be consistent.

Night Baseball. I love all kinds of baseball, but I love night baseball best of all. Ninety percent of all players probably prefer day ball. I still prefer playing at night.

I'd rather get up late in the day for a night game than get up early in the day for a day game.

Ted Williams. I love larger-than-life guys like Ted Williams. He once told me—and I was surprised to hear it—that he was really sorry that his relations with the Boston press and other writers hadn't been better. He would have treated them differently, he confided, if he had it to do all over again.

Ted still insists that the mark of a really distinguished hitter is his ratio of walks to strikeouts. In Ted's case it was 3 to 1, a truly fantastic figure. How many hitters in any era, including today, come close to this remarkable Williams standard?

Whenever I think about Ted Williams, I recall one of my favorite pieces of baseball writing, from the typewriter of John Updike. Composed after Ted's last game in 1960, it celebrates Williams's final home run. "Like a feather caught in a vortex, Williams ran around the square of bases at the center of our beseeching screaming . . . he ran as he always ran out his home runs, as if our praises were a storm of rain to get out of."

Hustle. I'm partial to guys who play the game as though it were their last game, and I guess Pete Rose, "Charlie Hustle," is the epitome of one. On any team you'd care to name, Pete could be the manager and also play three infield positions and two outfield positions. Charlie Hustle guys always appear to exude endless enthusiasm for the game. Even when they do poorly, they seldom earn boos. That's unfair, of course, to hustling players who often don't appear to be trying hard. Charlie Hustle players, after all, are guys with some ability and style. But the fans' perceptions reward them, even if there are times when they shouldn't be rewarded. A Gilbert and Sullivan lyric says it all, I think: "Things are seldom what they seem; skim milk masquerades as cream."

My all-time Charlie Hustle team includes only guys who have had to do more because they were gifted with less.

FIRST BASE: At first we'll put Rose, who probably has never been booed in a home uniform. (On the road, that's another matter.)

SECOND BASE: Steve Sax. Obviously, there have been many better players to play the position, but none who try harder to play it well.

SHORTSTOP: Larry Bowa. He's a sulker and perennial underdog, cut twice from his high school baseball team, irascible as hell; but Bowa's traits helped him play better. He always fought himself, but his abilities came gushing through anyway —a real rarity. One time he destroyed a washroom with his teammate Buddy Harrelson's bat. Some guys said it was the best swing he had all season. Runner-up: Tim Foli, a.k.a. "Crazy Horse."

THIRD BASE: Don Hoak, old "Canvasback." Always a fighter on a fighting Pirates team, he could be bleeding halfway to death, but he would tell other players not to tip off his manager. One time in 1960, he had a lawn mower accident and suffered a very, very deep gash in his foot. That night he had to play a doubleheader. After the first game he came into the clubhouse, took off his shoe, and there was blood everywhere. He had Band-Aids haphazardly put on this cut that really required stitches. He looked at teammate Bob Skinner and his only comment was "Don't you fuckin' go tell anyone about this." Then he went out and played the second game. Died young.

CATCHER: Gary Carter, first-class competitor who plays hurt. Usually, guys on this kind of team don't have as much talent as Gary, but he does belong here for his hustle. It's a puzzle to me how he failed to project this attitude in Montreal.

OUTFIELD: Tony Gwynn, Paul Blair, Curt Flood. They have—or had—talent, sure. But it's what they did over and above that talent that places them on this team. Curt was one of the underrated guys in the game. He could go 0 for 15 and still pull for the other guys, a very rare quality in baseball—and in life. The ultimate team man. Baseball can use more guys like Curt. Earl Weaver once said of Paul Blair: "He never made a difficult catch." There was a game in 1986 where Gwynn made three assists against the Mets in the first five innings. Those were the best plays I've ever seen in such a short period of time. With all three of these guys, their techniques improved because of sheer hard work.

Talent. Hustle is great, but obviously you need talent to be a major-league ballplayer. These are the most talented players I've run into.

THE PLAYERS: I love the various differences—social, racial, educational, economical, cultural—among the men who play baseball. Guys come from all backgrounds and environments; sometimes they're rich, sometimes poor, lousy, fancy, seamy, enlightened, or ignorant. You'll get a math whiz like Davey Johnson, a painter like Curt Flood, a Yalie like Ron Darling, an offbeat counterculture type like Bill Lee, a straight arrow like Dale Murphy (maybe the nicest guy in the game), a recluse like Steve Carlton, a born leader like Willie Stargell. These differences are what make the locker room so much fun to be around.

I'm going to stick with those men I have seen and played with and against who I think filled out their uniforms and the record books as few before them have done. I never saw Ty Cobb snarl at a pitcher or sharpen his spikes in the dugout. I never saw Babe Ruth hit a homer, except in those grainy old movies where the camera caught him trotting almost daintily around the bases, his beer belly propped up by his celery-stick legs.

I never saw Lou Gehrig, the Quiet Hero, who died the year I was born. I never saw Dizzy Dean, who started broadcasting in St. Louis that year, too. And the last game Lefty Grove ever pitched came a few months before my own arrival in 1941. Sadly for me, the stylish Joe DiMaggio remains a name immortalized in a Paul Simon song. I never saw him play, either. The year I was born he ran off his unmatchable fifty-six-game hitting streak, while Ted Williams, whom I also never saw play, batted .406. Hey, that was some year to be born, wasn't it!

All of these players are generally considered sure things on anybody's all-time all-star team. But to be fair about it, I can't nominate them for my own team. I can't pick Stan Musial, either, because when I played with him those last years of his remarkable career he wasn't exactly the Stan Musial of the early years. And because I played most of my games in the National League and broadcasted mostly Mets and Phils games, I'm going to stick with those National Leaguers I've seen and know. Otherwise, a team like this—my dream team —wouldn't make too much sense. You don't choose a team like that from yellowed newspaper clippings.

FIRST BASE: Those two Willies, McCovey and Stargell, were both explosive hitters. But Stretch McCovey, with 531 homers hit over twenty-one years, also had deftness with the glove that astounded many observers. The first time I looked up at Stretch from my squat position, he was, in truth, a gentle giant. He hit the hardest ball I ever called for, off Alvin Jackson in 1966; I don't think it's come down yet. The fellow who hit the second-hardest ball I ever called for was Stargell. In 1971 he hit a backup slider from Jim Bunning into the right field upper deck tunnel in Philadelphia. He hit it a ton.

We may be forgetting Keith Hernandez here. Keith is the most artistic fielding first baseman I've ever seen. But let's face it—with Keith you don't have the threat of the long ball. Keith doesn't give you the Willies.

SECOND BASE: The best defensive second baseman I ever saw was Julian Javier. Nobody could take Julian out on a double play. He cheated on the double play so much that his nickname was the Phantom. I know there'll be an argument here for Bill Mazeroski, who had the quickest release on a double play ball of any second baseman I've ever seen. But you could take Maz out of a double play, even though you had to go through his tree trunk legs to do it. The glove was almost an appendage to Maz's body, but a slight edge to Javier.

THIRD BASE: As he goes on year after year, providing invulnerable defense and hitting homers at a pace that will inevitably push him over the five-hundred home-run plateau, Mike Schmidt offers a degree of consistency matched by few players and never matched by a third baseman. No contest.

SHORTSTOP: Have you ever seen anyone in the field any better than Ozzie Smith? At times he appears to be playing shortstop on a trampoline. Defensive genius and improved hitter. Maury Wills gets an honorable mention here because he opened up baseball's eyes to what speed can do for a team.

OUTFIELDERS: Willie Mays was the best ballplayer I ever saw, period! What he's done has been chronicled. But to show you how he could get the psychological edge, too, check out this story. In 1963 he came up to me before a game, during batting practice. In that famous high-pitched voice of his he said, "I've seen you block the plate. When I was younger, I cut up catchers. I once sliced up Del Rice from his knee to his asshole." And then, with that puckered smile of his, he said, "But I don't do that anymore."

I'll also take Frank Robinson in my outfield. He was invaluable to any team he ever played for. Big hits, stolen bases, long home runs, a high average, and the ability to field like a demon. There wasn't anything Robby couldn't or wouldn't do on a ball field. More than anybody I've ever played against—and this is the general consensus of guys who played with him—Robinson was a genuine leader on and off the field.

Hank Aaron, of course, was a great hitter who became a fable in his time and the conqueror of baseball's most cherished record, the Babe's 714 home runs. He never failed to put the fat part of his bat on the ball, the way they tell you to in the classroom. Once Lew Burdette and Warren Spahn, the Milwaukee pitchers, sneaked a look at a bat that Hank had used for half a season without cracking. All of the dents on the bat—places where Hank had hit the ball—were in exactly the same place: the "sweet part." Pretty good evidence of how Hank was seeing the ball.

Billy Williams, whose nickname was Sleepy because he appeared to be drowsy until the ball was about a dozen feet away, swung the bat as if it were a switch.

From 1963 to 1970 he was in the lineup every day for 1,117 consecutive games, a model of desire and consistency. He hit over .300 five times and had 426 homers. There's no way he doesn't rate as one of the best outfielders I've seen.

Then, of course, there was that ultimate competitor, the remarkable Roberto Clemente. If you saw him run the bases, hit, and field that right field corner, you'd never forget him. He's now part of the social history of Puerto Rico, where they revere his memory. Intense, prideful, aggressive, Roberto kept getting better with each year. Is there anyone who could rifle a throw to the bases any harder or more accurately than Roberto? Roll out the adjectives; they all apply to Clemente. The only thing he couldn't do was hit with the kind of power that Mays, Aaron, and Robinson could.

CATCHER: There's no competition for Johnny Bench. Enormously strong as a thrower and hitter. The transfer he made of the ball from the mitt to the hand was as smooth and unimpeded as I've ever seen. For pure defense, Jerry Grote belongs on the team. His hands were lightning quick; that was the key to Grote. Johnny Roseboro may have been the toughest man blocking the plate I've ever run into—that man was a human brick wall.

Gary Carter is close but slightly inferior in each category to Bench. Gary would have had a shot at Bench's level if not for all the injuries.

PITCHER: It's too soon to think about Dwight Gooden, but he's clearly been better than any pitcher's been for his first three years.

"Gooden may not be invincible," says Chuck Tanner, Atlanta's manager, "But he's the closest I've ever seen to it."

From the left side, if you're going to go with durability, it's hard to pick against Warren Spahn. But Spahn was going out as I was coming in. I could see the signs of his greatness, but I didn't see him in his prime.

Okay, you say, forget durability. Go for sheer talent. Gotta be Sandy Koufax, who, over a concentrated six-year period, had the most impressive stats ever in the history of the game.

But I've got to go with Steve Carlton. One of the remarkable things about Lefty is not only his durability but *how* he remained durable. Example: He struck out nineteen Mets in 1969. Fourteen years later he struck out sixteen Cubs virtually the same way. He didn't have to resort to any trick pitches. The *quality* of his durability is astonishing.

The three candidates for my all-time right-handed pitcher are Bob Gibson, Tom Seaver, and Juan Marichal.

Marichal, the Dominican Dandy, threw, as Roger Angell once wrote, "like some enormous and highly dangerous farm implement." Masterful with his control, he could throw one of four pitches over on any count. He's Pete Rose's toughest right-hander, but not mine.

Seaver: powerful and daring. What made Tom so fascinating was that he rarely fooled you. You knew what was coming, but you still couldn't catch up with it. It's as though you needed a ladder to get on top of his fastball. I don't think anyone ever broke down or defined the art of pitching any better than Tom.

But the edge here goes to Gibson. What puts him over the top is the irrepressible aggression he brought to the position. Though a remarkable athlete, Gibson can't be categorized as artful in his approach. He was as vicious and unyielding a competitor as I ever saw. His year in 1968 remains unmatched.

Screw-Ups. If I could single out one trait I don't like about many players, it would be their irresponsibility—not showing up on time for appointments, not returning phone calls, not paying bills on time, refusing to do the big and little things in life that people are obligated to do. No, I'm not stereotyping here. It's just that I know too many guys in baseball who, out of ignorance, arrogance, immaturity, or too much money in their jeans, behave this way.

Curt Simmons, that wise lefty who put in so many winning years with the Phillies' Whiz Kids and the Cards, used to get very frustrated with some of the failings of his fellow players. "If it's something good," he once told me with more than a touch of irony, "trust ballplayers to screw it up."

That's an overstatement, perhaps, but there's more than a little truth to it. Spare me from the guys who don't appreciate how much this incomparable game has done for them.

The Wave. I'd like to get some respite from the Wave, that unfortunate fan concoction that's washed over our ballpark shores the past few years. Yes, I know the fans seem to be having fun with it, but there are times when some of the participants in the Wave get pugnacious and unruly. Too many beers can do it, or too little respect for other people's rights.

I watched the Wave get out of hand one day in 1985 at Shea and, employing a fishy metaphor, I said that "a couple of barracuda have surfaced in the Wave."

Maybe the fans will tire of this behavior in the years to come, but unfortunately it seems to be gaining rather than losing momentum.

Batting Practice. Baseball is without doubt the most difficult sport in the world to play well. The most difficult part of this most difficult sport is hitting a baseball with consistency.

I once watched Kareem Abdul-Jabbar, one of the finest athletes in the world, taking some swings against a pitcher in a pregame exhibition. Sad to say, he looked totally out of his environment, even uncoordinated. Imagine calling Kareem uncoordinated!

I love to watch batting practice in spring training, and I love to watch it before every game that I broadcast. I get close to the batting cage and turn my back to it, then close my eyes and try to guess who's hitting by the *sound* of the hits. Try doing that when you come to the game early sometimes.

The All-Star Game. There are few things more satisfying for a major-league ballplayer than to be acknowledged as one of the best in his trade. Selection to an all-star team at midseason gives a player such recognition. Yet there are players who for some unfathomable reason take this honor lightly. A few years ago Garry Templeton, now of San Diego, thought he was worthy of being the starting National League shortstop. Named to the NL squad, but not as a starter, Garry uttered the Ali-esque statement, "If I ain't startin', I ain't departin'."

He wasn't the first or last to bypass the All-Star Game, for one reason or another. But his pithy quote epitomizes the attitude of some players, who would rather take three days off than put in an appearance in baseball's midsummer showcase. I don't understand it and never will.

Baseball Realities
—Good and Bad

Sometimes the best deals are the
ones you don't make.
—BILL VEECK

The following quote appears in *Willie's Time: A Memoir*, by
Charles Einstein:

In 1947, Jackie Robinson's first year in the majors, the St.
Louis Cardinals decided they would not take the field
against a team that included a black player. "If you refuse
to play," president Ford Frick of the National League told
the Cardinals, "you will never play another game of major
league baseball." The Cards played. Fade out, fade in, and
now again it is 1964, with Barry Goldwater saying you can
not legislate what is in men's hearts, and at the height of
Goldwater's campaign for the presidency, white and black
players hugging and kissing one another in celebration of
their World Series victory over the Yankees.

The final out is made, and that is a white catcher from
Memphis exploding from behind the plate like a cork
blown from a bottle to throw his arms around the black
pitcher who made the dream come true.

I was the cork blown from that bottle.

In a ballplayer's life there's nothing that can equal the euphoria of being part of a world championship team.

It happened to me for the first time back in 1964, when I was twenty-two years old. That tumultuous locker room scene is still as clear in my mind as if it happened last season.

I'd been a major leaguer with the St. Louis Cardinals from the time I was seventeen. That year, in a goose bumps finish, the Cards won the National League pennant on the final day of the regular season. Then we went on to win a pressure-packed World Series, with Bob Gibson hanging in to beat the Yankees 7–5 in the seventh game.

Now, with the whole delicious drama over, I was back in the Card clubhouse, savoring every moment of it.

To the victors belongs the noise, and boy, was it noisy. Amid the beer and champagne showers and the chaotic jostling in the crowded quarters that had been our home throughout an incredible season, the Cards were getting used to being champs.

Some of us meandered down to the ramp that led from the dugout to the locker room in old Busch Stadium. It was like a bridge, and the fans could walk underneath it. We congregated there and watched the excited throng. Banners were popping up. It was an adoring, maniacal crowd; it was uncontrolled insanity. I'd never seen anything even *remotely* like that kind of adulation. Five years earlier I'd been in high school, playing in front of 350 people—and most of them had been members of my family!

Back in the clubhouse, I could (and still can) hear Bob Gibson saying "I love you, man!" and I can see Dick Groat, our shortstop and a former college basketball player at Duke, taking crazy jump shots across the clubhouse, using little hunks of cracked ice instead of basketballs. And there was Mike Shannon with a grin wider than a Halloween pumpkin's, and Bill White smiling like I'd never seen before.

I remember Bob Uecker, without a stitch of clothing on, dancing to the dumbest song I'd ever heard—"Pass the Biscuits, Miranda." He was dancing all by himself, somehow putting modern moves to this idiotic song that, for some reason, had been the 1946 Cardinals' rallying song. Uke could dance, too.

But me?

I still hadn't made a single move to take off my Cardinals uniform, even though the two red birds on the shirt front were drenched in a catcher's honest sweat and champagne.

Like some benevolent despot, I waved and shouted to the fans who had gathered to pay their loud respects. These folks hadn't had a St. Louis winner since 1946, and they were loving all of this as much as I was.

All the while a clubhouse guard, Doggie Lynch, kept reminding me that it was time for me to close up shop, put on my clean clothes, and get over to Musial's with the rest of the guys.

"Come on, come on," Doggie kept urging me. "Everybody's goin' over there. Let's go!"

But I looked at him with a blank stare. I felt certifiably looney and didn't understand why he was trying to break up my fun. I felt like Scanlon in *One Flew Over the Cuckoo's Nest* when Jack Nicholson threw him the fishing pole. I had that same vacant stare. Was Doggie trying to break up the greatest moment of my life?

There was more.

That night there was a party at Stan Musial's restaurant, Musial and Biggie's. As we arrived, Diane Taylor, the wife of one of our pitchers, Ron Taylor (who later played for the World Champion 1969 Mets and became the team physician for the Toronto Blue Jays), went around asking everyone as they arrived if they'd seen Ron. We had enough trouble keeping up with ourselves; no one had any idea where Ron was.

About two hours into the party, still no Ron Taylor. Fearing the worst, one of the guards was sent back to the clubhouse to see if he could dig up a clue to Ron's possible whereabouts.

Now, picture this. The guard goes back to the dark clubhouse—which looked as if a typhoon had hit it—and flicks on the light. The first thing he sees is a pair of feet sticking out from under a pile of clothes. Attached to the feet, lying peacefully, contentedly, is the rest of Ron Taylor, who'd done just a tad too much celebrating.

After giving Ron a quick shower, the guard did get him to Musial's party, and I'm telling you, I've never seen a guy before or since who looked so much like a blocked punt.

A few days later there was a Main Street parade in my honor in Memphis. Some fans marching in the parade hoisted signs proposing me for president. More madness! That winter, after things settled down somewhat, the Pasadena Rose Bowl Committee invited Bob Gibson and me to join the Rose Bowl Parade on a float. The other players were to be represented by plastic figures, but the battery would be live. I'd heard of beautiful young women exhibiting their charms in this manner, and even of whales on a flatboat. But Gibby and me! Al Fleischman, from the ad agency representing Budweiser and the Busch family, called me and told me I could bring along my wife, too, at their expense.

I said, "I'm not married."

He said, "Well, get married!"

Three minutes later, I called Anne and proposed.

There were two more World Series for the Cards and me in the sixties, one of them a victory in seven games over the Red Sox in 1967, with Gibby winning three games and me batting a whopping .125. People in New England still think that if Lonborg had had one more day's rest he could've beaten Gibson in that seventh game. Lonborg was so dominant that year, I'm not sure they're wrong.

In 1968 there was a painful series loss to the Detroit Tigers in seven games, after we'd led three games to one. Remember Mickey Lolich's winning three games? Gibson's seventeen strikeouts in game one? Mickey Stanley's coming in from the outfield to play shortstop? Curt Flood's getting stuck in the mud? I batted .333 with one homer. That series setback happened seventeen years ago, but I still think about it today. It was like a bad dream.

After the Cards lost that Series, Bob Burnes of the *St. Louis Globe-Democrat* endorsed the quaint theory that our team had been defeated by its own excessive materialism.

According to him, we were more interested in our clothes than we were in winning! It was the most scathing personal attack on a team I've ever read. And talk about an absurd notion! The idea that we were putting more emphasis on our Nehru jackets and gold chains was totally ridiculous. Talk about grasping for straws. This was an unfair journalistic ploy trying to explain our loss. The simple truth was that Detroit deserved a lot of credit for coming back. I mean, did we win in 1964 and 1967 because we dressed like shit?

Sixteen more big-league years were to follow, making me, as the trivia buffs will inform you, one of only seven modern-day players to play in four decades, from 1959 to 1980. I'm the only modern-day catcher to do it. As one wag put it, I went in one era and out another.

In baseball, as in life, there are good and bad memories. Obviously, I prefer to dwell on the good, though I won't ignore the other side. I was the first—and am still the only—catcher to lead the majors in triples, with my thirteen in 1966. In the 1967 season, when Orlando Cepeda, the Baby Bull from Puerto Rico, was the first unanimous MVP choice in our league's history, I came in second. It was his 280 points to my 136. Hell, I even finished ahead of third-place Roberto Clemente that year.

I had the thrill, too, of being behind the plate for two no-hitters, one by Rick Wise of the Phillies in 1971, the other by Bill Stoneman of Montreal in 1972. What irony that in all those years I never caught a no-hitter thrown by Gibson or Carlton! In the All-Star games of 1966 and 1967 I had three hits in three at bats—a *perfecto!*—and scored the winning run in the tenth inning of the 1966 game in front of a hometown audience in St. Louis.

Again, for the trivia-obsessed, I hit in every position, from leadoff to cleanup to ninth. And if you want me to load on more stats, I wound up with a grand total of 1,387 games behind the plate, which puts me around twenty-third on the all-time list for durability and suffering.

I have the highest batting average for National League catchers in World Series play—.311, with twenty-three hits in seventy-four at bats, over three Series.

Topping it off, they renamed the Double A baseball stadium in Memphis McCarver Memorial Stadium in May 1977. Tug McGraw once asked me why they called it a memorial stadium, since I am still alive. I told him the name referred to my arm, which had died ten years before.

Which reminds me, I did promise a few of those unpleasant realities, too.

Number one is that I never had a strong arm. I always had to work as much as I could on my throwing. Believe me, no one put in as much futile time trying to strengthen his arm as I did.

One of the reasons ballplayers are so sensitive to criticism of their abilities is that a lot of them work really hard to improve. And when you don't improve it's frustrating as hell. White-collar workers can, for the most part, cover up their day-to-day work errors. But try throwing out a runner and having your throw look like an infield fly or having the shortstop call for a fair catch. I can joke about it, but, believe me, to this day I can get uncomfortable thinking about some of my weak throws. It's a little like a southerner's making fun of his preacher—*he* can do it, but don't *you* do it.

I feel as if it's an obligation to make this kind of admission. And I'm not through.

I didn't hit for power. Ninety-seven home runs in twenty years is not exactly in Ralph Kiner's league. I hit the top half of the ball; I had no lift on my swing. People think that power is only strength. Not so. You need strength, but there has to be lift. I was strong. For instance, I'm a stronger man, physically, than Graig Nettles. But Nettles has over three hundred home runs because his style of hitting is based on lift.

These days I'm not exactly haunting the Hall of Fame (I got 16 votes for the Hall in 1986, only 303 votes short of making it—wow, what a close call!). And maybe my bubble gum cards, with me in my pre-seventies crewcut and exhibiting oversized ears, aren't going for a thousand bucks. But, folks, I've been there; I've been through it. I've been down, I've been up, I've heard the cheers and jeers.

One of the most painful realities of playing baseball is getting traded.

After the 1969 season I was traded from the Cards to the Phillies. It was one of those blockbuster deals, as the newspapers like to dub them, involving a lot of big names. Outfielder Curt Flood, who had been one of the finest defensive players in the National League and for the Cards for almost a decade ("His glove was the place where triples went to die" could have applied to Curt, even if it was Shoeless Joe Jackson for whom it was originally written), was the headliner in the deal, along with me. Also in the Cards' package were Byron Browne, an outfielder, and relief pitcher Joe Hoerner.

In return the Phillies sent Richie Allen, a marvelous player, to St. Louis, along with infielder Cookie Rojas and pitcher Jerry Johnson.

In 1969 I had hit .260 with seven homers and 51 RBIs in 138 games, slightly better than my 1968 performance. But even though we won three out of the five pennants from 1964 to 1968, we finished a paltry fourth in the first year of divisional play. Ted Simmons was to blossom, in 1970, into the Cardinals' number-one catcher, and primarily because of my haunting bugaboo—throwing—I became expendable.

Flood refused to report with me to the Phils, preferring to challenge baseball's reserve clause in a celebrated test case, which forced him to give up his 1970 season and his $100,000 salary. He suffered two losses in the lower courts and a 5–3 setback before the U.S. Supreme Court, but there's no doubt in my mind that Curt's action got the ball rolling toward freeing players from the shackles of the ninety-year clause that could tie them to a team against their wills. Those million-dollar contracts of today exist in large part thanks to Curt Flood. But how the battle cost him. After missing the 1970 season, he played about a month and a half in 1971 for Bob Short's Washington Senators. Then he more or less faded away into baseball oblivion.

Since Curt didn't join the Phils, the Cards had to send another player. Initially, that player was to be Mike Shannon. But he developed nephritis, which eventually caused his retirement. So they sent first baseman Willie Montanez to Philadelphia.

Think about this trade for a second. Cookie Rojas, in the

spring of 1970, was sold to Kansas City for $20,000. Jerry Johnson was basically given to the Giants that spring. Dick Allen became the only player ever to hit more than thirty home runs in Busch Stadium—and he missed over six weeks of the season—but he was then traded to the Dodgers for Ted Sizemore and Bob Stinson. Stinson, before ever playing for the Cards, was sent to Montreal for nothing. So Sizemore ought to be proud. Over the course of one year he was, in essence, traded for Tim McCarver, Curt Flood, Dick Allen, Byron Browne, Joe Hoerner, Mike Shannon, Willie Montanez, Cookie Rojas, Jerry Johnson, Bob Stinson and a little cash.

When General Manager Bing Devine broke the news to me about my going to Philly, he said it "hurt" him to do it. That's like a father dangling a razor strop in front of his four-year-old son and saying, "This is going to hurt me more than it'll hurt you." *Bullshit!* Since St. Louis had been my baseball home since my rookie year in 1959, it had to hurt me more than a little, too. But I kept telling myself that that was the way things were in the land of baseball and that being traded was nothing personal.

My wife, Anne, may have had the most practical reaction to the trade, considering that our two daughters, Kathy and Kelly, were four years old and twenty months old, respectively, at the time of the switch.

"We always had the same baby-sitter and the same grocery man," said Anne. "Now we'll have to make other arrangements."

To this day I'll always think that the trade contributed largely to the disintegration of the Cards in the seventies, but that's baseball, too. With the exception of Brock and Gibson, they totally dismantled that club over the space of two and a half years. We all wished we could have stayed with the Cards. We thought we could win. But it wasn't to be. If you go around in life looking for fairness and trying to analyze whether people are getting what they deserve, you're wasting your time. Fairness, to be blunt about it, simply doesn't exist in this world, and I don't say this with any residual bitterness.

By 1972, after an injury year in 1970 and a .278 season in 1971, the Phils figured it was time for me to move again.

At the start of 1972, after forty-five games, I was batting only .237, and the June 15 trading deadline was quickly approaching.

On that night, a couple of hours before the Phils' game started, I received a phone call out of Houston from the manager of the Montreal Expos, Gene Mauch, a man with a reputation for winning lots of games without winning any pennants.

"What would you think about playing third base for me?" Mauch asked.

"What?" I was incredulous.

"If Mike Shannon can do it, you can," Mauch responded, with persistence. "I'll get back to you." And that's the way the call ended.

A half hour later, Frank Lucchesi, the Philly manager, called me into his office.

Lucchesi was trying to avoid looking at me as he talked, but I insisted on staring at his face. (He was a guy with whom I hadn't always had the most congenial relationship. One time, after he had banned the customary two cases of beer on a charter flight on an off day, I pulled him aside in a hotel lobby and told him that the players deserved to be treated as adults. What the hell would cutting off the beer ration prove to anybody? I asked him.)

"We just made a trade," said Lucchesi. "We traded you to the Expos."

"For whom?" I asked. He had probably never heard the word *whom* used.

Lucchesi paused for a moment. "John Bateman," he said finally.

"And?"

"Well, there'll probably be another minor leaguer involved," Lucchesi lied. He knew, and I knew, that it was a one-for-one trade. He was simply too embarrassed and ashamed to admit it.

"If you didn't get any more for me than Bateman," I growled, "you got fucked!"

Naturally, Lucchesi didn't appreciate hearing my estimate of the trade. But I had to say what I did.

With game time still more than an hour away, and while

I was still wearing my Philly uniform with the number six on the back, I opened a can of beer.

"I guess this is the earliest I've ever had a beer," I said to a Philadelphia sportswriter. "You think the Phils will retire my number? Or did they get tired of my number?"

When a guy is traded off, as I was, he often reacts the way I did. People say take it like a man. What does that mean? How would you feel in your business or occupation if you were summarily shipped off in exchange for a character from another firm? (There's not really any comparable experience in the "real world.")

At least the Phils didn't issue any treacly statements about their team's being family, and they didn't suggest that the Philly organization was another version of Lasorda's Dodger blue.

In baseball, getting traded represents just one more psychological hurdle for a player. Sooner or later, ballplayers have to get acclimated to the idea, but it's never easy.

From 1972 to 1975 I was something of an involuntary nomad, a pale rival of the irrepressible Kurt Bevacqua, who, during the seventies and eighties changed his baseball venue almost as often as he changed his sweatshirt. ("Journey-proud" is what Vin Scully calls such peripatetic characters.)

In November 1972 Montreal traded me back to my old stamping grounds in St. Louis for Jorge Roque, an outfielder from Puerto Rico with a lifetime batting average that hovered around .150. Boy, there was a trade that really shook the baseball world! I played first base in seventy-seven games for the Cards, batting .266. To say the least, it wasn't my natural position, and I didn't provide any threat to the reputation of Keith Hernandez. I was trained to *block* balls thrown in the dirt, not catch them. At first base, I blocked a helluva lot of balls, but I didn't actually catch too many.

We were winning one game 8–1 with a runner at second, top of the ninth, two out. A ground ball was hit three steps to my right; I should have fielded it but, of course, didn't. Fully realizing there'd be no play at the plate, I thought it a good time to try to figure out how I missed the ball. José Cruz, the right fielder, however, had other ideas. Trained to hit the cutoff man—me—that's exactly what he did . . . right in the back!

Bobby Wine, the first base coach, fell to his knees laughing as I yelled out to Cruz, "That's the first time you've hit the cutoff man all year!"

Batting .217 with zero home runs in September 1974, I was sold by the Cards out of the league to the Red Sox (I'd been put on waivers in August). I took this move about as hard as anything I'd ever been subjected to in baseball. When the Red Sox picked me up, I hadn't the slightest notion they had any interest in me. In fact, I thought I was being traded to Oakland. When the Cards took a flight to San Francisco, I went with them, fully expecting to transfer across the bay, because that's what I'd been led to believe by Bob Kennedy, the Cards' liaison man. When we got to San Francisco, I called Anne and said, "I need you." I did, too, because I was pretty depressed about leaving the Cards, who had a shot at the pennant that year.

Anne flew from Memphis to San Francisco and we had dinner that Friday night. The next morning, I got word that I was heading not to Charles O. Finley and company, but to the Green Monster in Beantown. So Saturday, Anne and I flew back to St. Louis to pack up and move out of our house there. Then we drove six hours to Memphis. The next day, I flew to Baltimore to meet up with the Sox, then five games ahead in first place. And, boy, did I inspire that club. Monday, a Labor Day doubleheader, the Red Sox lost both games—1–0, 1–0. Following an off day on Tuesday, Jim Palmer shut us out 5–0 on Wednesday.

I was miserable!

I was with the Sox until the end of the 1974 season and then for the first three months of 1975. In 1975, the Red Sox were a team fighting for the pennant. Eventually, they went to the World Series against Cincinnati, with the sixth game of that Series turning into one of the most exciting games in history. (Remember Carlton Fisk's body-Englishing the ball into fair territory over the left field screen for a home run?)

But I wasn't around either to enjoy that Series or to be a

part of it. The Sox released me in June, only a few days after Darrell Johnson, the manager, had assured me I was going to be around as long as he was. My release, according to Boston writer Peter Gammons, was based on Manager Johnson's "fear that McCarver might get his job."

In truth, I had as much interest in getting Darrell's job at that time, when I was just thirty-three years old, as I had in presiding over the Bureau of the Budget. But there it was: I was gone again. It became a bit easier for me to take a little later, when the Red Sox voted me $4,400 of their World Series money—not too bad for a guy who'd played in only eleven games for them that year.

Less than two weeks after the Red Sox let me go, I signed with the Phillies. That's when I began a whole new catching career as Carlton's aide-de-camp. In addition, my life as a baseball Gulliver was over at last.

I was with the Phils until the end of 1979. Then, in a unanimous three-part decision (involving Ruly Carpenter, the Philly owner; Paul Owens, the GM; and Dallas Green, the manager; but excluding me), I retired. I started to work on Philly TV during the 1980 season, employing my flea market of baseball notions, but I was reactivated, at my request, for the last month of the Phils' pennant drive. And, yes, I was eager to become a four-decade ballplayer.

L'envoi, as they say in Montreal, means farewell. My valedictory game came for me on the last day of the 1980 season, when Dallas Green sent me in to pinch-run for Pete Rose. The Phils had clinched the division the day before and Pete was the only regular who had insisted on starting—naturally.

After replacing Rose, I stayed in the game. My last hit came in that game, off a screwball thrown by Steve Ratzer. It was a double. To show you how my priorities had changed, for one last time I cranked up from my southpaw stance and pumped a line drive into right field. When I wound up on second base, I tipped my hat toward the Philly broadcast booth —Richie Ashburn, Chris Wheeler, Harry Kalas, and Andy Musser—and shot them a big grin.

No mas.

After the Ball Is Over

If what you did yesterday still looks big to you, you haven't done much today.

—WID MATTHEWS
FORMER CUBS GENERAL MANAGER

Many athletes think there is no life after baseball. The dreadful thing to contemplate is that for many of these guys that proves to be correct.

Picture the professional athlete. He has been something special to his family, his friends, and his neighbors since he was in his teens. Then, almost overnight it seems, his career is at an end, and it all slips away, and the bright lights fade. He has nothing to fall back on except those shining memories.

Many stories and books have been written about athletes who have spent their lives basking in the glory of their past herohood. You could call this behavior a prolonged adolescence or simply a failure to grow up. There are a number of unflattering depictions of one-time sports heroes who have failed to make a proper transition into the life of the "real world." Sure, the challenge of adjustment can be rougher than all hell for the ex-baseball hero. But a guy has to face it in the same tough, competitive way he performed on the diamond.

The author James A. Michener has recognized the plight of the ex-athletic idol. "What happens to the boys of summer," he once asked, "when they are forced to become the men of winter? The athlete lives in a world the rest of us can scarcely imagine. That any survive to live reasonably decent lives is a miracle."

When Tommy Heinsohn, the former Boston Celtics basketball player and coach, retired, he commented that he felt almost addicted to the game he loved.

"I believe there's something almost chemical about it. You're used to being up, you're traveling all the time," he said. "You're preparing for games, you're playing in games. It's the same year after year after year. It's all part of your being. Then it ends. The routine is gone. The up is gone. There's this awful down. You get depressed. It's like falling off a cloud."

Memory is selective. It can distort and exaggerate truth. In the memories of many ex-players, their prowess as performers increases with each year they're away from the scene. They become prisoners of their past. Despite their desperate efforts to make that past alive again, their fame and reputation can sink like a stone.

A guy has to reject living in the past and get out there and become productive and involved in the real world. He can't expect to make a career out of signing autographs at car dealerships and shopping mall openings. I don't want to become a scold or an evangelist on the subject, but take it from me— that's the only way out of the doldrums (or, as Philly manager Frank Lucchesi used to say, "the doodlums").

Ballplayers are extraordinarily competitive human beings. Most of the players I've known were aggressive men who literally ached to win. It didn't make any difference if they were competing in a coin-tossing contest or a card game—they just burned to come out ahead.

Dr. Stephen Ward, a psychiatrist and former Pitt football star, said some years ago that "an athlete faced with failure becomes enraged. He is given to new peaks of effort. Defeat is indescribable anguish, a chaotic hell."

Even if Dr. Ward was overstating the case somewhat, there's no doubt in my mind that most people aren't competitive the way athletes are. After the course has been run, and when they get into the real world, the trick is for ex-players to harness and exploit that almost desperate compulsion to compete.

Okay, a player lives and struggles for years in and for himself and his sport. In my case, I did it from the time I was eight years old, when I started to play baseball in the local Rotary League in Memphis. One day it all began when my dad, who coached the team, sent me out to play right field. When I was ten years old, I became a catcher for the first time, and pretty much stayed on my haunches until I retired, at thirty-eight years of age and after 1,909 big-league games.

Surprisingly, I never suffered a serious leg injury in all that time, and my fingers, unlike those of most catchers, don't resemble a passel of broken pretzels. However, I wasn't lucky enough to escape injury completely. I missed the first week of the 1965 season because of a broken finger—it was stepped on by Jimmy Lefebvre—and in May of 1970 I went on the disabled list for the only time in my career when a sharp foul ball off the bat of Willie Mays broke my right hand—or, as the doctor's docket had it, the fourth metacarpal bone on the back of my right hand.

As fate would have it, that broken hand was sustained in a relatively unimportant game. San Francisco was ahead of us 9–2, hardly a situation compelling enough to break your hand about. I was then in my first year with the Phils and batting nicely at .287.

When I went into the clubhouse, a Doctor White took a look at my hand—which looked as if about half a golf ball was lodged between my thumb and forefinger—and said, "Aw, hell, that's just displaced." And with that, he took my forefinger and pulled on it. I almost passed out. I screamed as loud as I could possibly scream. It later turned out that the good Doctor White was a bit off in his diagnosis. The bone was completely crushed—just shattered. The X ray looked like a grenade going off—the pieces of bone looked like little pieces of shrapnel.

In the same inning, and only a few minutes after Mays's foul ball smashed up my hand, Mike Ryan, the Phillies' second catcher, also got his hand busted when he made the horrendous mistake of colliding at home plate with the mountainous Willie McCovey.

When I went to a San Francisco hospital with the Phillies' trainer, Don Seger, a young woman at the receiving desk said, "We've been expecting you, Mr. Ryan. We'll take care of you right away."

"I'm McCarver," I tried to explain. I hadn't the slightest notion that Mike had been hurt, too, since I had left Candlestick Park without seeing or hearing about his accident with McCovey. Obviously, someone on the Phils had phoned ahead to tell them a Mr. Ryan was coming. Somehow or other, they'd just forgotten to tell them about me.

When Mike and I finally got together at the hospital, like a couple of birds with wounded wings, he laughingly confessed something to me.

"You know, Tim," he said, "I've gotta tell you that I always secretly wished that you'd break a hand or a finger. Now it's happened to me *and* you!"

After we were repaired, Mike and I flew back to Philadelphia, separately from the rest of the team. A stewardess came by, saw our hands in their casts, and solicitously asked how our injuries had happened.

"Vietnam," Mike said without missing a beat.

This seemed to solicit an inordinate amount of sympathy, so we began to elaborate. We went from big-league catchers to platoon squad leaders who'd led their soldiers on a mission of glory. We had her crying so hard she couldn't serve the rest of the passengers. I don't know how I didn't crack up as Mike wove his part of the tale. But I didn't. And I managed to become quite a hero myself in the telling.

The broken hand, buried in plaster, kept me out for sixteen weeks, and I missed 110 games. By the end of the season, I felt as if I truly did deserve the Purple Heart.

Ballplayers are taught to be hotly competitive right from the start. They learn quickly that they're better at doing physical things than most other kids. They know that they can hit the ball on the fat part of the bat more consistently than their friends of the same age can. They know they can make more contact. They know their arms are stronger. They know they can throw better and run faster. They know that they're *different*.

They know something else, too—that the major-league scouts are watching them as they progress through high school, American Legion ball, the Babe Ruth League, or whatever is in vogue in their area. They're aware that these people are examining their every move, and this, naturally, encourages even further their latent competitiveness.

By their very presence, these veteran scouts are a constant, dramatic reminder of the substantial financial rewards that are out there for the plucking.

Yes, almost everything in their immediate environment is saying to these young people that fame and fortune are just an arm's reach away and that it's their talent, their competitive drive, that's going to make it or break it for them.

No ballplayer is ever really prepared for the afterlife—a life on the bench, where he isn't scrapping and battling anymore and the crowd isn't there anymore. Now, all of a sudden, he's expected to go out in the world and act as if he'd always had a nine-to-five job.

A few years ago Bob Gibson and I were staring at some pictures of the Cardinal teams of the sixties that hang in the press room at Busch Stadium in St. Louis. *Sports Illustrated* had once featured the 1968 Cards team on its cover, with the salaries of the players printed on an overleaf. (Those salaries added up to less than a million bucks, a figure that included the wages of a guy like Gibson, who, in 1968, won twenty-two games and lost nine, had an ERA of 1.12, and pitched thirteen shutouts! Today, the *average* salary approaches four hundred and fifty thousand dollars.)

"Boy, that team could really play," I said to Gibby.

For a change, Gibby agreed wholeheartedly with me. "They sure could," he said, almost wistfully.

"The most interesting thing about those guys in that picture," I continued, "is that almost every one of them is successful out of baseball. It's unusual for a team that was as successful as we were on the field to repeat that success after their playing days were over."

That Card bunch was, for the most part, a very intelligent

group. The players were able to use their competitive attributes in the outside world. For instance, in the broadcasting business alone that Card team produced a covey of talented, confident guys.

Let's start with Bob Uecker. (He wasn't around in 1968, but he was there in 1964, when he was my roommate in St. Louis and the funniest guy I've ever seen or heard.) Today he has a book to his credit, years of broadcasting for the Milwaukee Brewers behind him, and he's recognized everywhere because of his commercials and TV series.

Uke, not exactly a Ruthian slugger, once announced that his top thrill in baseball was the time he wangled out of a rundown. And if you haven't yet caught him in that TV commercial where he's sitting all alone in the remote, empty upper deck of a ballpark while mindlessly second-guessing umpire calls down on the field, you've been on Guam too long.

Gibson, too, has been a broadcaster, and he's coached for the Atlanta Braves. Base-stealing champ Lou Brock has been on the air, and so has Mike Shannon, who, along with Jack Buck, is the voice of KMOX radio in St. Louis.

Curt Flood, a portrait painter who did some work for me when I opened my Memphis restaurant in 1967, has done some broadcasting, too. In New York, Bill White, our slick fielding first baseman, remains a highly respected and popular broadcaster for the New York Yankees' games.

Roger Maris, who died fighting cancer in 1986, owned a Budweiser distributorship in Gainesville, Florida.

Julian Javier has accumulated a good deal of wealth in the Dominican Republic, where he's part owner of a winter league team. Dal Maxvill, the understudy to Dick Groat in 1964 and then our regular shortstop in the pennant-winning years of 1967 and 1968, is now the general manager of the Cards.

Ballplayers are used to being cheered and booed from the time they are teenagers, so it's natural to seek such responses after leaving the playing field. When you've lived in a veritable goldfish bowl for over twenty years, it's tough to lead a quiet existence afterward. Even after a half dozen years in the TV booth, I still seem to need the audience's immediate response to what I say, how I say it, and what I do.

I always used to get a kick out of reading that sportswriter cliché, "in the twilight of his career." It makes the turmoil of retirement from baseball seem a bit more lyrical than it is. But there's no doubt that at such a time problems of an emotional and psychological nature can grip some guys in a hard fist.

It's true that many former players pass into a life of boredom and mediocrity after the shouting dies. I'll tell you one practical reason for this: They're just plain tired out. They're tired of driving between the white lines, of going as hard as they can. They've busted their asses for a game, which is the way it should be and the way most of them would want it to be. And now many of them think the public owes them something—not the least, a living.

Owners of major-league sports franchises are taking meager steps to solve the ballplayers' plight in their after-baseball lives. I don't mean to sound like I'm talking about a criminal's rehabilitation, but this is long overdue. Not everybody, when he gets out of the game, is financially secure. First of all, most players aren't superstars. Most of them aren't "set for life." Most ballplayers get out of the game when they're in their early or mid-thirties and they want to go on to lead productive lives. Not all of them know how.

It's a sad thing when those who once made headlines in the sports section wind up adorning the sensationalized headlines of other sections.

Enough.

A Long Season
in a Small Booth

The successful broadcaster must
be daring; he must not be bound
completely by the chains of
tradition.

—RED BARBER

In spring training of 1980 at the Phillies' Jack Russell Stadium
in Clearwater, Florida, I squeezed into a TV booth for the first
time. I was in good company, next to the old pro himself,
Richie Ashburn.

I looked down on the neat greensward, where I had spent
a good part of my life, and I thought that this was where I
belonged.

"This is a lot easier than squatting, isn't it?" said Ashburn
with a chuckle.

"I'm not sure yet," I answered.

"Are you nervous?" Ashburn asked.

"Not really," I answered.

And it was true. My heart wasn't beating any faster than
usual, but my mind was already searching for the right word.

I worked just one inning that day. Nothing very unusual
or important happened in those few minutes, either to the
Phils or to me. But my new career had begun.

I did think I'd have some interesting things to say about
the game of baseball. I thought I'd be able to take some of those

insights and opinions that I had expressed in locker rooms and dugouts over the years and convert them into fodder for the fans. But always there were those reservations in the back of my mind: Was my voice acceptable? Did I know how to prepare? Would I blurt out the wrong things? You never know until you do it. Now I know what to do because I've done it. But I sure didn't then.

More than anything else, I came into broadcasting with the idea that I owed it to the listener to be as honest as possible. And to the player to be as fair as possible. I came into it, too, with a mouthful of opinions, most of them gripped the way a terrier grips a meat bone. As *New York Post* writer Phil Mushnick once wrote, "McCarver is as opinionated as any five unemployed inhabitants of Wrigley Field's bleachers." Phil's right. I *am* too opinionated. But I've tried to tone that down. I've worked at it. It's a constant process, actually, of work and introspection. I realize that my opinions to some are interesting but to others are annoying. The only thing I can really do is trust my instincts and try to be honest with *myself*.

There's one thing about this business: If you think something's wrong, you ought to go ahead and say it.

I don't think the primary function of a broadcaster is to be cautious and protect his ass.

Venturing out there—"first-guessing," or saying what will happen before it happens—takes some guts. But, after all, isn't that what broadcasters get paid for? The reason I use the term *first-guessing* is that I don't like to second-guess. The biggest thing a broadcaster can give his audience is the various options of what can happen on a ball field. That's what I try to do. If those options don't materialize, so what? I've still done my job. I also try to set the tone for what's to come, not simply to criticize after the fact. If you criticize only after something's happened, that's second-guessing, and I hope I've made it clear that I hate that. I sure got enough of it from managers when I was catching. But if you make a statement *before* some action occurs, you definitely have the right to refer back to it when the action's over. As long as criticism is consistent and knowledgeable and fair, it's not only interesting, it's essential.

There have been times when some of my observations

have gotten old buddies kind of wrought up. It used to hurt when that happened, because I, like them, took it personally.

In my first year of play-by-play broadcasting with the Phillies in 1980, my credo was put to the test. It caused a problem between a good friend of mine, Mike Schmidt, and me.

Schmitty had just connected with one of those towering belts that have come to be his trademark. But instead of going over the fence, the ball ended up hitting the top of it. When the smoke cleared, Schmitty had barely made it into second base.

My judgment as a broadcaster was that Mike had settled for a double when he should have had a triple.

"Schmitty, like most sluggers and home run hitters," I said on the air, "likes to gaze fondly on his product. Like an artist holding his thumb up, on their first step out of the batter's box, these hitters like to gaze admiringly at their piece of work. Consequently, their first two or three steps, they don't bust out of the batter's box; they act like tourists in New York City for the first time, gazing up constantly and not concerned with where they're going." Therefore, I added, he was only able to reach second base.

I thought that was an accurate description of what my eyes had just seen and that I'd provided the motivation for Schmidt's behavior.

Mike hadn't heard what I said, but his friends had. The gist of my remarks was quickly relayed to him. It was also edited. By the way, this is a separate problem. Once a friend or a member of a player's family gets through interpreting your on-air comment, it rarely resembles the original in meaning—or sometimes even at all. Anyway, to put it mildly, Schmitty didn't like whatever it was he heard.

The next day around the batting cage he was chilly as an igloo toward me. I went over to him to explore the situation. I don't like such confrontations, but if you're going to be in this business and try to maintain some kind of objectivity, they're a very important part of your work.

"Don't ever say anything that implies I'm not hustling out there," Schmitty said, looking me straight in the eye.

"I never said you weren't hustling," I rebutted. "I was just trying to report why you only wound up on second base."

He was obviously concerned that listeners would perceive him in a bad light as a result of my comments, and I understood his sensitivity.

"Michael," I continued, "do you think you should have been on third base?"

"No," he said.

"Well, I do." And I told him why. Basically, it was the same stuff I said on the air, told in a slightly different way.

"Maybe I *could* have been on third," he admitted, "but I still don't think you should have explained it that way."

We were at an impasse. Neither of us was satisfied, but at least the antagonism wasn't allowed to fester and, like most things, our problem eventually went away on its own.

It's too bad when this sort of thing happens between old friends, but once you get a mike in your hands, it comes with the territory. It also happened once with Bob Boone, another guy for whom I have infinite respect and affection.

In my first month as a Philly broadcaster I noticed that Boonie seemed to be favoring his knee while catching in the bullpen. He appeared to be limping slightly. It convinced me he had some kind of knee problem, so I talked about it on the air.

It didn't take long for Boonie to get back to me about what I had said.

"I don't like anyone giving my medical report in progress," he said, in his typically civil manner. It isn't Boonie's style to get mad at people or to hold grudges.

In retrospect, I don't think my reporting was wrong or damaging to Boonie. I also think he had a right and an obligation to speak up about it.

Another friend I offended, to the point that he even wrote about it in his book *Bats*, is Davey Johnson, the Mets' manager. In an early season game in 1985 Davey nominated Ray Knight to pinch-hit for Howard Johnson when a lefty pitcher went to the mound. I suggested that Knight was a poor choice because he was in a slump.

"It seems to me," I said, "that Davey may have gone to Ray Knight because he's more worried about Knight's feelings than he is about winning or losing a game." I went on to say that sometimes, in order to win many future games, it would be reasonable to assume, a manager needs to instill confidence in a batter. It may be a bad strategic move at the time, I said, but it's a good psychological move for the future.

Knight popped out, but that's not the point; I try not to be one of those I-told-you-so guys.

When Davey later heard, through Mets hitting coach Bill Robinson, about what I'd said—edited, of course—he was pretty burned off at me. "Even your best friends will say things that may undermine what you have going. . . . there are a lot of wolves waiting to tear you to pieces at the drop of a hat," he wrote scornfully in his book.

Davey even took me aside at spring training in St. Pete in 1986 and let me know what he thought about what I'd said.

"You're not responsible to anyone for what you may say on the air, Tim," he said. "Nobody's around to second-guess you and your opinions."

"That's not true," I told him. "I have critics the same as you."

"Let me finish," he insisted. "How the hell do you know what's in my mind when I make my decisions!"

"That's my job," I told him.

"But how do you know?"

" 'Cause that's my *job*."

"But you *don't* know."

"It's my *job* to know."

The newspapers played up the "spat" with Johnson for a few days—that's their job, too. It was suggested by Jack Lang in the New York *Daily News* that my exchange with Davey was pretty heated and that it was an "eyeball-to-eyeball" jawing session.

The fact is that, from the first day I met Davey in spring of 1977, this is the way we've always talked to each other. Described as "heated discussions" by other people, they're just simple conversations between two strong-minded men—no more, no less.

As Steve Zabriskie puts it: "Timmy, you enjoy the give-and-take of being adversarial." I don't always, but there are times when you must.

Ballplayers who expect to reap the benefits of praise

should also be willing to tolerate criticism. They *should* be, but it isn't easy for any player to accept such a premise. And it isn't easy for an announcer to follow such a policy without alienating, at least temporarily, guys who have traditionally been friendly with him.

Flash forward to game one of the 1985 World Series. I was in the ABC booth with Al Michaels and Jim Palmer. Ozzie Smith of the Cards took a whopping lead off first base and stole second without a whimper or a challenge from Kansas City's normally talented defensive catcher, Jim Sundberg. There was a runner on third, Jack Clark.

Surprised that Sundberg hadn't made any effort to throw Ozzie out, I commented about it. "By not throwing through at all, that's just like giving up," I said.

Many millions heard the remark. In due course, what I'd said got back to Dick Howser, Kansas City's manager.

The next day, Howser, who is the quintessential low-key guy, pulled me aside.

"I want you to know," he said, "that on this team we don't ever play give-up baseball."

"I didn't say you played give-up baseball. I said it was a give-up play. There's a big difference."

I had no argument with Howser. He wanted me to know how he felt about his players, and that's a legitimate enough defense in my book. Also, in fairness to Dick, I didn't have the time to explain every little detail of my criticism on the air. If I had had the time, I would have said that Jack Clark was a slow runner, so Sundberg had the luxury of throwing to try to nail Smith. If Vince Coleman had been on third, I probably would have kept my mouth shut.

I feel very strongly that it's part of my job to show up on the field after I make my remarks. I have to make myself available to Howser, Sundberg, or anybody else who might want to express himself or bitch about what I said. I'll always listen. Otherwise, grudges are held.

I was emotional as a player, and I guess I'm emotional as an announcer. But you must understand that the job isn't a witch-hunt. Professional announcers are not paid for character assassination. However, repeated praise with no criticism is pure fluff. If players could only understand that credibility is all. My making justifiable criticism when it's called for validates the praise I'm more than willing to heap on them when they deserve it.

I keep repeating to myself: Try to be fair and try to describe what has really happened. Respect the listener and try to keep it light. Explain what happened as best you can, but don't dwell on the guy who made a misplay or a mistake.

On the other hand, if a guy can't run hard for ninety feet four times a game, I've got to say something. I know players will resent that, too, but how do you think thirty thousand people who paid eight bucks each to see the game feel?

There are times when the light touch, or what you think is light, can get a bit heavy, especially when a guy feels he's been victimized.

When Manny Trillo, a friend of mine from my Philadelphia days, was second-basing for San Francisco in 1984, I noticed one afternoon that he didn't choose to join a hurry-up confab at the mound. Knowing that Manny's roots were in Venezuela, I said, tongue in cheek, "Trillo isn't out there with the others because he doesn't speak English."

Oops. Trillo didn't take the remark with the same light attitude I had intended.

"My English is better than McCarver's arm ever was," growled Manny to a writer in response.

Oftentimes, a tongue-in-cheek remark needs the announcer's inflection to show that he was teasing. Whoever repeated my comment to Manny didn't—and couldn't—capture either my inflection or what he hadn't seen, my body language—the cocked head, animated hands, and smile in the eyes.

Every now and then a broadcaster will mangle a word on the air. I've done it lots of times. One time when I misused a word, I volunteered, "Well, those things happen when you're educated in the South." Then I let the thought trail off.

Later I thought I'd better explain what I regarded as a

facetious remark. I didn't want anyone to think I was engaging
in foolish stereotyping. "I was just poking fun," I explained.
"Feeding into the northern stereotype that all southerners are
backwoodsmen raised in a hole. I do like to say things tongue
in cheek, and sometimes they don't come across quite as I
meant them."

As a former catcher, and a rather loquacious one at that,
I was probably destined to wind up in the broadcasting aerie.
What is it about catchers that brings them into the TV booth?
Why have Joe Garagiola, Bob Uecker, Johnny Bench, and oth-
ers ended up as voluble—too voluble, according to some de-
tractors—broadcasters?

Theorists might have a field day with that one, but I don't
think it's too much of a mystery. Catchers-turned-announcers
are doing what comes naturally. As announcers they're watching and participating in ball games in much the same way as
they operated as catchers. The only difference is that they're
not squatting 150 times a game or getting their fingers busted.
(One other difference is that they're doing it from a press box
that's about two stories higher than where they used to be
perched.)

Catchers are also experts on the results of pitches. Since
pitching is such a vital part of the game, it would follow that
someone experienced with handling pitchers could relay those
thoughts to the viewer.

The one man most responsible for getting me into broadcasting is Lew Klein, president of WFIL in Philadelphia, who
"discovered" my latent talents.

Lew and I were at a luncheon press conference one day
in 1969, the year before I played in only forty-four games for
the Phils because of my broken hand. My mouth wasn't broken
that day, however, so I was asked to say a few words to the
luncheon crowd.

Lew insists I said something so funny that day that he
immediately envisioned me as a TV broadcaster. I don't recall
what I said, so I don't know if it was as funny as Lew thought.
But I do remember hearing Lew say, "If you can talk that well
in front of a group, you might do very well on the air." It's
interesting to note, however, that not all on-air broadcasters

are good public speakers. A lot of them aren't nervous in front of a camera or a mike, but people can terrify them. It is odd how you can get so used to talking to a camera. It's almost as if that camera becomes a personal friend. By the way, I don't think I am a particularly good public speaker.

Anyway, when the 1970 season started, I contracted to do thirty-six pregame shows for $100 a show. I was going to co-host it with Richie Ashburn, who had been in the business for eight years. The show was cleverly called "The Ashburn and McCarver Show." Each show lasted ten minutes. The idea was for me to talk about my daily playing experience, but since I was injured I wasn't playing. Thus, I didn't have an awful lot to say. Then and now, I'd rate the show a disaster. But it was also a start.

In 1975, when the Red Sox released me, Anne and I shipped everything back to Memphis, including seven trunks and the dog, and then, looking like your basic band of gypsies, drove to Philadelphia. I chose Philadelphia because I had the opportunity to audition for channels 3 and 6 there. One audition was done with Jessica Savitch—first she interviewed me, then I interviewed her. I'd say that those interviews—and the whole audition—were about as disastrous as the Ashburn and McCarver show. I was in no rush to play the rest of the season —I was getting paid for the entire year no matter what—but Bill Giles, then business manager of the Phils, convinced me that if I wanted to play the next year it would be a lot more difficult if I sat out these additional three months. So I agreed to sign on with the Phils as a pinch hitter and backup catcher.

I initiated a couple of crash efforts to break into broadcasting at that time, basically because I was forced to. I knew that my career in baseball wasn't going to last forever and that I'd better be prepared for my future. Ballplayers are usually shocked into thinking about their future. Subtlety doesn't work. It's mostly because it's almost impossible for a twenty-five- or thirty-year-old athlete, or even a thirty-five-year-old athlete, to accept the fact that he's not invincible. It's tremendously difficult to envision when you're young that your skills will one day evaporate and your body will let you down. For a lot of guys, those skills and that body are all they have.

I signed my 1976 contract with the Phils ten minutes after the 1975 season was over. I was not exactly dealing from strength at that point. When the 1976 season started I was one of three catchers. But after opening day I was one of two, because Dave Parker crushed Johnny Oates into the ground trying to score from third base, and separated Johnny's shoulder. This gave me a reprieve—it was as if the governor had called right before the switch was to be pulled. Not only did I get to play a lot more than I normally would have, but this really opened up the beginning of the Carlton-McCarver relationship. I would not have caught Lefty nearly as much then if Oates had been around.

We won the division that year, and I discovered I could still play baseball. I'd proven my critics wrong. It was extremely satisfying, probably the most satisfying thing in my career, to show the world that I was the master of my own baseball fate once again.

After the 1976 season, Peter O'Malley called and offered me a four-year contract to sign on as the Toronto Blue Jays' announcer. But I wanted to play, and unlike it had been during the season before, my negotiating position was quite strong.

Bill Giles, trying to keep me with the Phils, countered with an offer for a two-year broadcasting contract beginning after my playing career was over. This seemed to be the best of both worlds. I could still play (and, in fact, play with a hefty raise in pay) *and* I had security for that tough transition period when my playing days were over.

To further prepare for my future in broadcasting, I contracted to co-host a children's show during the 1977 and 1978 seasons. My co-host was an ex-Lutheran minister, Carter Merbrier. His wife, Pat, made the puppets for the show, which was called *Captain Noah and His Magical Ark.* I'd appear once a week, shin guards and catcher's mask on, to do in-depth material with such guests as Chickie the Orangutan, a mongoose, a boa constrictor, and a nurse from the Board of Health who talked at some length about the dangers of influenza.

At the end of the show I would stand around with the guests and sing the following classic:

Red and yellow and pink and white,
purple and orange and blue;
We can sing a rainbow,
sing a rainbow, sing a rainbow, too.

Believe it or not, all this time Lew Klein and Gene Kirby kept purring nice things in my ears. They continued to assure me that I was not one-dimensional, which really helped me, especially coming from people I respected.

Gene Kirby had been an executive producer for NBC and had also worked with Dizzy Dean, Peewee Reese, and Buddy Blattner when they were broadcasting baseball in the 1950s. (Kirby had practically caddied for the incorrigible Dizzy on CBS's "Game of the Week.")

In 1980, when it was all over for me on the field, I went after a TV career in earnest. That winter I took my "spring training" for the broadcasting business. I'd sit there at Channel 17 watching countless videotapes of Philly games that had been shot during the season just ended. As the games went on, I announced along with them. If you want to get tired of your own voice really quickly, try that some time. Chris Wheeler, one of the Philly announcers, often came by to kibitz during those practice sessions. He'd often make pointed critiques about my style and approach, which at that time would have rated about a C-minus, with an A for effort.

The first time I ever had to do this, Wheeler and Fred Waskoff put a tape on, pressed the start button, and said, "Talk about what you see." I could see, but I'll tell you what . . . I sure couldn't talk. Sweat started pouring from everywhere. I panicked. They coaxed me along until eventually I came out with a few words. They were inaudible, but at least they were words.

I've got to admit that there were plenty of days when I didn't want to show up for those sessions. But I kept returning, three or four days a week. It was a classic exercise in tedium, but I was learning a good deal and I was headed in the right direction.

I started doing the Phillies' games in 1980, as my contract with Bill Giles stipulated. It didn't take me long to realize what a lucky guy I was. I loved being in the booth. I loved being as close to baseball as I'd been before, although I immediately felt the separation between the guys on the field and me.

Here I was, after fighting *with* these guys between the white lines one year, all of a sudden expected to publicly criticize and comment on their abilities. I can well understand the difficult transition Rusty Staub had to make in 1986, when he went from being one of the true stars in the game to making objective comments about his Mets teammates. Subjectivity to objectivity overnight—it's tough, boys. Try criticizing your friends, family, and co-workers on a daily basis. See how they like it. Then try broadcasting that criticism to millions of people. Think you'd stay as popular as you are now?

I don't want to give the impression that you're paid only to criticize. But part of the job is being honest—and, as I've stressed before, you've got to say what you perceive to be the truth.

Another part of the job, which is not as easy as it looks, is trying to keep up your level of enthusiasm. I've been called ebullient. A couple of TV critics have even said that I'm a "What, me worry!" kind of person. Not true. My worries are similar to those of other people, but I don't let them get the better of me. On the air I'm a reporter, no question about it. But anyone who doesn't understand that announcing baseball games is at least as much entertainment as it is pure reportage just hasn't the proper formula. I don't claim to be totally objective. None of us are. But I do generally think that my job is to convey the whole range and the beauty of the game. You and I are going to go on a journey—that's my broadcasting approach. The journey will not necessarily be a totally happy one. There should be joy and excitement, but also tears. I do guarantee you that it'll be an entertaining journey, however. You will remember it.

I learned a lot about broadcasting during my first season with the Phils, but the one instruction Gene Kirby gave me turned out to be the best nugget of wisdom about broadcasting baseball I ever heard.

"Don't talk through the goddamn pitch," Kirby said to

me, at a time when I was doing just that. The advice was as valuable to me as the admonition given by General Putnam to the home team during the Battle of Bunker Hill in the American Revolution.

"Don't fire till you see the whites of their eyes," General Putnam told his pitchers.

Kirby gave me other pointers as well—slow down in the booth, don't talk too much or too quickly, and, for heaven's sake, don't gush and exclaim while the pitcher is doing his thing.

Baseball is essentially a leisurely, subtle game. There are no clocks ticking away to circumscribe the action. There's always plenty of time for a point to be made, an anecdote to be told, an insight to be provided. There's no reason to do it when the viewer is trying to concentrate on the action.

If you serve long enough in the booth, there is no way you're not going to mangle a few sentences, render bad judgments, say things you wished you hadn't said. Should there be a fine for announcers who commit verbicide? Should boo-boos in the booth go unnoticed and unremarked? You be the judge and jury. What should the punishment be for uttering such well-worn clichés as the following:

"Strawberry can be an *awesome* hitter."

"The Mets' play has been *outstanding*."

"*Basically*, this is a good ballclub."

"Ozzie Smith *executes* very well."

"Roger Clemens is trying to *stay within himself*."

"Valenzuela is pitching with great *velocity*."

"Carter is oh-for-three and three-for-ten *on the season*."

Okay, here's my verdict: hanging by the tongue!

It's easy to criticize others, though. *I* probably should have been hung—well, at least severely chastised—during the 1980 season for a bad habit I developed. Whenever Andy Musser would say something I liked or agreed with, I'd say, "Good point." I must have said the words "good point" fifteen times a broadcast over the first two months of the season. That's nine hundred times! I kept saying it until a close friend of mine, a lawyer and a wordsmith, called and said, "A point with which you are impressed is not necessarily a good point."

That cured me of the habit. It was a good point.

Then, of course, there are the malapropisms and solecisms that sometimes squirt out during a ball game. As New York Mayor Fiorello La Guardia once said about his own mistakes, "They're beauts." Well, I've had some real beauts myself.

For example, a few seasons ago I described George Foster as being "the Cadillac of a Mets two-run rally." Now you know I meant to say the word *catalyst*, but in a moment of exultation and absentmindedness, that's the way it emerged.

One day in July 1985, with the Mets playing Houston in the Dome, Bill Doran of the Astros tried to steal second base. Gary Carter made a deft throw to try to nail him.

"Doran drugged his front leg," I said. When I realized what I had said, I started to giggle. Hell, I was getting into the same league as Dizzy Dean.

In the sixth game of the 1986 playoffs, Davey Johnson made a move, putting Lee Mazzilli in left field and Jesse Orosco on the mound. He also had Mazzilli batting in the number-nine spot and Jesse hitting sixth. Keith Jackson, my ABC cohort in the booth, explained what had happened, then turned to me and said, "Tim, why did Davey do that?"

Well, I was a bit unprepared. So I did what I often do: I started talking, hoping I'd figure out what was going on before I *stopped* talking.

"That's what's known as a double switch," I began. "Well, it's not really a double switch. It's a modification of a double switch." With every word I said, all I kept thinking was, *Deeper —I'm getting in deeper.*

"Davey's doing it for defensive purposes only," I went on, "although there are offensive ramifications." Finally, I just threw up my hands and said, "I guess I surrounded that explanation, didn't I?"

All Keith said was "Yup."

I once got Tim Wallach of the Montreal Expos on CBS's "Sixty Minutes" by mistakenly calling him Mike Wallace. Valenzuela came out Venezuela one night. Writhing has been wreathing, as in "wreathing in pain." In 1986 Howard Johnson made a play at third base where the ball took a bad hop, hit his arm, and trickled into his glove. A brilliant image came into my mind as we watched the replay.

"Sometimes an infielder, instead of catching the ball

cleanly in the glove, is forced to handle the ball as a mother
would a baby. Watch how Howard *smothers* this ball."

Ralph Kiner turned to me and quietly said, "I believe you
meant *cradle*."

And I said, "Right! *Cradle.* Cradle. Cradle." Somehow I
figured that if I said the word *cradle* enough times, they'd
forget my "smother" imagery. "Right! Cradle! Cradle!"

Speaking of Ralph Kiner . . .

I had been a Mets broadcaster for about a month in 1983
when Ralph introduced me rather enthusiastically as follows:
"Fans, now I'll turn the play-by-play over to my good buddy,
Tim MacArthur."

I looked at him. "Ralph, my name is McCarver."

"What did I say?" Ralph asked.

"MacArthur," I answered.

"Well, that's pretty close," Ralph rationalized.

Ralph has done a job on some other names, too.

To show you how Ralph can brilliantly turn things like that
to his—and the broadcast's—advantage: At the end of the same
game, which the Mets lost 9–1, I said to Ralph, "You know, we
were talking about MacArthur earlier, and he once said,
'Chance favors a prepared man!' And the Mets weren't prepared tonight."

Ralph, realizing we were ready to cut to a commercial,
came back with, "MacArthur also said, 'I shall return.' And
we'll be right back after this message."

Another time, in 1986, I was reaching for a little excitement in the midst of a boring game. I pointed out that there
were two outs, the count was two-and-two, and there were two
men on.

"And look at this," I said, feigning a feverish pitch of excitement. "The batter just fouled a pitch off in front of *two*
photographers."

In his low-key, somber manner, Ralph dryly responded,
"And that's *too* much."

When Gary Carter hit an extra-inning home run to start
off the Mets' 1985 season with a win, Ralph was so ecstatic that
he greeted Gary on his postgame show by calling him Gary
Cooper.

On occasion Ralph has misnamed Darryl Strawberry as Darryl Throneberry, Gary Carter has been Gary Cooper, and Ryne Sandberg, the Cubs' second baseman, has been everything from Sandbag to Rhineberg to Ryne Duren.

When Ralph converted Sandberg into Duren, I reminded him that Duren, a former relief pitcher who once terrorized batters with blazing fastballs that appeared to have little sense of direction, once hit a guy with a pitch—only the guy was in the on-deck circle.

"That was *me*," Ralph said.

On one of our game telecasts I listed the names of famous double play combinations. Inevitably, I came to Tinker to Evers to Chance, a Chicago Cubs trio that was probably greater in legend than in reality. Franklin P. Adams's famous poem, written in 1908, has considerably embossed the legend.

"I once recited Adams's poem," said Ralph, "and the next thing I knew I received a letter from Evers's niece. She said his name should be properly pronounced EE-vers and not EH-vers, as it has generally been pronounced all these years."

"That would spoil the poem," I told Ralph. Whereupon he launched into a recitation of the poem right there on the air.

The next day a critic inquired whether the poem had been recited with the aid of a teleprompter or from a handy book of poetry. Ralph, the man who occasionally mixes his Strawberrys with his Throneberrys and his Quisenberrys, rattled off the nine-line poem again without a bobble. The performance won him a standing ovation in the normally hard-crusted press room.

Steve Zabriskie arrived in the Mets' booth the same year I did. He came up with this beauty on July 5, 1985, during a game, by the way, that started on July 4. This was the classic nineteen-inning game won by the Mets over the Atlanta Braves 16–13. The fireworks, scheduled to go off after the game, did indeed go off—at 4:01 A.M., when the game ended—alarming, as Skip Caray, one of the Braves' announcers said, the cardiac unit at nearby Grady Memorial Hospital. Totally exhausted by the sixteenth or seventeenth inning, Lenny Dykstra made a put-out by catching the ball with his cap askew. Zabriskie said, "Sounds like a southern fraternity—Cap

Askew." Thereby the New York branch of Cappa Cappa Skew was formed.

Most people are suckers for pets and for animal stories. However, you don't know where they might lead. Fran Healy, another gentleman with whom I work, is another one of these catcher fellows who has gone into broadcasting. One day he mentioned that once in the winter league an outfielder refused to field a ball that dropped near the left field line because there was a barking dog in the area.

"Some people are afraid of dogs, especially when they make noise," Healy suggested.

"Did you ever see a pig wandering in the outfield?" I asked. Healy said he hadn't.

"Well, I remember many years ago a pig was walking around in the outfield," I began, "and when the next batter hit a ball right in his direction, the pig got to the ball before the center fielder and swallowed the darn thing!"

"What happened?" Healy said.

"The batter ran all the way home," I replied, "and they called it an inside-the-pork home run."

Healy came back at me with another animal story. "There are a lot of wacky guys who have turned to pitching," he said, looking around to make certain there were no pitchers hiding in our booth. "One of them I know, Bill Fall, liked to eat live frogs, without garlic."

"That's entirely understandable," I said, again with a straight face. "He just wanted to get more of a hop on his fastball."

Richie Ashburn, whom I worked with in Philadelphia, can be a gadfly, a character who often dresses with his uncles' (or somebody's) throwaways. The only Philly ever to win the National League batting championship twice, Richie is a highly individualistic guy, with his cocky tweed caps, his pipe, his sweaters, and his unending stream of fast-delivered quips.

Once, in 1972, Richie was interviewing Steve Carlton, who was still talking to the press. "So," Richie said, "I hear you're going' hunting with your old buddy McCarver after the season. Where you goin'?"

"We're going up into Alberta," Lefty told him.

Ashburn's reply—on the air—was, "Don't believe I've ever run into her."

Another time I was going on and on about Bob Walk, a recently recalled pitcher, who'd started out six-and-one that year.

"It's interesting," I pointed out, "as good a year as Walk is having, he'd still be pitching in the minor leagues if it wasn't for the injury to Larry Christenson."

So far so good. Unfortunately, I kept going.

"Speaking of L.C.," I went on, "he just got back from his home state of Washington. And he brought back two bags of volcanic ash from Mount St. Helens." I then described, in detail, these two bags that Christenson had been showing around the clubhouse. One bag's ash was coarse, almost the size of hailstones or golf balls. The other bag contained ash from the explosive side, fine and powdery.

Without batting an eye, Ashburn said, "I thought if you'd seen one piece of ash you'd seen 'em all."

Do I have to tell you that I almost fell into a coma?

Then there's the Winder, Don Drysdale, the Hall of Fame pitcher, White Sox announcer, and pitching coach, who probably threw more unreported spitballs than any pitcher of his era outside of Gaylord Perry. Reporters still ask Drysdale today whether he ever "wetted up" the ball, and he always says that his mother told him "never, ever," to put his "dirty fingers" in his mouth.

One night I was in St. Louis with Drysdale, Bob Gibson, and Duke Snider, now a broadcaster for Montreal. Duke looked around at us and then said pointedly, "There's lots of knockdown pitches in this booth." He might have added that there were a few spitters there, too.

There's no telling who will make the transition from player to broadcaster. Drysdale did it and did it well, but Sandy Koufax didn't make it. NBC liked Sandy, but he was uncomfortable and quit.

Working the booth is fun most of the time, but it can also be tough and very frustrating. I'm talking now of spending a whole season covering a loser. That's exactly what I was subjected to in 1983, when I joined Kiner and Zabriskie on the

Mets play-by-play. When I got to Shea, I hoped fervently that things would get better. Certainly it makes the job more pleasant to cover a club that's in serious contention and has a fighting chance to win.

But we had no such luck that first year. The Mets finished dead last in the Eastern Division of the National League, with a 68–94 record, slightly better than their 65–97 of 1982. Ralph attributed the vast improvement to my presence. Thanks, Ralph.

Constant defeats, even if you're up there in the booth and not responsible for what's happening on the field, can be a real downer. I kept trying to remind myself that things would get better. It was particularly tough because the Phillies—whom I'd just left—went all the way to the Series that year. This doesn't mean I'm rooting for the team I'm covering. It just means it's a lot more fun covering a winner than a loser.

Some broadcasters have worked in the booth for losers almost all of their lives. Jack Brickhouse did the masochist bit for the Chicago Cubs from 1948 to 1981. There wasn't a winner for him in all of those years.

As the Mets kept losing in my first season in the booth, it was my job to remain equable. An attitude of optimism and serenity was advisable under the circumstances. And for most of that frustrating season I think I kept my emotions under control.

But then, one foul day in Atlanta, about halfway through the season, the Mets blew sky-high in the eighth inning. With the help of four walks and an unspeakable throwing error, they managed to lose still another ball game.

After the game was over, I sat quietly, all by myself, in the booth. I watched attendants sweep peanut shells and empty cartons. Then I slowly wended my way down to the press room, which emptied out so quickly you'd have thought a tornado hit town.

With not a soul in sight, I suddenly began yelling at the top of my lungs—at the walls, at the bottles, at the pictures on the walls. If someone had walked in on me, he would have hustled me into a straitjacket.

When I got through with my primal scream, I felt better.

It was therapeutic. It helped me to survive the season. I recommend such behavior to all announcers who suffer through those long Augusts and Septembers when their clubs do little more than show up, the flag races heat up for everybody else, and the audiences melt down.

Again, I'm not paid to be a rooter, but by midseason of 1984, it was a pleasure to be broadcasting for the Mets. Not because they were winning, but because I was able to talk about a more interesting brand of baseball and a group of truly talented young players. I even got to work a potential no-hitter, with Gooden on the mound. He went into the seventh inning against the Pirates and appeared to be on the verge of the first no-hitter ever registered by a Mets pitcher. (There have been six no-hitters thrown *against* the Mets.)

For years there had been a cherished but somewhat silly baseball tradition that potential no-hitters should never be reported by announcers. This nonsense probably was rooted in the fact that teammates of a pitcher with a no-hitter in his grasp didn't want to put undue pressure on him by talking about it in the dugout. "Is it possible," Red Barber asked, "for a pitcher to be blissfully unaware of what he is doing?"

When Red opted to announce that the Yankees' Bill Bevens in the 1947 World Series against the Dodgers was actually working on a no-hitter in the fourth game (now celebrated for Cookie Lavagetto's ninth-inning double that broke Bevens's heart and his string—his heartstring), Red almost caused his sidekick, Mel Allen, to faint dead away.

Instead of adopting the traditional mum's-the-word approach to incipient no-hitters, I chose to be upfront about it. Well, I figured it was something to talk about, not hide.

So as Dwight kept throwing zeros, I invited everyone to tune in. "Gooden's got a no-hitter going," I said excitedly. "Get on the phone and call all your friends!" I wouldn't be a bit surprised if we even increased our audience over the next inning or so—or until Dwight lost his no-hitter.

Did I jinx Gooden? Oh, come on with that stuff! I was just doing my job—reporting. I got a ton of mail, though, calling me a Mets hex, among other things.

.   .   .

Over the last couple of years, in addition to covering the Mets, I've also appeared on national TV with ABC. I was paired off with Drysdale on backup "Monday Night Baseball," and I acted as roving center and man-in-motion interviewer during the 1984 League Championship Series between the Cubs and the San Diego Padres. In 1985 I teamed with Al Michaels and Jim Palmer on the Kansas City–Cards World Series, and in 1986 I covered the memorable Mets-Astros playoff series with Keith Jackson.

Before last year, ABC's policy on their baseball coverage was that no announcer who followed a team could cover that team on a national broadcast because they thought it presented a conflict of interest. That policy is no longer in effect, which is why I was able to do the 1986 playoffs. The danger, in ABC's opinion, was that the announcer would be biased in favor of the team he regularly covered. My feeling in 1986 was also, arguably, an inclination to bias—but I was also worried that I'd bend over backward to give the Astros credit. I was concerned that my favoritism would work *against* the Mets.

When I was "the man in the stands" for the Cubs-Padres games, I couldn't help but get caught up in all the revelry. Even though I'd done some NBC "Game of the Week" broadcasts in the early 1980s and some games for ABC in 1984, this was my first broadcasting experience with postseason play. What a scene, too. Wrigley Field in Chicago. Wow! Carl Sandburg once wrote that Chicago is "the city of the big shoulders." Well, as I wriggled and wended my way through Wrigley's bleachers, I needed big shoulders. I talked to the famous bleacher bums, players' wives, Chub Feeney (then National League president), Commissioner Peter Ueberroth, Bill Murray, Bill Veeck, and I took my first trip inside Chicago's scoreboard. This was one of the few times I'd ever seen a game from the stands.

And those stands were really rocking. Even as a nonpartisan observer I got chills and goose bumps in response to the noisy support the Cubs were getting from their loyalists. The foot-stomping, hand-clapping, and hollering reached such a level that I was convinced the place was going to fall apart. Wrigley seemed to be shaking and quaking under my shoes. I kiddingly told Kevin Mulligan, a *Philadelphia Daily News* columnist, that I wasn't going to do many upper-deck interviews because I was afraid to be caught up there when the place came tumbling down.

We moved to San Diego after the Cubs won the first two games. The high point of my roving in that National League series was when the Padres staged a seventh-inning uprising in the decisive fifth game. They had just tied the game and had the lead run prancing threateningly off first base. While the hometown San Diego fans were roaring, the long-suffering Cub fans across the nation must have been considering mass suicide.

As I hung out at the railing of the Cubs' bullpen, the TV camera shifted to me. I remarked that Steve Trout, a big lefty who had started and won the second game, was warming up rapidly in the hope that he could march in to rescue Rick Sutcliffe, the Cub pitcher.

I told viewers at that juncture of the proceedings that Trout was not accustomed to coming in in relief, that he hadn't had much time to warm up, that Manager Jim Frey had possibly gotten him up too late, and that he was "not readily available" to bail Sutcliffe out of trouble. (By the time Trout did trudge into the game Sutcliffe had already yielded four runs and the National League pennant.)

As things developed, my observations were on target. But I was dismayed to read later that a few folks thought that ABC, when they cut away from the game action to me in the bullpen, had cracked the game's tension. One critic suggested that the information I had divulged could have been offered just as easily from a broadcaster in the booth. Further, it was remarked that what ABC had done that day was typical of TV: They had chosen to intrude on their own coverage. Couldn't a good ball game, the critic asked, stand on its own merits?

I simply don't buy the suggestion that what ABC did was a rude and unnecessary intrusion. It's up to the producer, the director, and the talent to decide when (if at all) it's proper to cut away from a game and do some kind of insert. These decisions have to be made on the spur of the moment—and under tremendous pressure. They have to be spontaneous. Unlike print reporters, we don't have the luxury of erasers on the ends of our pencils. We make a decision—as we did in the Cubs-Padres game—and it's irrevocable. To tell you the truth, I think it's pretty amazing how often the producers and directors make the *right* decision. And I think we made the right decision in 1984. I believe I managed to give an insight that might not have been as apparent from upstairs.

I was told I would be in the booth for the 1985 World Series between the Cards and Kansas City only ten days before the games began. Talk about knee-knocking apprehension. I was fully aware that you don't put your auditions on the air. I don't have the marquee value of, say, Jim Palmer or Reggie Jackson or Tom Seaver, so a second chance was probably out of the question. And I knew that. I worked with Al Michaels and Jim Palmer, both excellent and knowledgeable at handling a ball game. Al is the consummate professional, the perfect anchor for such a big event. Jim, an articulate and knowledgeable pitcher, also has a subtle sense of humor. I thought we were different enough to be good. There are many people who still think two is company in that booth and three is a crowd. I happen to think that while the repartee may flow better between two—if the announcers are dissimilar, but complementary, in their talents—three in the booth can work. The bottom line is, I'm an employee. If they say work with two, I do. If they say three, I work with three.

Along about the eighth inning of the sixth Series game, with the Cards leading 1–0 and seemingly on the road to a tenth Series victory (their second in four years), I went down to cover the "winning" locker room. ABC had already set up a platform for us in the Cards' locker room, and I was prepared to join a champagne-flooded flock of Redbird players as well as Manager Whitey Herzog.

But a funny thing happened while I was in the Cards' locker room. In the ninth inning, Kansas City miraculously pulled the game and the World Series out of the ashes. A 1–0 win for the Cards metamorphosed into a 2–1 Royals win—with the help of a safe call by umpire Don Denkinger at first base (the replay showed that the runner had been clearly out) and Jack Clark's catatonic misplay of a pop foul by Steve Balboni near the Royals' dugout. (The Cards, mind you, had not blown a ninth-inning lead the whole year. But they hadn't only blown this one, they had outrageously kicked it away amid an unprecedented outburst of surliness.)

So I didn't get to interview the winners on that tumultuous night, and ABC had to get their platform off the premises before the losing Cards came in from their dugout. Never in my life have I seen a bunch of guys work so rapidly to get rid of props. I was still on the platform when they started to dismantle it.

The next night, as millions of sadists will recall with some glee, the Cards fell apart completely in mind, body, soul, and base hits. Kansas City swamped them, 11–0, with a fuzzy-cheeked new father named Bret Saberhagen chloroforming their bats and with the Cards' Joaquin Andujar erupting like a volcano.

When Andujar blew his stack at umpire Don Denkinger, earning himself an ejection after an explosive exchange, I commented on TV that I wasn't sure he'd ever recover professionally from the incident.

Next to me, Al Michaels nodded his head. "I think you're absolutely right," he said.

With the final game horror show concluded, I had the assignment—perhaps the most difficult of my broadcasting career—to that point—of interviewing Whitey Herzog in his gloomy headquarters.

What made the mission a little easier was the fact that Whitey and I were friends. What's more, I truly felt compassion for the man.

Going on live, before an audience of millions of baseball fans who had just been witness to a classic exhibition of self-destruction, couldn't have been an easy task for Whitey.

Under the circumstances, I thought he handled it very well. He comported himself with restraint and didn't duck out, either on the interview or the questions. He could have opted to do both.

I flung the one question at him that I figured most fans must have been conjuring at that moment.

"Will Andujar be back with the Cards next year?" I asked.

"Yeah, he'll be back," Whitey answered.

Of course, Andujar didn't come back. By December the Cards had traded him to Oakland in the American League. But when Whitey told me Andujar would be back, I think he was telling the truth as he saw it. What he failed to reckon with, in those few moments after that hectic evening, was the unyielding attitude of the St. Louis front office. They wanted Joaquin out of their sight.

Like anybody in this business, I have detractors. What I try to do is keep both the criticism and the praise in perspective.

One way to keep things in perspective is to pay attention to fan mail.

Even though I haven't weighed my fan mail recently, or tabulated the yeas and nays, I feel I'm on the right track with most of my listeners. But not everyone has nice things to say. Two of my favorites came from folks who seemed to have very little use for what I did and how I did it.

"Bring back live people who sound like human beings and not encyclopedias," one nonadmirer wrote. "Your voice is as interesting and live as the Sahara Desert. You are a Monday-morning quarterback wimp, a marshmallow mouth."

The second was a postal card featuring a picture of Sigmund Freud's psychiatric couch. The message: "Please be prompt; the doctor is waiting."

I've been listening to some people badmouth baseball for years. For a while, some years ago, it was popular to pronounce final rites for the game. It became chic at that time to say that baseball was boring everybody to death, that it was too slow-moving, often tedious, and had too few moments of excitement and suspense. People had all sorts of prescriptions for speeding things up, for altering the pace of the game, for putting more emphasis on hitting, for changing the basic rules (some guys even wanted to make two strikes you're out, three balls you walk—that sort of nonsense).

You don't hear too much from these critics anymore. Sure, there's not much to satisfy those who prefer an atmosphere of frenzy and violence and shoot-'em-up activity to the subtleties and nuances of baseball. But for me this game will always be the ultimate game. It's cerebral, yet easily understandable. You have to have patience to watch it and to play it, and that requires involvement, commitment, and devotion on the part of player and fan. It's typically American, because it reflects how most people work. People do routine things, day in and day out, as well as they can. And over the course of time it's those things that really matter. It's not the occasional brilliance that wins. The ability to perform the basics—the fundamentals —all the time is the essence of baseball.

Baseball is a beautiful game to watch and to play. It's a game without limitations of time. With no clock to govern it, its action ebbs and flows, producing big and little surprises. It's a game of great respect and fondness for its past, yet its fans are always "waiting for next year."

In baseball you lose and pick yourself up and carry on from one day and one week to the next, just as in real life you pick yourself up and carry on from one day to the next. There are bad days and good days, bad months and good months, bad years and good years.

That's life. That's baseball.

Mets 1986:
Living It

When my co-conspirator, Ray Robinson, and I decided to create this handy little baseball guide a year or so ago, we also thought it would be interesting to include a personal sketchbook of the 1986 Mets season. These ruminations promised to go from the flowers-that-bloom-in-the-spring to the somnolent, lazy, crazy days of midsummer, to the gut-twisting pressure of the playoffs, to that final reward of the long season —the World Series.

My observations were recorded daily, as the events transpired. There were no hindsights or second-guesses. I had no way of knowing, at any time, whether the Mets would win 108 games or lose 108 games. I wrote as the games were played out, as the slumps came and went, as Davey Johnson kept munching on his stomach pills, as the emotional roller coaster sped to its frenzied finish.

1986 was clearly the Mets' "next year." In 1985, on the day the team was eliminated from the pennant race, they received a standing ovation from their fans. Such unvarnished affection set a pressure-filled stage for 1986, truly the year of "great expectations."

I had no way of knowing or foreseeing last March, as I embarked on this writing odyssey, that the Mets would, indeed, emerge as National League champs after an almost unendurable confrontation with Houston's Astros and "Dread" Scott. Nor did I anticipate their incredible World Series come-from-behind triumph against the Red Sox, finally accomplished in late October, as millions of fans prepared to hibernate around their hot stoves—waiting, as always, faithfully and longingly till yet another "next year."

We began the year in earnest on March 9, a seventy-two-degree Sunday afternoon in St. Petersburg, Florida. Some kids had climbed up on the outfield fence of Al Lang Stadium and were paying (the wrong word to use in this context) as much respectful attention to the proceedings as those other nonpaying fans, the seagulls. Under slightly overcast skies, the stadium was sold out. And why not? Dwight Gooden, the phenom himself, was scheduled to work three innings. All hands had been picking the Mets for first place in the National League East, and the Cards, their foes that day, had been named as a close runner-up. These were teams that enjoyed going at each other, even in spring training.

Dwight went his three innings, giving up a couple of hits, a couple of inaugural strikeouts, no walks, no runs. That's what the people had come to see. The annual spring baseball ritual gets more popular every year, and Dwight isn't doing anything to discourage it.

In 1985, the Mets had a fictitious pitcher, Sidd Finch, invented by George Plimpton for the April Fool edition of *Sports Illustrated*. Well, in 1985, Dwight Gooden was a real-life Sidd Finch. Talk about great expectations. Gooden was 24–4 with a 1.53 ERA. How can you improve on that record?

Watching him pitch against the Cards, several things popped into my mind: Will Davey Johnson continue to use Gooden every fifth day? Will Gooden pitch more than nine innings if needed (Davey's never let him go past nine)? My guess is Davey will continue to be equally prudent with Dwight's right arm. But what if they're in a down-the-stretch dogfight for the division? When does a great talent such as Gooden go from boyhood to manhood?

. . .

When I was a catcher, spring training seemed to never end. Now, as an announcer, it passes oh-so-quickly.

For the players, spring training in Florida revolved around the pre–Vero Beach and post–Vero Beach trip—because St. Pete is a four-hour bus ride from Vero Beach. A hot and not-too-pleasant four-hour bus ride. But a catcher has to make *all* the trips. You never know when an extra catcher will be needed. That's why spring training seemed interminable.

I go over to the Mets' complex and I see catchers catching balls in the dirt. It stirs up memories of the grueling catching process, the pain. I feel like a retired chairman of the board who comes back to his company years later. It's an odd feeling because you remember the decisions, the deals, and the hard work it took to build the company. There's a great satisfaction in the success of the company—and in your own past—but you don't regret being out of it.

I hear Mel Stottlemyre, the Mets' pitching coach, yell, "Hey, I need another catcher over here to warm up a pitcher." Not me, boy. As a catcher, you really get to *hate* pitchers in spring training. They require all that work and they always need an accessory.

Contrary to the regular season, when the players are so unattainable, so unreachable, in spring training these demigods come to life. You can practically reach out and touch them. For the fans, spring training is much closer to their childhood visions of baseball. The game is played on a field, for one thing, not in a huge, impersonal stadium. The players smile and sign autographs. It's fitting that spring training takes place in what is largely a retirement community, a place for older folks. For the ballplayer, preseason assumes that slow, leisurely, almost regal pace. It's only when the season starts that the pace picks up—the pressure begins, the pain mounts up, the winning and losing becomes meaningful.

Winning and losing in spring training is not that important. What is important is that the Mets reached Opening Day without any major injuries. Despite that, however, they got off to a sluggish start—they went two and three to begin the season.

Then came the sonic boom—they reeled off eleven victories in a row.

My April thoughts about the Mets are centered pretty much on the potential of Darryl Strawberry. We basically know what Carter, Hernandez, and Foster can do—even though I *hate* to think that way. You always read that in the press: "Pencil in Keith for a .300 season" or "Count on Gary Carter for his usual thirty home runs." I don't like that because it minimizes their accomplishments. When they reach their goals, everyone tends to simply say, "Well, that's what they were *supposed* to do."

The point is, however, Carter and Hernandez have performed for a long enough time that we know what their limits are, more or less. Keith will not hit thirty-five home runs. Gary Carter will not steal thirty bases. So in my view Darryl is the only Met who might make a quantum leap forward in overall production. But he's hard to calibrate. He busted twenty-nine homers in 1985, despite seven weeks on the bench with an injured thumb. Some people, including Manager Johnson, think Darryl's numbers could be astronomical if he puts it all together. I agree.

Darryl has made a relatively fast start, with five game-winning hits in less than a month, and he's beginning to look like the player everyone thinks he can be. But there is still that nagging inability to hit lefties. And, of course, as long as he is nagged by them, opposition managers will keep pitching them. By the way, Joe Garagiola, who has observed how bundled up Darryl looks when he arrives at home plate—with his batting gloves, wristbands, doughnut on his left thumb, etc.—made me laugh the other day. He said Darryl could be mistaken for "a sporting goods store looking for a sale."

Everyone is saying that Bob Ojeda, who came over from the Red Sox in a November trade, is shaping up as the John Tudor of the 1986 season. Okay, so he is so happy to have escaped Fenway Park's leering green monster in left field that he practically runs out to the mound each time he pitches for the Mets. So he's left-handed; so they both have good change-ups.

Still, don't you get sick of the constant comparisons? It takes away the individuality of the players. Ojeda *isn't* Tudor. Anyway, during Tudor's first season in the National League he was a .500 pitcher with Pittsburgh. I guess comparisons are inevitable, but they're so unfair.

With the team rolling along, not even an occasional rainy evening can stop them. On the night of April 22 it poured all night long, but the Mets outswam the poor Pirates, 7–1, at Shea. Ojeda said afterward that the game had been played "under marginal conditions." That understatement led me to believe he could probably pitch underwater—especially since the Pirates were swinging at him as if *they* were underwater. There's a great line, by the way, about Larry Bowa. Dick Ruthven once said that Bowa, a switch-hitter, swinging left-handed looked as if he were swinging underwater. A great image, and one I don't mind borrowing to describe the Pirates.

I maintain that it is never wise to judge a player by how he fares in either April or September. A team, however, is another matter. The Mets are out of the gate almost as quickly as the 1984 Tigers. There's an old saying that a team is never as good as they think they are or as bad as they look. But the Mets are looking great and thinking they're great. And their remarks to that effect are causing a bit of resentment around the league. The mudslinging's beginning, and things are heating up rather early.

The eye-opener—the Bloody Mary—of the young season is Kevin Mitchell. He's from a ghetto in San Diego, and his younger brother was killed a few years ago in a brutal street fight. Wanting to avenge his brother's death, Mitchell was ready to quit baseball and return to the streets. Several of the Mets' higher-ups prevailed on Kevin, and eventually he decided to stick it out. You've got to hand it to the kid. He's overcome a lot to become an early candidate for Rookie of the Year. He's also one of the more popular players on the club, with a marvelous sense of humor. I think you've got to have a sense of humor and be real loose to assume the kind of role Kevin has had shoved on him. He's become something of an all-around handyman for Davey Johnson, as versatile as a baseball Thomas Jefferson (that's not to confuse him with Stanley Jefferson, another promising farm apprentice of the Mets).

In one April game against the Cards, Davey put Kevin in at shortstop, a position he had scarce familiarity with, and the young man handled six chances with aplomb (although he did botch a throw to the second baseman, leading me to believe he really wasn't a natural at the position). While a national TV audience watched, Kevin also hit a single and a home run against the old Mets nemesis, John Tudor.

As the Mets took those four straight from the Cards, Kevin, a third baseman in Triple A with Tidewater in 1985, was a definite factor. Unheard of before the season, he was playing a role in his team's drive for the pennant. And make no mistake about it—even this early in the season, this was a pivotal series in the pennant race. As the battle for Stalingrad stopped the momentum of the Germans in World War II, it seems to have turned the tide of the 1986 season. The Mets have clearly become the team to beat. And the Cards now know it's not going to be so easy to beat them.

I think Davey has the guts of a burglar to start this kid at short, but it only underlines the kind of manager he is. He wants more punch at shortstop and he's willing to gamble to get what he wants. Earl Weaver once said, "The experimenting stops after the All-Star break." Maybe so. But Davey's attitude is "if you pay them, play them." And he's shown he'll play anyone anywhere.

You see, Johnson likes to have his players in competitive situations. All of his players. Think about it. There's Wally Backman and Tim Teufel at second, Howard Johnson and Ray Knight at third. It appears to be happening in left field, too, with George Foster and Danny Heep. And when Mookie Wilson came off the disabled list in early May, the same competitive situation developed with Lenny Dykstra. I'm convinced that this is healthy, because as Ralph Kiner keeps saying, it's important for a manager to know how to handle players who play every day, but it may even be *more* important to know how to handle those players who *don't* play every day.

Speaking of Kevin Mitchell, you'll still hear jokes made at a rookie's expense, even though there's nowhere near the kind of hazing that used to go on. In 1959, my first year, I was with the Rochester Red Wings, and Dick Rand, an old catcher, sent me into the clubhouse to get the key to the batter's box. I innocently asked him where it was, and he told me it was "next to the glove stretcher." The hook was set and I bit.

A couple of days later, I was in the bullpen and Howie Nunn, a pitcher, wanted to bet me five dollars that there were between twenty and thirty thousand people in the stands. Knowing that Red Wing Stadium held only eighty-five hundred, I again bit. I had to pay off—as he explained to me, he had meant exactly what he'd said: There were between *twenty* people and thirty thousand people.

It didn't stop there. Nunn gave me a chance to get even. He said he'd run me for five dollars—double or nothing. Well, I knew I could outrun this old fart. The game was going on, but we lined up and took off out of the bullpen. I raced to the finish line while Howie just kind of jogged casually along. When he finally caught up to me, he said, "Pay up."

Incredulous, I said, "What do you mean? I won?!"

"I just said I'd *run* you," Howie told me happily. "I didn't say I'd *beat* you."

I paid up.

I can't tell you how many guys paid for the way I was treated in my first year. Every bat boy in the National League who sees me still comes up to me and says, "Hey, there's a new kid over there. Tell him to go get the key to the batter's box." I was gotten, I got them, now they want to get the new kid on the block. It's neverending and only fair.

That's the way rookies used to be treated, but as Willie McCovey told me not too long ago, "When you go into a clubhouse these days you have a hard time telling who the rookies are and who the veterans are. The rookies talk as much as the veterans. That's a little different from the time Bobby Bonds came up to the Giants as a rookie and thought his only mission in life was to carry my stereo or Mays's stereo around."

Oh, the innocence.

During a game this year, Vin Scully told a story about a manager who was talking to a rookie pitcher about location.

"You've got to learn to pitch inside," explained the manager.

A look of despair came over the rookie's face.

"Ya mean you're gonna trade me to Houston?" the rookie wailed.

The surprising home run power of Ray Knight, who hit six homers in a dozen games (in 1985 he had six in ninety games, thus encouraging the Mets' front office to try to trade him or ship him off to a desert island), has been as much a highlight of the early going as the uniformly magnificent work of the pitchers. By the way: a Lee Mazzilli for Ray Knight trade—straight-up—was turned down by Pittsburgh. At least that's the rumor. And at this point the Mets must be glad that the Pirates refused to deal.

The most crucial single blow of the first weeks was struck by the Mets' other third baseman, Howard Johnson. People, especially the press, are always searching for a team's moment of truth, a watershed event that turns things around. Hojo's smack is my favorite watershed.

Hojo began the year platooning with Knight. When Ray started to imitate Ralph Kiner, it looked as if Hojo were out of luck and out of work. But in the first game of that April set with the Cards, Manager Johnson asked player Johnson to try short-stop for the evening. In the ninth inning, with the Mets trailing by two runs, Howard hit a clutch home run to tie it up. Eventually, George Foster won the game with a single in the tenth inning. But it was Hojo's homer that gave the club a life and propelled the team to its eleven-game winning streak. Like the proverbial farmer, Hojo had killed the cow to feed his family. And the Met family went on to prosper.

Boy, the 1986 baseballs are hopping out of parks like jackrabbits! All the evidence to support this statement isn't in yet, but guys like Kirby Puckett, Bill Almon, and even pitcher Rick Aguilera are getting too much distance with too much consistency not to make me suspicious. In May, Tony Gwynn of San Diego hit a game-winning homer in his home park against Jesse Orosco—in spite of the fact that he cracked his bat! Darryl Strawberry hit a 3–2 pitch, a curveball, out on his front foot, which meant that his power was spent. Where'd he hit it? Ten rows back into straight-away center field in Fulton County

Stadium in Atlanta. Sure, Darryl's strong, but he's not *that* strong.

Is the ball smaller and bound tighter than in other years? It certainly appears that way.

Stan Musial commented to Red Schoendienst the other day in St. Louis that he never in his life had seen balls come off the bat the way they are this year. An experienced observation from a trained eye.

Incidentally, although Strawberry never complains about any pain in the thumb he injured in May 1985, he still has it bandaged every day he plays. You've got to wonder if it still bothers him.

If you ask him about his thumb, he says, "I don't think about it much." You've got to take his word, but still, there's that bandage.

I'd like to add another note here about Ray Knight. After 1985 he must have felt like the rabbit who lost the foot that people carry around for good luck. But in 1986, wow, is it different! From the start of the season Ray has looked and hit like a new man. How did it happen?

Well, for one thing, his health is a hundred percent, and that can do a lot for a man, especially one who has been beleaguered by difficulties with his body. You can't play the game well when you're hurt—it's tough enough to play baseball when all your parts are functioning perfectly.

But there is another thing with Ray. He has a remarkably supportive wife. Most baseball wives are emotionally supportive to their husbands in their own way, but Nancy Lopez, Ray's wife, is special. She's an outstanding professional golfer, and as an athlete she's quite aware of the process of hitting golf balls. She can relate to Ray's experience as a player and analyze what he does or doesn't do. She told Ray that in golf you play one hole at a time, with one swing at a time, and you concentrate on that one situation only. Relating that to baseball, Nancy suggested to Ray that he should concentrate on one at bat at a time, one fielding play at a time. Her suggestion appears to be working.

Outside of Knight's remarkable turnaround and Hojo's big

hit against the Cards in April, the key element for the Mets has been their "table setters" at the top of the lineup. (I *am* going to toss something in with a bit of hindsight here: The phrase "table setters" was just a tad overused during the 1986 season, playoffs, and World Series. In fact, if I hear the phrase even once during the 1987 season, there's a good chance I'm going to hang myself with a piece of piano wire. I mean, who's managing the Mets—Julia Child?) Dykstra and Wally Backman have repeatedly contrived to get on in some way—every time you look up it's Dykstra and Backman, first and third.

Well, Dwight Gooden was named Pitcher of the Month for April.

This, despite a somewhat rocky off-the-field existence. Remember, he had an ankle injury before spring training that was turned into an unsolved mystery; he missed the New York baseball writers' annual dinner—he just didn't show up; he missed a spring training game because of a traffic accident that may not have been a traffic accident and got fined by Davey Johnson; then there was a flap at a La Guardia Airport car-rental place, where someone was supposed to have thrown a drink in someone's face and somebody is supposed to have called somebody else a bitch.

Believe it or not, Dwight had a rather reasonable response to all this. "Maybe I should sleep on a cot in the clubhouse," he said.

Later, after some of the unnecessary tumult and shouting died, Dwight added, "I'll have to learn to cope with all of this, day by day. It's not always going to be easy."

All of this stuff makes me realize once again how difficult it is to be a star in New York City. Despite everything, Dwight seems to have a good grip on things and a mature perspective about himself and the turbulent world around him. I think he can keep things in balance. It's said that New York is tough on its sports heroes. But, even though some players, from Mickey Mantle and Roger Maris to Ed Whitson and Butch Wynegar, had their difficulties, there are those who have handled it well. Tom Seaver, for one. Ron Guidry and Catfish Hunter, for others. Reggie Jackson even thrived on it. To tell you the truth,

I think the adulation and the rewards that come with playing in New York *far* exceed the trials and tribulations. Sure, players take knocks from the New York media, but they're also overpraised, overpublicized, and often overpaid. Over the long run, I think Dwight can handle it. A pitcher has to control not only the ball but his emotions as well.

In early May I filled in on ABC, broadcasting an Expos-Dodgers game. Johnny Bench was my broadcast partner. On the same afternoon that I did the game with Johnny, the Mets lost to the Reds, 3–2, for Gooden's first loss. Oddly, the Mets had won eighteen out of nineteen before Dwight's defeat, while the Reds had been mired in the cellar, which seemed to surprise a lot of observers. The Mets had won nine in a row at home, too, before Pete Rose's liner over Backman's head drove in three runs and did them in.

Is it possible the Mets will fall victim to premature hyperbole? It's mid-May and even the perceptive guys, such as Chuck Tanner of Atlanta, are humming tunes about the invincibility of Davey's club.

"Those scouts should start scouting the Mets for the playoffs," Chuck announced. Is he trying to throw the whammy into the Mets? Or is he giving his true opinion?

On the Mets' first trip to Dodger Stadium, Gooden was ahead 3–1 in the sixth inning. With runners on second and third, the game was stopped by home plate umpire Bob Engel. A car's headlights were mysteriously shining in through the center field fence.

When play resumed after ten minutes, Gooden threw a curveball to Greg Brock, who singled to right field, tying the game. The Dodgers eventually won the game, though Gooden got a no-decision. Most important, rumors of Doc's vincibility have begun to surface. Last year, with a two-run lead, you could wrap it up if Dwight was on the mound.

While we were out on the West Coast, *USA Today* printed one of their interminable daily sports lists. This one listed Steve Boros's five favorite books. Boros, the San Diego Padres' manager, is considered somewhat of a baseball intellectual. Unfor-

tunately, his team isn't up here to read—their record is fading
rapidly. Fifth on Steve's list of favorite tomes was *A Farewell
to Arms.* It sounds like an apt description of the Padres' pitching staff.

Up in San Francisco the Mets were faced by the Giants and
their manager, Roger Craig, who could easily be mistaken in
appearance for the late Lyndon Johnson. Roger, who once lost
twenty-four games with the Mets in less happy times, has had
his Giants playing winning baseball in his first year as boss man.
People have actually been coming out to the Candlestick Park
tundra to see what's going on.

Roger is still the same loose, confident guy I played with
back in 1964 on the Cards. Now he's earning lots of attention
for introducing the split-finger fastball to his entire pitching
staff. He's also doing something with his catchers that I don't
agree with. He insists on standing in the dugout and flashing
signals to them, prescribing exactly what his pitchers should
throw. They say he did the same thing with Lance Parrish and
the Tigers in 1984, when he was a Detroit coach.

In my opinion, what Roger is doing is unsound for two
reasons. First, you can't instill confidence or develop a
catcher's self-reliance with such strategy. Also, any catcher
knows more about what a pitcher is doing than anyone else,
including his manager. Remember, a catcher is and should be
an expert on results. Second, it could be pretty darn easy to
pick up the signals the manager is sending.

The Giants have a young catcher, Bob Melvin. What's
Melvin going to learn this way? Can he be trained properly or
learn anything from such tactics? I doubt it.

Solly Hemus used to call pitches for Bob Gibson early in
Gibson's career. Gibson says he remembers one such inning:
Fastball—the hitter popped up. Solly proudly flashed another
sign. Slider—a ground-out to third. Hemus, chest expanding,
signaled for another slider. Billy Williams of the Cubs
promptly parked it on the right field pavilion of old Busch
Stadium. When Gibson looked over for another sign, all he saw
was the once proud Hemus getting a drink of water. Managers
always drink water when they're not thirsty.

. . .

When the Dodgers came to Shea later in the month, the Mets won three in a row. George Foster hit a grand-salami on the first pitch thrown by relief pitcher Tom Niedenfuer. Ray Knight, the next Met batter, was immediately and solidly hit on the left elbow. Both benches emptied and television viewers got to see a better fight than you'll usually see in network bouts.

Almost everyone knew, of course, that Tom deliberately tried to hit Ray, even though he was quoted as saying he wasn't. But you have to say that.

Sending "messages" to batters is certainly a venerable baseball custom and is generally accepted as permissible behavior. The tradition of keeping hitters honest is an old one. But depending on whom you're rooting for, hitting the next batter is not usually considered kosher. The theory being that the prevention of home runs is much more ethical than hitting a batter out of anger over a previous home run. Plain and simple, it's bush to hit the next guy. That's why Knight charged Niedenfuer.

Such unpleasant incidents happen in baseball. It's a myth that baseball is a nonviolent or noncontact sport. When frayed tempers get out of hand, grown men become warriors.

There were some surprises in the first two months, but I don't think anything has been more satisfying to the Mets than the performance of Bob Ojeda. The Mets traded for consistency and got brilliance.

Ron Darling has also been winning, in spite of a few unscheduled home run pitches. While Ron keeps dancing through the raindrops, Davey Johnson delivers avuncular lessons to him about getting ahead of batters. Some folks suggest that the Johnson-Darling relationship is sort of symbiotic, almost a father-son sort of thing. Some compare it to the Weaver-Palmer relationship. Davey has gone public, saying that Ron's hard to watch because he falls behind so many hitters. But, as of June 1, he's got six wins and no losses.

Wally Backman continues to play superb ball. His on-base percentage is tremendous, largely because he'll do anything to get on base—walk, bunt, try to beat out a little dunker down the line. A San Diego writer described Padre Tim Flannery as having "extraordinary will, with ordinary skill." That goes double for Backman.

On a perfect June day the wily Whitey Herzog issued a communiqué to the world announcing that the National League East struggle was already over, that the Mets were going to win, that the whole thing was a *fait accompli*. It looks as if Whitey is precariously close to throwing in the towel and going home. I am totally surprised by this early announcement.

Naturally, Whitey made the sports headlines with that prediction. I have to wonder what the White Rat is up to. Has he really divined that after some fifty-five games the Mets have already clinched it? Is he trying to lull Davey and his boys into complacency? Is it meant as a wake-up call for Tommy Herr, Willie McGee, Jack Clark, etc.? Or does this shrewd baseball strategist actually figure that the Cards have had it?

There is a rumor that Whitey recently held a clubhouse meeting with the Cardinals. He was concerned because he thought his players were making too many excuses. Typically, Whitey said, "Guys . . . when you're horseshit, you don't have to make any excuses. And you guys have been horseshit!"

There is no way that Davey is buying Whitey's message. Most of the Mets just shrugged the whole thing off, attributing it to Whitey's frustrations. Danny Heep may have summed up the Mets' feelings best when he said, "He's trying to give us false security."

On the other hand, with the Mets zooming off to their best won-lost start in their twenty-five-year history, the general euphoria around New York has gotten so out of hand that many fans are expressing rage and impatience when the Mets lose *one* in a row!

One of the Mets who hasn't shared in the general prosperity of the first two months is Gary Carter, though I think Gary is indispensable to the team's success. One of the remarkable things is how well the Mets are doing without great production from Carter. Though he's driving in runs, he isn't hitting for a high average and he is having a tough time throwing out runners. In my opinion, because of the knee surgery he had in the 1985 off-season, I think he's favoring his knee. As a result, I believe he's hurt his shoulder. That's what happens: When you compensate and favor one part of the body, you're bound to screw up another part. Then it starts to weigh on the mind.

"You can get so much advice from everyone, as I have," Gary told me, "including advice from Davey, Bill Robinson, the fans who write such well-meaning letters. But in the long run what it boils down to is that you have to work it out for yourself and by yourself. Nobody can do it for you."

I say amen to that. You can give a guy like Carter a dozen tips on what he's doing wrong—weight shift, hands in improper position, opening up too fast, not striding into the ball, pulling away too much, swinging at bad balls, etc.—but he's the one who's got to resolve it.

I can recall a time when I was experiencing a similar hitting famine. I took extra batting practice until my hands became sore and bleeding and my arms literally hurt from swinging. Dick Sisler, my kind batting coach, watched me patiently, instructing me occasionally on certain nuances and discussing things that chiefly had to do with hand-to-eye coordination. It was a long and painful process. At the end of it, Sisler, who had a pronounced stutter that was often the butt of jokes that he made about himself or others made about him, looked me squarely in the eyes.

"T-t-timmmy," he asked, "c-can you h-hit?"

"Sure I can," I answered quickly and with conviction.

"Then s-s-s-swing the b-b-b-bat."

Let me tell you: It boils down to that. If you know you can hit, swing the bat. Keep it simple.

Gary Carter knows that.

A lot of people are asking questions out loud: Are the Mets ready to dominate baseball for a few years the way the Boston Celtics have done in basketball and the way the Chicago Bears threaten to do in football?

The question is legitimate, I believe. But, talk about prematurity. There are still, at the beginning of July, a hundred games to go, and everybody who's been around baseball knows this kind of talk can sink a lot of dugouts.

But there's no escaping it. Strange and exciting things are happening to the Mets in their newfound wonderland. Tim Teufel, who bats mainly against southpaws as he fills in for Backman, went up and pinch-hit a home run with the bases loaded against the Phils in extra innings. On another day, Strawberry won a game with a ninth-inning single against the Pirates after Keith Hernandez had been purposely passed. The book theory is that the lefty on the mound for Pittsburgh would do the usual job that lefties have been doing versus Darryl. As of this moment, nobody feels that Darryl owns any southpaws, but he appears to be making a better effort to make contact against them.

In another game with the Pirates, Dwight struck out thirteen, his season's high. It was his best performance of what has been up to now an uneven year, but he still didn't get credit for the win. Dwight's been struggling for the past month. Joe Garagiola recently cracked that "Dwight's leading the league in headlines that ask, 'What's up, Doc?' "

Everyone has become a Dwight-watcher, including me. The search is on to find out what's wrong. The one thing I don't think is wrong is Dwight's concentration. As he prepares to pitch, Dwight still reminds me of a Japanese chef carving a flower out of a carrot.

I continue to get a big kick out of watching Lenny Dykstra do his job. He's got more nervous tics up there at bat than an old hound; when he chokes his bat you'd think the wood would scream. He's got those anxious fingers and seems as nervous as a hermit expecting company. But he's really made himself an important element on this club. In one game with the Padres, Lenny bunted safely with two strikes on him, catching everybody by surprise, including us in the booth. Even though he got a base hit, it was a bad play. To be successful, a bunt should be pushed down the first- or third-base line. But when you've got two strikes on you, you can't risk bunting down the line— it's too chancy that the ball will go foul and you'll strike out. With two strikes, you've got to bunt in the middle of the field. When you do that, you not only take away the element of surprise, you make it much easier for the pitcher to field the ball.

Even though there are mostly pleasant developments around the Mets' encampment, on June 11, when the Mets faced the Phils, there was a personally painful (to me) incident. The Mets pummeled Steve Carlton in the first inning with three runs. Then they got another in the second inning. Ray Knight added further embarrassment with a homer in the third.

Watching the Phils manager, John Felske, yank Lefty in the fourth inning, after Kevin Mitchell hit a bullet over third base, was a sad event for me. I appreciate that reporters are expected, among other things, to be objective, but I'd be a liar to say I wasn't suffering along with Carlton. Not to be too melodramatic about it, but on the air I referred to A. E. Housman's famous poem about an athlete dying young. Housman says it's better for an athlete to die young than to confront the downside of his career.

Lefty certainly isn't dying, though his career is on the downgrade now.

With his eventual release from the Phillies, I was besieged by people inquiring about my reaction to the event. I did twenty-two interviews and eight on-cameras. My general theme was that I don't believe that athletes owe it to anyone to bow out gracefully. To me it's graceful and the epitome of class for an athlete to fight like a wounded tiger when they are trying to tear the uniform off his body. Maybe I get too emotional about it—and perhaps my own experience colors the way I think about it—but history does tell us that many athletes who have been prematurely counted out do come back for that one last hurrah.

In early July the Mets are leading the universe in almost every department, including outfield collisions. The outfield sometimes resembles a replay of Pork Chop Hill. Instead of catching flies, they are dropping like flies in left field. Hojo got hurt, Dykstra was almost hurt, and Foster almost made the infirmary list. It makes you wonder whether the outfielders are bothering to communicate with one another out there as they grope for fly balls. The left center field area, between the left fielder, center fielder and shortstop, has come to be known as the Bermuda Triangle. When fielders converge on a pop fly in that area, they rarely emerge intact. Howard Johnson's arm is broken, which means that Davey must employ Rafael Santana as the Mets' shortstop.

Even at midseason, Santana is still hitting less than .175. But I'll say this again about Davey Johnson: If he's got a hitter whose batting average is lower than the temperature at the North Pole, he won't jump all over him. Santana doesn't have good range, but he does have soft hands and remains a more-than-adequate defensive shortstop.

Maybe the most imperfect thing that has occurred, as the 1986 season rolls along, is the failure of the Redbird Machine of 1985. Did anybody anticipate that the Cards would collapse like a pricked balloon this year? This was the team that beat out the Mets in 1985, with most of its players experiencing career seasons. The Cards were first in batting average and runs scored in 1985, and had a pitcher, John Tudor, who couldn't lose over the last part of the season. Now they are last in runs and batting average—an "accomplishment," going from first to last in both categories, that no team has equaled in a century.

It's mid-July of 1986 and the Cards are trailing the Mets by over twenty games. They are already being written off by their own manager, Whitey Herzog. Was their downfall a carryover trauma from the World Series, when they blew sky-high over Umpire Don Denkinger's sixth-game call and then watched the Vesuvian explosion of Joaquin Andujar in the seventh game?

Whatever it is that's ailing the Cards, their season in microcosm occurred in a June 30 game against the Mets in St. Louis. In the first inning Vince Coleman led off with a triple. He remained stranded there as Ozzie Smith struck out, Tommy Herr popped up, and Willie McGee, the league's leading hitter and MVP in 1985, hit meekly back to the pitcher. At that moment you could have said, as I volunteered on the air, that Busch Stadium had metamorphosed into *Ambush* Stadium. But it was the Cards who were being ambushed, not the enemy.

In the same game Coleman stole four bases—speed had always been the Cards' most valuable asset—but Vince never came around to score. The Cards were shut out, 7–0.

The Cards' situation approaches the comical, if you're not a Card. You have to laugh to keep from crying. If they're lucky, they might hit sixty home runs over the whole season.

The KMOX call-in show in St. Louis has been receiving hundreds of beseeching phone calls urging the team to do this or that, pitch this guy, fire that guy, presumably assassinate somebody, etc. When a visiting team arrives in St. Louis these days, the most judicious behavior is to tiptoe into the city, beat 'em up on the diamond without causing any unnecessary arguments or incidents, and then quietly leave town, perhaps even buying them a tall drink on the way out. When a team such as the Cards is in the doldrums (or, as Frank Lucchesi used to say, "the doodlums"), you don't do anything to wake them up if you can help it.

Some time has to be spent discussing Keith Hernandez, whom I believe to be the Mets' MVP.

For the first time, Keith made it to the All-Star Game as the starting first baseman. Talk about overdue.

Defensively, he is simply state-of-the-art. He's the Baryshnikov of first basemen. Baseball is a game where, if you do the routine things spectacularly, you win more games than doing the spectacular things routinely—because few athletes have the talent to do spectacular things routinely. Keith has that kind of talent.

What's always a tough hop for most guys is somehow ironed out by Hernandez. On what's usually called a "good effort" by announcers, when first basemen fail to come up with the ball, the play is almost always simply an out when Keith's in there to make it. How many guys make the cutoff like Keith? How many have his arm? How many save errors the way Keith does consistently, game after game? How many first basemen, by their positioning, allow a second baseman, who may be weak going to his right, the luxury of not *having* to go to his right? Well, Hernandez, who plays far over toward second base, does that for Backman.

From an offensive standpoint, he's not "offensive" at all. One criticism of Hernandez is that he doesn't have a lot of power (he's never hit more than sixteen home runs). But Keith is the kind of consistent clutch hitter who relies on "big" RBI production as compared with "multi" RBI production.

As an example, a lot of one-run games are won by key hits in the middle innings rather than by big three-run home runs late in the game. Keith is a spectacular middle-inning hitter. Especially with the type of pitching the Mets have, Keith is the perfect hitter. You've heard the baseball adage, "Keep 'em close, I'll think of something"? Well, the something the Mets think of is usually Keith Hernandez.

When he's between the white lines, I marvel at how he can block out everything except what's going on in the game. It's almost as though Hernandez's relaxation is his business. You've heard that business can be some men's mistress, but with Keith it's even more than that—it might be his marital partner. He even loves, cherishes, and obeys first base.

When he came back from the Pittsburgh drug trial in 1985, he went five-for-five in his first game. When he balked at the commissioner's edict this year in spring training—Keith had to pay a hefty fine and donate time to community service or be suspended for a year—he was under tremendous pressure. Yet he got off to one of the fastest starts of his career. That all stems from the total respect he has for his business.

If I had to write a book about Keith Hernandez, I'd title it *In the Game*. That's the one phrase that Davey Johnson uses more than any other when describing Keith—he's always "in the game." It's also the one thing Davey expects Keith to teach the younger players. And I think he has.

The speculation has continued about the supposed diminution of Gooden's talents. When Dwight gave up an 0–2 home run to Lou Whitaker of Detroit in the July 15 All-Star Game, the gossip about him gushed like Niagara Falls. Fans everywhere were talking about him.

Without analyzing all of Dwight's stats, which clearly show his strikeout numbers down and runs against him up, one thing was certain about Gooden at midseason. He was throwing more pitches out of the strike zone and was getting behind batters more frequently than he did in his marvelous 1985 season. I don't care how good a pitcher happens to be—he can't keep pitching from behind and get away with it unscathed.

It also seems to me that Dwight has been "wild high" just enough this year to lose many of the batters he victimized in 1985. Also, hitters have been much more selective in swinging at that borderline high fastball. The speed is still there, no doubt about it. The radar guns generally pick up Dwight's pitches at ninety to ninety-six miles per hour. But the radar gun is, for the most part, bullshit. It's the pop at the end of a fastball that counts, not how quickly the ball gets to the plate. Dwight's movement just isn't there. Remember: Movement, location, and *then* velocity. It's no wonder that Gooden is having problems, because what stands out right now is velocity.

Whatever ails Dwight, the Mets have come halfway with a glowing 59–25 record, for a .702 winning percentage, plus a robust thirteen-game margin over second-place Montreal. It's the fattest All-Star break margin since divisional play began in 1969.

The Expos have been playing exceptional ball, but the major speculation around the Mets has to do chiefly with the margin of victory at season's end and whether Gooden, Fernandez, Ojeda, and Darling can each win twenty games. At this stage, these are their numbers: Fernandez has twelve wins; Ojeda, ten; Gooden, ten; and Darling, nine. Fernandez has also been exhibiting the most overpowering fastball in the National League.

Darling made a delightful remark the other day.

"On any other pitching staff," Ron said, "I'd be the shining star. On this one I'm the caboose."

With a bullpen headed by McDowell and Orosco, the Mets look unstoppable.

The All-Star Game was held in Houston. Rick Cerrone (no relation to Rick Cerone, the former Yankee catcher) of the commissioner's office invited me to emcee the All-Star Game media press conference, held the day before the game.

"One of these days," I remarked at the conference, "Darryl Strawberry is going to hit a ball farther than anyone has ever seen. I hope I'm there to see it."

Prescience is part of my job as an announcer, but I mean, *really* . . .

That same afternoon, in a home run contest at the workout in the Astrodome, with about fifteen thousand fans on hand, Darryl unloaded on a ball that hit the public address speaker some 200 feet high and 350 feet from home plate. If the speaker hadn't been there, the ball might have gone through the roof—and I mean that! I've never seen anything like it. When the crowd realized where the ball had gone, there was a spontaneous roar, followed by a standing ovation for Darryl.

Speaking of fifteen thousand fans, that's about what the Astros are averaging per game. The Astrodome has been a place that the Astro fans are, even with players such as Glenn Davis, Kevin Bass, Bob Knepper, Nolan Ryan, and Mike Scott fighting to capture the National League's West Division, staying away from. Is a puzzlement, as Yul Brynner said in *The King and I.* Though maybe it isn't so puzzling, since Houston is such a football town.

It was great fun broadcasting the fifty-seventh All-Star Game with Al Michaels and Jim Palmer. Clemens was positively superb, and so was Fernando Valenzuela, whose five straight strikeouts rekindled memories of Giants screwballer Carl Hubbell. Gooden gave up a two-run homer to Lou Whitaker, and it was a fairly dull game until knuckleballer Charlie Hough of Texas came in to pitch the seventh and eighth innings. I could really empathize with catcher Rich Gedman's first experience with Hough's butterfly of a pitch.

The American League won, 4–3.

I got to spend the entire week in Houston since the Mets opened the second half of the season at the Dome.

It's rare that I get to spend so much time in one place in one sitting. It was particularly nice because Anne came down for the whole week. We had a really relaxing time. It broke the schedule up nicely, and now I feel refreshed and ready for the rest of the season.

Jack Buck took two weeks off to do the Irish Derby in Ireland and told me how relaxed he was when he came back. Mets GM Frank Cashen told me that when he was with the Baltimore organization he used to give the Orioles' broadcasters a week to ten days off each season so they could refuel for the homestretch. I heartily approve. One of the things people simply don't understand is that baseball is a seven-days-a-week job. I can't tell you how many times people say to me, "What are you doing for the July Fourth weekend?" or "What are you doing on Labor Day?" or even "What are you doing this weekend?" I'll tell you what I'm doing—going to the ballpark!

I suppose it's a little strange for people to really appreciate that what they do for fun is *work* for me. Even at a cocktail party, let's say, I like to talk about things other than baseball. Because talking baseball at a party is like talking business. It's odd, I know. People go to the ballpark on weekends to relax, so they can't understand sometimes why *my* being at the ballpark is draining or exhausting. But it's like my saying that I'm going to hang out in your office for the weekend—just for fun.

The Mets started the second half by blowing out the Astros 13–2.

The next night, it had to happen!

The Mets, after going 110 games without suffering a shutout—a streak dating back to September 11, 1985—have finally been whitewashed. A neat job it was, too. The shutout surgery was performed by lefty Bob Knepper. The odd part of the blanking is that Knepper had failed in seven previous attempts to win his eleventh game. Go figure it! Especially after the Mets had exploded for those thirteen runs the night before.

Only one team in history—the Yanks of 1932—had ever gone a full season without being shut out. The Mets had gone halfway, and now had finally succumbed. It was no tragedy, of course, but it was one of two events that occurred within twenty-four hours that had the baseball world—and plenty of people outside that world—gossiping and wondering.

On Saturday night, July 19, in Houston, four Mets—Tim

Teufel, Ron Darling, Bob Ojeda, and Rick Aguilera—were arrested after a fight at a local bar called Cooter's Executive Games and Burgers. A couple of days earlier Teufel's wife had given birth to their first child, and Teufel was theoretically out celebrating with his buddies. But he allegedly wound up scuffling with some Houston gendarmes, uniformed police officers serving as security personnel at Cooter's. The four players were picked up at 2:00 A.M., a smidgen past Davey Johnson's curfew time, then spent eleven hours in a holding cell before bond of $8,000 was posted for each of them. Teufel and Darling are charged with third-degree felony assault, which could carry sentences of two to ten years in jail and a $5,000 fine if they're convicted. The charges against Ojeda and Aguilera could call for up to a year in jail and a $2,000 fine.

There were, of course, varying stories about what happened. The newspapers, especially the more sensational tabloids, are having a field day with this chewy item. One memorable headline was the screeching one-liner "THE BOYS OF SLAMMER."

Trying to make light of this nocturnal brouhaha, some of the other Mets stuck adhesive tape vertically on the four players' stalls, suggesting, of course, with a minimum of subtlety, jail cells. Also displayed on each player's stool was a beer can, a plastic cup labeled "tequila," a bar of soap-on-a-rope, a cigarette, a razor, and a box of matches. Gallows humor? Not really. Not in a clubhouse. Again, it's a different world. Stuff like this is just grist for ballplayers. The seriousness of this sort of thing has nothing to do with life in the clubhouse.

There's no desire on my part here to minimize what these Mets are supposed to have done at Cooter's. But it's my impression that in the "olden days" such brawls were not regarded with quite the seriousness that this one was. Perhaps the fact that the police were involved puts a different face on it from the usual barroom scramble.

One thing to keep in mind: A normal barroom patron, after a few too many drinks, would like nothing better than to take a swing at a ballplayer. Johnny Edwards once said, "You've got to eat shit in bars." What he meant was that you've got to take whatever they hand out in that kind of a public place. When a guy has too much of that "loudmouth soup" in him, you've simply got to walk away. Most ballplayers, as they get older, learn to stay away from confrontational situations like these. But it's tough when you're young.

The oddest thing about this whole incident is that of all the guys in the National League, Darling, Teufel, Aguilera, and Ojeda are probably the least likely to ever get involved in this kind of fight. Not just on the Mets—in the entire league!

The clamor over Cooter's had barely subsided when the Mets enlisted in the Punch Bowl at Cincinnati, with Ray Knight the featured player for the second time this year.

On the night of July 22, Eric Davis, a young Redleg with enormous ability, stole third against the Mets in the tenth inning of a game that had been tied in the ninth after Big Dave Parker made an error on a fly ball that he misjudged. Knight, playing third, objected to the safe call. Eric had practically uprooted the bag in his slide, but the slide was clean. Pushing and shoving ensued, and as Knight put it, Eric said something bad and, brother, he wasn't whistling "mother!" This was followed by a punch thrown by Knight; then all hell broke loose. Both benches emptied as if the players had all been shot out of a circus cannon, and one of the longest (fifteen minutes), bitterest fights I've ever seen in baseball got going.

Knight got the heave-ho when the track was cleared. So did Kevin Mitchell, who was kicked so hard in the ribs he was spitting up blood all night. Eric Davis and Mario Soto got the heave, too. I remember yelling on the air, "This isn't a game, it's a crisis!" This all led to one of the strangest finishes any of us have ever seen.

Because Davey was shorthanded—Strawberry had been tossed out of the game even before the fight began—relief pitchers Jesse Orosco and Roger McDowell kept switching from the mound to the outfield (yes, the outfield), with Jesse actually making one nice catch of a line drive to right field. On one occasion, Jesse and Roger actually hit back-to-back. (When has that ever happened to two pitchers?) And Gary Carter played some third base for the first time in eleven years. As a matter of fact, he was involved in a 3-5-4 double play started by Keith Hernandez—something I've never seen before.

The fight served to reinforce the already prevalent feelings around the league that the Mets are chronic brawlers and battlers, and that charge of arrogance is resurfacing. But have you ever heard anyone accuse a last-place team or a noncontender of being arrogant? No way! It seems the Mets are becoming the Los Angeles Raiders of baseball.

An interesting aside to the fight was George Foster's noninvolvement. In "the macho nonwimp world of baseball," wrote Ira Berkow of *The New York Times*, "it's supposed to be incumbent upon a teammate to run onto the field in support of your teammate" when a fight breaks out. For the most part, that's what happened in Riverfront Stadium. But when I looked down at the glaring violence on the field, almost as glaring was Foster's absence. I'm not saying it was right or wrong of George, I'm just saying it was strange of George. Obviously, several Mets criticized George for his decision.

If you think that the Mets have gotten punch-drunk from this succession of events, it's not so.

They just keep winning. The lead went to thirteen over the Expos, then fifteen, and now it's nineteen. There's definitely a light side to things, too—there always is with a winner.

Darryl decided to cut off all his hair, with the help of Kevin Mitchell, who performed the tonsorial honors. I told Darryl, "The next step is waxing."

Darryl said, "Yeah, I've heard of that."

"It's painful, though," I said. "But I think that's the next thing—waxing and buffing."

We talked about Darryl's new look on the air. I started going on about how I didn't understand why we had hair on our ears. "I get the head," I said, "and I understand the nose. But what's hair doing inside our ears?" Steve Zabriskie had no idea where I was going with this. In fact, neither did I. But there's one thing that's certain—I still don't know why we have hair in our ears!

With the Mets galloping off to a seemingly insurmountable lead that even confounds Davey Johnson, everyone, including me, makes jokes about it. When the Mets drop a game or two in the standings, I say it's like a loss of eight pounds or so by William Perry, the Chicago Bears' Refrigerator. Who'll notice? After the Mets lost four in a row to the Cards—their longest losing streak of the year—Ralph Kiner dismissed the whole series as "spring training games." ABC's broadcaster Keith Jackson suggested that "you'd have to be camping outside of Bogotá not to know that the Mets are running away with it."

What impact, if any, does this have on the other clubs in the league? Whenever there's such a margin between first place and the also-rans, what happens to the fighting instincts of the other teams? Do they go catatonic through the remaining games on the schedule? Do they simply give up and wait till next year?

No. I believe that the competitive instincts of ballplayers make them play and play hard. One equalizer in baseball is that the individual will always play hard—because of his own individual stats. It's a healthy form of greed. In this respect, pride and greed go hand in hand.

The fangless Cubs just put together four wins over the Mets, two at Shea, now two at Wrigley. I can't help thinking that they are playing the Mets as if they are back in 1984, vying for the pennant.

While in Chicago, we got word in the booth that George Foster made a statement to Jim Corbett of the *Westchester News* implying that his fortunes had declined on the Mets primarily due to racial reasons.

In my opinion, Foster isn't making a very good case. Shortly before Foster's emotional outburst, Davey Johnson had turned over George's left field job to Kevin Mitchell, who is a black man. George also insinuated that white men such as Gary Carter and Keith Hernandez have been generally favored by the Mets as role models and thus were used in commercials and various promos, but I think he's also distorting the truth there. Dwight Gooden and Darryl Strawberry are also favorites of the club in this area. All you have to do is turn on your TV set to see constant images of these two young men. In print and on the tube, they are wonderful merchandisers of their own talents and abilities, as well as the Mets' image. Just a few years past their teens, they have practically become cult heroes.

On the general issue of race relations on the Mets, my own perceptions are that the air is healthy. This is not a management or team of racists or bigots. Davey Johnson doesn't care about color when he makes out his lineup card.

We interviewed Jim Corbett on the air to verify that Foster's statements were accurate. He stood by his story.

We also interviewed Davey Johnson, who was visibly upset by Foster's accusations.

The Mets are trying to decide what to do with Foster. My guess is he'll be released. The combination of this new controversy and the fact that he's having a lousy year will probably push the Mets to that point.

George Foster was released today, two days after his statements hit the papers.

I believe that if George had kept quiet, the Mets would have let him finish the season. You never know, but I think he would have stuck around.

The broadcasting team—but especially me—was criticized in the press for not giving editorial commentary about the Foster situation. It's tricky. I can understand the criticism, especially because I usually editorialize about anything and everything under the sun. But in this particular instance, I feel my job was to report, not editorialize. It's a judgment call. It may be wrong, but I'll stand by it.

Irrevocably out of the race after only a half season, the Cards struggled into Shea Stadium in mid-August for a six-game series, including two doubleheaders.

The Mets dropped four of those six games, which is not all that important at this point. What *is* important is that the Mets have lost Gary Carter to the disabled list for fifteen days. Taking what for him was a holiday, Gary was playing first base on Saturday afternoon in place of Hernandez and tore a ligament in the thumb of his left hand as he sprawled for a ground ball. I've always said Gary was the least dispensable man on the Mets' roster, and now my theory will be put to the test. Ed Hearn will fill in until Gary returns. Even though Keith is the MVP, Gary is the least dispensable. It's a strange thing—but

Carter is tougher to replace. Even when you have a guy like Hernandez, it's easier to replace someone at first base. It's the position that dictates indispensability—and the difficulty of finding an All-Star-level catcher is what makes Gary's injury so tough to take.

Some folks are hinting that sitting it out for two weeks will give Gary a chance for a well-earned rest and that he'll return to the lineup stronger than ever for the so-called September stretch drive. That remains to be seen.

The extended Cards series was also an inauspicious half week for Strawberry, who simply couldn't buy a hit. At one point he went oh-for-twenty-four, causing Steve Zabriskie to describe Straw as being "in a deep, dark forest." Whatever forest, swamp, or dungeon he is in, Darryl appears to have lost his way in the strike zone. In the ninth inning of one game, when Darryl was called out on strikes with two on base and the Mets trailing 3–1, he threw his helmet and bat precariously close to the umpire. A study in frustration, Darryl was also out a hundred bucks for his loss of control.

In the game during which Carter hurt his thumb, Lee Mazzilli hit a home run to tie the game in the ninth. It was Lee's first right-handed home run in some five years.

Maz has replaced Foster on the team. His return had a positive impact on the players, but an even bigger impact on the fans. The Shea faithful were thrilled to welcome back their one-time hero.

With the noncontenders upholding the game's virtue and integrity, how about the Mets' own intensity factor at this stage? That is the question asked of me most frequently as I travel around the country doing my broadcasts.

Well, I believe the Mets have in some mysterious way taken on the personality and character of their manager, who is, to put it mildly, a ruthless competitor. I don't mean that to be a negative appraisal, either. It's just that Davey, the ultimate competitor, does not believe in letting up, even for a moment—in cards, in golf, and especially in baseball.

In an August series with the Dodgers, when the Mets

swept all three games (something they hadn't accomplished in Chavez Ravine in eighteen years), Davey Johnson played every inning to the hilt. Each game was much more important to the Dodgers, for they are still fighting to remain a factor in the National League West against Houston and San Francisco. But watching Davey's constant involvement with lineup shifts, pinch-hitting strategies, and the use of Roger McDowell, a ubiquitous presence out of the bullpen (he still looks to me like an Eagle Scout pigging out on bubble gum), you might have thought that it was the Mets fighting to stay in contention.

There's Johnson, eighteen or so games ahead, slightly betraying his emotions, removing his cap and putting it back on, rhythmically chewing his cud, slyly raising a nervous finger along the side of his face, all the while staring fixedly at the occupant of the mound.

Every place you go, all anybody talks about is the Mets' four starters. Two guys who may have been forgotten about—though not by the players—are Orosco and McDowell. McDowell is on a pace to set a Mets all-time appearance record. Orosco, while not quite as consistent as Roger, appears to have recovered from the nagging elbow problems he had in 1985. The two combined are giving the Mets the most devastating lefty-righty bullpen combination in the league.

It's getting to be "countdown time" for the Mets in the Eastern Division, and they are probably already preparing in their minds for one helluva clubhouse celebration. The newspapers and we on the air are starting to carry those portentous magic numbers, a happy omen for the front-runners and an equally sad signal that the months and days of the long season are winding down.

In the booth recently there's been a lot of good-natured joshing about my being on the cover of *Esquire*'s September issue. Ralph says that the clothes they had me pose in "were already worn by somebody else," and Fran Healy asked me if *Esquire* wanted all those snazzy clothes to be returned. I'm now "Cover Boy" to my intimates, which, I guess, is far better than the "Bush" they used to call me when I first arrived in the big leagues twenty-seven years ago.

How can anyone really dislike being the pictured image on thousands of magazine covers? I'd be a hypocrite to say it annoyed me. Hell, I wouldn't have posed for it if I'd felt that way.

Yet, there's a troubling aspect to it, which I think about sometimes. I've been reading *Intimate Strangers*, a book by Richard Schickel, which deals with the current American preoccupation with celebrities. One of the points the book makes is that many people "out there"—the unfamous, you could call them—think they really know all those faces, like mine, that they see on TV, in the movies, and in magazines. They build up fantasy relationships that aren't too healthy for all parties concerned. According to Schickel, people want a piece of you. They also come to expect certain behavior from their celebrity "friends"—graciousness, attention, humility, kindness—many traits that can't be supplied by the celebrity.

I'm not certain I've got the whole relationship—and my own responsibilities in it—all figured out. I end up saying hello and being as courteous to people as I've been all my life. I enjoy being recognized, but I can be disturbed by gratuitous insults, usually flung by people trying to make a point or two with their pals. A lot of times, a celebrity is put in a no-win situation. If you do something—let's say, something simple such as giving an autograph—you're *supposed* to do it. If you don't give that autograph—or make that personal appearance or smile at someone who starts talking to you while you're eating dinner—you're a prick. I'll tell you, the whole thing can be disturbing, and I'm still trying to figure it out.

The beat goes on. It's now late August and the Mets have returned home to Shea.

Perhaps the whole near-mythic season of the Mets—the Mets' phenomenon—was captured in the play that ended the last game of the West Coast trip. The Mets, leading 6–5 in the last of the eleventh inning at San Diego, pulled off a play in a few glittering seconds that should be repeated for years on late-night TV replays.

Here's what happened in less time than you can say Mel Ott: Garry Templeton doubled to start the Padres' eleventh. Then, with one out, Tim Flannery drilled a hard single to center field, where Lenny Dykstra, playing unusually shallow, pounced on it and made a good throw home to the waiting John Gibbons. John's a real hard-nosed guy, and he held his ground as the ball and Templeton arrived almost simultaneously. When Templeton crashed into him, the force of the collision sent the Mets' catcher on his back. But in a moment John was raising his right hand in triumph, showing that the ball hadn't been shaken loose by the force of the slide. Templeton was out.

While this was going on at home plate, Flannery, who later said he didn't believe Lenny was going to throw out Templeton, kept skittering around the bases. He passed second, heading for third.

Leaping to his feet, Gibbons quickly reacted to a shout of "Third base, third base!" He threw to Howard Johnson, who easily tagged out the onrushing Flannery. I was doing the play-by-play and, caught up in the action, screamed, "Just your routine 8-2-5 double play!"

There doesn't seem any way to stop the Mets from winning over 100 games. They stand a chance to equal or surpass the 108 wins of the 1975 Reds.

In the West, the Houston Astros appear to be making a strong run at winning the division for the first time since 1980. Charlie Kerfeld, the six-foot-six, 260-pound Houston right-hander, who hails from Knob Noster, Missouri (you gotta love that name!), has already hailed his Astros as a "team in a season of destination." If the Astros meet the Mets in the playoffs, as seems most likely right now, that'll make two teams of "destination."

Less than two months ago the baseball world was engaged in constant speculation about the potential of the Mets' pitching staff. Would Gooden, Ojeda, and company all end up with twenty wins or more? It now looks as if none of the big four starters will reach that level, although they are all bound to have excellent won-lost records.

In addition, the early nay-saying and head-shaking over Dwight Gooden's performance has, for the most part, withered away. It has withered simply because Dwight, over his last half dozen starts, increasingly resembles the Gooden of 1985. Columnist Barry Lorge of the *San Diego Union* said Dwight was throwing "a curveball that drops in on a right-hand batter as malevolently as a bill collector."

Pitching coach Mel Stottlemyre has worked with Dwight on his mechanics and his stride. But it's been Dwight's own grit and determination that've done the job.

As of September 2, Gooden's stats over his last seventy starts read 45–9!

Winning persists and so does the booing for Darryl Strawberry, who went oh-for-August at Shea.

Up in the booth the other day, Ralph, Steve, and I were talking about booing.

"Sometimes when they boo you," I said, "they're trying to tell you they really love you and are just disappointed in you. Kind of a 'you always hurt the one you love' mentality."

"That's not my kind of love," said Ralph. "You don't mind getting booed on the road; it's when they boo you at home that it hurts."

Ralph and I both recalled that we'd been booed when we played—few escape it. When Ralph went from Pittsburgh's "Greenberg Gardens" to Chicago's Wrigley Field in a June 1953 trade, he obviously wasn't appreciated quite as much in Chicago as he had been in Pittsburgh. The Cub fans were more partial to Ralph's veteran outfield sidekick, Hank Sauer, than they were to him, a mere newcomer on their scene. So he suffered some of those hurtful slings and arrows at the end of his career.

When my throwing was, quite honestly, ragged in the late sixties with the Cards, I, too, often heard from the boobirds. It doesn't give you a feeling of security. In Shakespeare's tragedy *Coriolanus* the old bard makes a point about one-time idols wailing about "the dissenting rogues." It is always a shock when those cheers for heroes turn to hisses.

But it seems to me that booing of players and managers

these days has reached a new level of intensity, a pastime to replace the national pastime itself. Ballparks have become enclaves of free-floating anger and frustration.

The mass abuse has come down on Strawberry's head as never before.

His called strikeouts have been accumulating; his long home runs are becoming more scarce. The home hero has become a target, in a year when everything else seems to be breaking the Mets' way. As the raspberries pour over Strawberry, one has to wonder about the ferocity of it. How counterproductive is it for the man, who, in the words of *The New York Time*'s sportswriter Malcolm Moran, has graduated to "designated scapegoat"—or, in the words of the immortal Lucchesi, "scrapgoat"—at the age of twenty-four?

In what has been billed as a preview of the World Series, the Mets played a charity game on September 4 in Fenway Park with the Eastern Division leaders of the American League, the Red Sox. It's the first time I've been in the ballpark since I was released in 1975. Some memory!

Most exhibition games, especially this late in the season, are pure drudgery. But not this one. We even televised it, and I must admit the whole atmosphere was fun and festive. Players shuttled in and out of the lineup, making the contest look like a battle of pinch fielders and pinch hitters.

If the Red Sox and the Mets do meet in the Series, Fenway will go bananas. You would have thought the Series had actually begun here; there were enough media guys on hand to cover a presidential inauguration. And if anyone cares, the Mets, as they have done so many times in the regular season, rallied in the seventh and eighth innings to win.

A couple of days after the Fenway exhibition, a Boston TV critic took exception to my coining of the word "Fenwave." He also called me a "motor-mouth" and a "laughing boy" in his column.

Even in exhibition games, people listen.

Back to the real season . . .

For whatever inexplicable reason—anxiety, panic, Chernobyl, indigestion, complacency, fatigue, mass hypnosis, boredom, gonfalonphobia (fear of pennants and banners)—the Mets' batters suddenly have taken a journey to Death Valley just as they appeared on the brink of tacking down the National League East title.

They lost two out of three to the Expos at Shea, playing some of their worst ball of the year. Montreal scored nine runs after two outs in three different innings in one of those losses. In another the Mets were shellacked, 9–1, with a stray ninth-inning home run by Strawberry after two outs, preventing a shutout by Bob Sebra. By the way, when Darryl hit his homer, his twentieth, the crowd cheered him almost as noisily as it had been booing him a few innings before. That reminded me of Dale Murphy's homer for Atlanta against the Mets earlier in the year, when the Mets were ahead 8–0. In that instance, the Atlanta fans cheered and applauded Dale until the place echoed. I love it!

Then, with perhaps as many as fifty thousand New Yorkers paying their way into Philadelphia's Veterans Stadium for a September 12–13–14 three-game series, the Mets again failed to clinch, as the Phils showed them nothing but clenched teeth.

When the third straight Philly win was in the bank, I chuckled an apology over the air to those Met fans who had made the trip from New York to sit in on the "pennant clincher."

"We promoted this thing and encouraged you fans to visit the City of Brotherly Love," I said. "It's our fault, right, Ralph?"

But Mike Schmidt came closer to the real reason for the bounce in his stubborn, second-place Philly team. "We didn't want the Mets drinking champagne in our face," the competitive Schmidt growled.

That champagne, which had been schlepped from Shea Stadium to Philly, went on to St. Louis. The magic number was still two. The Mets lost the first game to the Cards, then finally won the second and last game of the series. One thing happened, though, that demonstrated the animosity felt around the league toward the Mets. After they won the second game, the Cards' scoreboard flashed the following message (after the

Phillies won *their* game, thus ensuring that the best the Mets could do that night was clinch a tie for the division): "There will be no clinching or drinking of champagne tonight in Busch Stadium." This was a real gratuitous slam. I can understand competition on the field, but when it filters to the front office like this, it becomes tactless and tasteless.

Back at Shea, my wife, Anne, had her own thoughts on the Mets.

"This whole thing," Anne said, "reminds me of a girl who is pregnant and doesn't know when it's going to happen. She's going to experience a certain amount of pain and discomfort. But when it happens, and it will, she'll be enormously happy!"

Ralph liked this line so much he quoted it on the air—and gave Anne the credit.

The Mets, and Gooden, faced the Cubs on September 17 at Shea. In the ninth inning, Gooden, leading 4–0, gave up a two-run home run. Anne continued her metaphor.

"It's starting to look like false labor pains," she said.

But it turned out all right in the end as the Mets won 4–2, clinching the Eastern Division crown once and for all.

In the forty-five years or so that Vern Hoscheit has been haunting bullpens and clubhouses, the old coyote hunter from Plainview, Nebraska, has developed some pretty sharp insights about this game. As the bullpen coach of the Mets since 1984, Vern also has some notions about what makes that Mets pitching staff tick. Back in spring training, Vern, along with almost everybody else, was predicting a big year, a pennant year, for his disciples. But what set him apart from the crowd was that the man called the *exact* day that the Mets would clinch the Eastern Division: September 17. Really: the man actually called the day right on the button.

Keith Hernandez, who had the flu, didn't play in the clincher until late in the game, when he went in for defensive purposes —and mostly just to participate in this important ball game. But his role was ably filled by Dave Magadan. It was Dave's first major-league start; needless to say, it was a debut that did not go unnoticed.

He became an instant hero, with three straight singles that

knocked in two runs. When he came to bat for the last time in the hectic evening, Met fans greeted him as if he'd played first base all season and his name were really Keith Hernandez.

As Ralph and I waited in the Mets' clubhouse for the postgame victory celebration, we heard Steve Zabriskie say on the air that the Mets had turned "the inevitable into reality." What we didn't hear or see was the savage behavior by some fans who poured onto the field.

During the course of the game, the Mets had entreated the fans to please stay off the field when the game was over. But it was to no avail. The field was ripped to shreds, with large clumps of the playing surface being removed for souvenirs. One Met, Rick Aguilera, suffered an injury to his left arm when some overzealous hooligan jumped on his back from behind the Met dugout. In retrospect, one has to feel lucky that nobody else was hurt or maimed. Why do people think this is the way to celebrate?

While some fans ripped up Shea's turf, the Mets held their own party in the clubhouse. Ralph and I interviewed the victors and were inundated with the usual shaving cream and champagne bath.

Sure, the Mets had been expected almost from opening day to win—and they did, comfortably. So it was no Cinderella tale. But many of these young men had never experienced this thrill before. I could really understand their high spirits.

This was my eighth one of these celebrations, as both player and announcer, and I think it's interesting to compare the two roles. As a player, you feel an integral part of the joy. But as an announcer, even though you're part of the organization and really part of the traveling team, you're strangely on the periphery. You can't get vicarious pleasure from these things—you've got to do it yourself.

On the air, as champagne shampooed my hair, ran down my cheeks and into my eyes, Wally Backman told me it was great to be able to "come back to New York and clinch it." And Davey Johnson, surprisingly dry when I interviewed him, said he'd gotten "great contributions from all twenty-four guys." New York's Mayor Koch, in a tête-à-tête with Ralph, after arriving on the scene in the eighth inning, promised a ticker tape parade for the Mets if they should win the World Series. That's one political promise that's sure to be kept.

The Mets literally and figuratively returned to earth on September 18—the day after clinching—and to a diamond that somewhat resembled the rutted, desolate, potholed landscape that Alan Shepard and company must have seen when they landed on the moon. It would be unfair to overlook, at this point, the truly wondrous patching job that Pete Flynn and his ground crew have done with the hundred thousand square feet of Shea's playing field. They worked all night after the wreckers had done their sorry job—and damned if by noon of the next day the playpen didn't look that much the worse for wear: just a field with choppy green rectangles that sort of resembled an old, beat-up tweed jacket with elbow patches. It was probably the best restoration job since the Statue of Liberty.

The oft-heard slogan and promo, *A September to Remember*, has turned out to be more than hyperbole. Now it is actuality for the Mets. For the other clubs it is now just a time to play out the schedule, to look over the youngsters, to pad out attendance a bit, and to wait till next year.

It is audition time, too, for the Mets, since the rosters of all teams are now expanded to the approximate population of China. In the last two weeks of the season, Davey will be able to make more changes in the Met lineup than he could of a one-year-old baby in a bassinet.

It's Johnson's plan to play the youngsters, keep the regulars sharp, and most important, stay away from injuries.

But on September 25, at Wrigley Field in Chicago, the Mets had a major scare when Ron Darling tried to score from second base on Kevin Mitchell's sharp single to right field. Darling came bowling into Jody Davis, a catcher who can chew you up. Fortunately, Ron escaped with no damage.

In the final game the Mets got their 108th win, on a glorious day to end a glorious season. The Pirates were their victims for the seventeenth time in eighteen games. But a young and wild lefty pitcher for the Pirates, Hippolito Peña, threw a couple of pitches in the first inning that might have abruptly left the Mets short-handed and short-headed in the LCS. He almost decapitated Lenny Dykstra to start the game, then several pitches later hit Hernandez in the back. Only Keith's agility and instinct for self-preservation saved him for the playoffs.

Then, in the seventh inning, Strawberry and Timmy Teufel almost collided under an innocent fly ball to right field. By some fast side-stepping, Darryl saved himself for the big games to come. It was like Bobby Unser driving his car to the Indy 500 and getting into a crash on the way.

The last day of any baseball season can be very depressing for those players who have had unsatisfactory years. It's a time when they start wondering where they'll be the next year. On the other hand, it can be a time of contentment for those who have performed up to and beyond expectations. Ironically, as a team the Mets performed beyond all expectations, notwithstanding the preseason hoopla. But many individuals on the club did not have "career" seasons. One can only imagine what this club would have done if Gooden had repeated his 1985 performance, if Strawberry had hit those oft-promised forty homers, if Carter had had a high-batting-average year, and so on.

◆ THE PLAYOFFS

You've seen waste recycled. I think that's what's got to be done with fear—certainly where the playoffs are concerned. You can't help the fear that's funneled into you. What you can do is try to turn it into steam. Fear can bring out the best in people —if used correctly.

Rusty Staub says "there's nothing wrong with butterflies." It's probably a tipoff of a man's intensity and desire. It's only when those butterflies are let out of the cage and are uncontrolled that tension can hurt your play.

I was never as nervous in a World Series as I was in any of my three playoffs with the Phillies. Once you actually get to the Series, it's almost as if the pressure's off. You're there. You're a winner, no matter what happens. But if you lose in the playoffs, your season's forgotten. You're just another loser.

In this instance, the pressure's got to be greater for the Mets because they're expected to win. Expectations can dictate performance, and it's hard to remember a team where the expectations were so high.

Supposed to are words that have become ridiculously magnified in this country. A team is "supposed to" win. Well, it's not that easy to win. "Supposed to" is Hitler invading Poland. With valiant Poles on horseback attacking German tanks, it's legitimate to say a superior force is "supposed to" win. But when you're talking about nine guys competing against nine other guys in a game of baseball, although one team might have an edge in talent, it's impossible to decide who's "supposed to" win. The Mets have been installed as 8-to-5 favorites —and that's just simply ridiculous!

I think the Mets have a slight edge at best.

Before handling the first Mets-Astros game for ABC from Houston, I watched the first American League playoff game between the Red Sox and Angels on TV. What struck me about the game, aside from the fact that Roger Clemens proved the uncertainties of baseball by getting bombed for eight runs, was that some stray cuss words came floating over the air from Fenway Park. Even while Al Michaels and Jim Palmer were broadcasting, you could hear the profanities, in the true accents of New England. In the real world we live in, none of these verbal outcries should shock anyone. But a little later in the broadcast Al made a brief announcement about it that I thought was right on target.

"It's the price we pay," said Al, "for trying to get the presence and the sounds of the game." The clamor and exhortations of a ballpark crowd are a legitimate part of the baseball scene, it seems to me, even if some of the utterances are often harsh and abrasive.

Forgetting fan exhortations for a minute, broadcasters must also have an automatic censor. It's always amazed me that broadcasters, in their intensity, don't slip up and let loose with an improper phrase. You'd be surprised how many times it crosses your mind to approach the broadcast of a game like a beer-drinking fan. Well, if you don't have that built-in censor, quite simply, you can't be a professional broadcaster.

While I'm on the subject, I have to question the word *professionalism* to some extent. Too often that word implies a certain plasticity, a lack of excitement. Now, I'm not a graduate of the Columbia Journalism School. I have not been trained in broadcasting the way some members of the older generation have been trained. But I have a pretty definite idea of the role an announcer must play. *My* idea of professionalism is certainly not jumping up and hollering (as one announcer once did in a Baltimore Colt football game, saying about the receiver Raymond Berry, "He dropped the fucking ball!"). But neither is it to sit back, stay calm and cool, and avoid the color, the ambience, and the feel of the game. If that feel is a little bit rough—or funny or offbeat or colorful—so be it.

I guess the whole point of this tirade is that the playoffs bring a whole new level of emotionalism to broadcasters as well as to players, and we have to deal with our nerves and fears as well.

First Playoff Game, Wednesday, October 8, Houston: Dwight Gooden was good, Mike Scott was great—a long Glenn Davis home run in the second inning did the Mets in, 1–0. They kept complaining about what Mike was doing to the ball. I remarked on the air that the Mets were complaining too much about the illegal pitch and not enough about the legal pitch—the split-finger fastball. The more they lost their composure in the batter's box, the more becalmed the stoic Scott became.

The question on everyone's mind is, "Does Scott doctor the ball?" The answer is yes, of course. But so do a lot of good pitchers. You'd be surprised at the names. But methinks me knows too much.

Scott was the key figure in this game, stranding the Mets with his pitching and, incidentally, the Astros with his hitting. Every time he came up to bat the bases seemed to be loaded with Astros, but he couldn't drive any of them home. It would have made life easier for him if he had. In the eighth inning the camera picked up a wonderful shot of Mike's face in the Houston dugout. "The eyes are the windows of the soul," I said, as our cameras focused on Mike's features. "And Mike is the calmest soul in the ballpark." And he was.

The question now remains, Can Scott do it again to the Mets—once, or even twice, if necessary?

The most animated moment of the evening came when a furious Keith Hernandez argued a called third strike with home plate umpire Doug Harvey. I chose not to make a point of it on the air, and I'll tell you why. To take apart a competent veteran umpire such as Harvey, who has been calling 'em for over twenty-five years in the National League—and to do it in front of a national TV audience—seems to me unjust and unfair. If Mike Scott is so tough to hit, then it stands to reason he's also tough to call.

In my opinion, the ball was not a strike. But a lot of questionable calls go unquestioned during the season because it *is* the season. Why should I go to umpire baiting now just because it's the playoffs? But I think this does raise the issue of playoff pressure. Keith would never have responded the way he did in the regular season. But there's such a feeling of finality to every call in the playoffs, he overreacted.

Second Playoff Game, Thursday, October 9, Houston: The remarkable Nolan Ryan threw his customary seeds for a few innings, and the Mets couldn't touch him. Ryan has probably thrown close to fifty-five thousand pitches in his career, and over the last half of the season he's been striking out hitters the way he did it in his youth. Some doctors insist that Nolan should check into a hospital after the season for elbow surgery similar to the transplant Tommy John had. I pointed out, on the air, that these doctors, of course, have never stood up there with a bat in their hands facing Nolan. If they had, they might think twice about his need for surgery.

The Mets did get to Ryan in the fourth inning, when Hernandez and Gary Carter delivered key blows behind the usual bill of fare served by Dykstra and Backman. Those two guys, I pointed out, are a perfect ten: Lenny wears number 4, Wally wears number 6. Add it up.

Meanwhile, Bob Ojeda, probably the best deal made in these parts since the purchase of Manhattan, scattered ten hits among the Astros, but only one run. Final score: 5–1. A key play came early, when the very adept Ojeda tagged out Kevin Bass,

who was trying to come home in the second inning on Alan
Ashby's chopper. Ojeda went tumbling as if he were in spring
football practice but he grimly held on to the ball.

Before this game the Met clubhouse, even with the team
down one game to Scott, had a pervasively optimistic atmosphere that indicated everything would be just fine. You might
chalk that up to confidence, which is an ingredient you can't
define but you just have. However, I think it's due more to the
four-out-of-seven format, as opposed to the three-out-of-five
format that prevailed until a couple of years ago.

Speaking of Kevin Bass . . .

I had heard that he did a mean Sammy Davis, Jr., impersonation. Since I was doing the interviews before this game
while Keith was working on his opener in the booth, I asked
Kevin if he'd go on camera and do his impression. Off camera,
he asked, "Two hundred bucks?" And he smiled.

"I don't have any control over that," I told him.

He said, "I sure do like those shoes you've got on."

So I said, "Okay, pal, here's the deal: You do Sammy on the
air, I'll give you the shoes."

He looked at me in disbelief and said, "Nahhh." Then he
went to take batting practice.

Third Playoff Game, Saturday, October 11, Shea Stadium:
Early wake-up call. *Very* early: six-thirty, because the game
starts at noon today.

The first thing I did when I got up was put my shoe trees
in my shoes—the ones that Bass liked—and put them by the
door so I wouldn't forget them. Anne was looking at me with
one of those *"what* are you doing?" looks. It's hard for a grown
man to explain to his loving wife that he was giving his shoes
to somebody in exchange for a Sammy Davis impersonation.
It's especially hard to explain this at seven o'clock on a Saturday morning.

When I got to the ballpark, I again did the on-air interviews. When I came to Kevin, I said, "We made a bet the other
day. I kept my end of the bargain—" and here I presented him
with my shoes, size 10 1/2, same as his "—now will you keep
yours?"

Kevin did his impersonation. He also kept my shoes, which surprised me. I kept thinking he was kidding, that he'd give 'em back. Uh uh. Forget about it. I won't see them again till the Mets play the Astros in 1987—and they'll be on his size 10 1/2 feet.

As to the game itself . . .

Lenny Dykstra delivered an astonishing coup de grace in the last of the ninth inning. With Backman on first as the result of a leadoff bunt, Lenny shot one into the stands in right field. The Astros had led, 5–4, after a run in the top of the eighth inning. Darryl Strawberry had hit a three-run home run off Bob Knepper to tie things up earlier, setting off a crowd reaction that could be heard in Reykjavík.

The 6–5 victory for the Mets had to be doubly painful for Hal Lanier and his tough, unremitting ballclub. They protested long and loud that Wally had run out of the baseline on his bunt. The rule, of course, permits a runner to make his own baseline as long as he isn't avoiding a tag. But the Houstons lost that argument—and the game.

Television is truly a visual medium, and no words could express the crowd's reaction to Dykstra's dramatic home run.

Craig Janoff, our director, did something so brilliant that, to tell you the truth, it gives me goose bumps to think about it. After the shot of the crowd going absolutely wild, he cut to a camera set up in a helicopter. The camera just zeroed in on the Mets slogan, printed on the outside of Shea Stadium: Baseball Like It Oughtta Be.

We cut to a commercial without anyone's saying a word.

Fourth Playoff Game, Sunday, October 12, Shea Stadium: Trailing two games to one, it was a "must" game for the Astros, and Scott was up to the task, even on Sid Fernandez's twenty-fourth birthday. Sid pitched a good game, but a second-inning home run by Alan Ashby with a man on base was all that Mike needed. Ashby, about thirty hours earlier, had been in a state of emotional shock after calling for the pitch that Dykstra hit out of the park. Now here he was delivering at the plate and keeping the Astros very much alive in this series.

Right before Ashby hit his home run, he hit a foul ball two

rows into the extra seats behind third base. Both Santana and Knight went for it. At the last moment, Rafael appeared to call Ray off it. Neither of them could make the catch. The day before, one of our statisticians and researchers, Jerry Klein, had said to me, "Wouldn't it be something if those extra seats cost someone a ball game?" When Ashby's ball—which normally would have been caught—fell into those seats, I remembered Jerry's comment, and I repeated it on the air. Well, when Ashby homered, proving my remark prophetic, I was immediately proclaimed a visionary. I thought I'd set the record straight here—Jerry's the prescient one in this instance.

Speaking of talking, Scott had Mets batters talking to themselves. When the Mets finally managed to score a single run in the eighth off Scott, their first run against him, it was a moral victory. Mike had nursed and rehearsed this split-finger fastball that Roger Craig put him on to, and it's truly turned his baseball life around. Don't forget, these are no humpties he's pitching against. These are the Mets, winners of 108 games, considered by many the best hitting team in the National League.

Unscheduled Off Day, Monday, October 13: When the fifth game at Shea had to be called off because of dark and weeping skies, the players retreated to their clubhouses. If you had caught a glimpse of them as they swapped jokes, did crosswords, played cards, and engaged in other minor pastimes designed to while away the hours, you would have concluded that all of them were pretty cool characters. Scott, for example, was perfectly willing to conduct an informal seminar for the press in the vagaries of his now notorious split-finger fastball. Here was the biggest name in baseball as of this week, as laid-back as a hibernating bear, quietly working to appease the endless appetite of the journalists for additional information about a pitch that could well send the Mets home to a disagreeable winter.

"Anyone got a ball so Mike can demonstrate how he does it?" remarked a sportswriter.

Mike turned around to look into his locker.

"No balls here," he said with a grin. "I guess you can get

one from Davey Johnson. He must have a collection of them."
That's a joke, son. There were rumors circulating at that pre-
cise moment that Johnson was in possession of a bunch of balls
that were headed directly for laboratory observation. Do they
do biopsies on scuffed baseballs?

Umpire Doug Harvey, who looks as much like an Associ-
ate Justice of the Supreme Court as anyone connected with the
game, also came by to reassure the media that Mike Scott's
insouciance was well-deserved. In brief, Harvey insisted that
he and the other umps hadn't seen anything to disturb them.
Clean as a hound's tooth was Mike.

"These men are just trying to get to Scott's mind," Harvey
said.

Fifth Playoff Game, Tuesday, October 14, Shea Stadium: Before noon the black skies were still crying large tears and it
looked doubtful that the proceedings would get under way for
at least another twenty-four hours. The scheduled pitchers,
Nolan Ryan and Dwight Gooden, had not thrown a single
warm-up pitch at a few minutes before one o'clock. Then,
literally out of the clearing blue sky, at twelve-fifty, the announcement swept media headquarters that the game would
indeed begin at one-twenty. The chemistry of these playoffs
has been altered considerably by the wet weather. The outfield warning track looks soggy and mushy. The puddles out
there threaten to twist knees and turn ankles for any overzealous outfielders.

The lights were on well before the game, but there was a
warm, not unpleasant breeze; by game time it was sixty-seven
degrees. Thoughts of Scuffgate, the Right Scuff, were temporarily old hat, or maybe old sandpaper. Now the game once
again was the thing.

With only about one quarter of the seats occupied at the
start of the game, the hardy crowd let out a roar as the game
got under way. The first pitch was greeted as if Dwight had
already hurled a no-hitter.

This game was the thing, too. It turned out to be a twelve-
inning classic, with Ryan performing magnificently and
Gooden pitching through the tenth inning for the first time in

his career. The Astros thought that a second-inning decision by umpire Fred Brocklander at first base deprived them of a run. With Kevin Bass on third and one out, Craig Reynolds hit into a Backman-to-Santana-to-Hernandez double play. If Craig had been pronounced safe at first the Astros would have scored a big run, as things turned out. The TV replays could have been used in hearty support of Hal Lanier's protest. Reynolds was clearly safe.

The Astros did score the first legitimate run in the fifth, with Alan Ashby coming home. At that point the Mets were totally stymied by Ryan, who had struck out eight straining Mets.

But in the bottom of the fifth inning, Strawberry, seemingly a player of feast or famine, connected on a 3–2 pitch that just barely skidded around the right field foul pole for a home run. The score was 1–1. It stood that way until the twelfth inning, when Gary Carter, also fighting a postseason slump, singled up the middle to score Backman with the winning run. Jesse Orosco was the winning pitcher.

Now up 3–2, what's on the Mets minds is: Let's win the sixth game so we don't have to face Scott again.

Sixth Playoff Game, Wednesday, October 15, Houston: Now think about this for a minute.

The weather's been awful—bad enough that it's almost overshadowed the games themselves as a topic of conversation. The players are exhausted—and so are the reporters, the broadcasters, and probably the fans. For a player, this kind of travel is particularly draining. Back and forth between Houston and New York. Because the weather's so bad, you don't know how long you'll have to stay once you hit a city. You don't know how much to pack. You don't know, when you wake up, whether you'll be playing one of the most important, emotional games of your life or whether you'll be sitting around your hotel playing cards and ordering room service. On Tuesday, the Mets and Astros played an emotionally sapping game. The fan got to have dinner, go to sleep, and then the next day turn on the TV and watch game six, possibly not realizing that it was in a city sixteen hundred miles away from game five. For

the Mets and Astros, a normal two-hour-and-fifty-minute flight
took four hours. They got into Houston around midnight (2:00
A.M., New York time).

So there's bound to be a letdown, right? There has to be
a reflection of all this in the type and quality of baseball that's
played, hasn't there?

No.

Wrong.

That's why one of the best sayings in all of baseball is "Hey,
rest in the wintertime!"

Game six of the LCS was one of the greatest, most exciting, most thrilling baseball games ever played.

And as my valedictory for the year, it was a bitch to broadcast. Grueling but oh so memorable.

The sixth game, at the Astrodome, started at a little after
three o'clock, which made it unusual right from the beginning.
The thought running through everyone's mind was, Is the city
of New York *closed* now? We didn't know what was going on,
but we figured that offices were basically shut and that everything was stopped so people could watch the game. We didn't
know—until afterward—the extent of the mania. It turned out
that hardware stores and restaurants put TVs in their windows,
and, literally, people in the streets stood in line outside to
watch the last part of the game. Because it was New York—
despite everything, still the Big Apple—there was a great
sense, on the Mets, of "Wow, what must be going on back
there?"

Bob Knepper pitched for the Astros, while Bob Ojeda
worked for the Mets. Both left-handers are generally calm,
quiet men. But before this game Knepper seemed particularly
animated and jacked up.

In these playoff games both teams, especially the Mets,
sort of shadowboxed in the early innings. But in this one the
Astros came out charging and swinging—like a Mike Tyson
first round. They banged three runs across in the first inning.
Then, oddly, they switched to a squeeze bunt play that failed.
All my flags went up. How many times have managers
impeded a club's aggression? Well, pal, this was one of those
times. It's like a competent violin teacher trying to change a

child prodigy's style. I mean, let the guy—in this case, the guys —play. What Hal Lanier did, in effect, was throw a prevent defense into his offense.

As the innings went by, the Mets couldn't touch Knepper.

Halfway through the game, the Mets had established a new, unenviable record for strikeouts. By the eighth inning the Mets still were scoreless, and Knepper had retired thirteen men in a row. When Knight made it fourteen to start the eighth, he walked back to the dugout with a grimace on his face that said just about everything about the Mets' and his own increasing frustrations.

Tim Teufel finally got the second Met hit, but Santana hit into a double play—and you couldn't help but notice that banner out in left field that read "Bring on Mike Skuff." The Mets surely didn't want to face Scott in a seventh game, but, trailing 3–0 in the ninth, it looked as if they were going to have to.

However, to lead off the ninth, Lenny Dykstra crushed a triple toward right center. Billy Hatcher, the center fielder, was shading Dykstra toward left center. I can't tell you how many games have been lost because center fielders shaded hitters one way or the other instead of playing straightaway. Curt Simmons put it best: "Doubleday put 'em there for a purpose."

Mookie Wilson followed with a handle hit over Doran's head at second base. Hernandez doubled, scoring Mookie, to make it 3–2. Still nobody out. Knepper, bewildered with the sudden turn of fortune, came out of the game and Dave Smith came in. Carter worked a walk, as did Strawberry. After a disputed 2–2 pitch, Ray Knight hit a sacrifice fly to right field, and the game was miraculously tied at 3–3.

The relievers took over until the fourteenth, when Aurelio Lopez yielded a leadoff single to Carter. Strawberry walked. Ray Knight, who had not had a sacrifice bunt since 1983, tried one, but Carter was thrown out at third. Bad play. However, Backman singled to right, and the Mets led 4–3.

Jesse Orosco came in to pitch the fourteenth, after Mc-Dowell had retired fifteen in a row. Orosco had already won two games in relief. He got a quick first out, then Billy Hatcher came up. The first ball that Hatcher hit went foul. As a catcher,

I was saying, "Stay away from this guy." On the air, I said, "If you're gonna make a mistake, make it away, because mistakes away to guys like Hatcher become singles. Mistakes inside become home runs." Well, Orosco's mistake was inside, and no sooner had I gotten this out of my mouth than *BOOM!* Hatcher tied the game with a home run along the left field foul pole.

Houston's fans went bananas. But Orosco got the next two outs.

In the sixteenth inning the Mets broke through for three runs with a leadoff double by Strawberry sparking what appeared to be the finishing touch. Darryl's hit fell just in front of Hatcher, who obviously was playing too deep. Knight then singled Darryl home; Backman walked. Knight came home on a wild pitch; Orosco sacrificed, and Dykstra singled Wally home.

With one out in the bottom of the sixteenth, I was told to get down to the Mets' clubhouse. Figuring the game would be over almost immediately, I ran. I actually hurt my knee. Here I am, a catcher for over twenty years, and I never had a real knee injury. But racing for ABC almost did me in.

And as I ran through the stands, I began to realize that this game wasn't over. Not by a long shot.

With one out, Davey Lopes walked, Doran and Hatcher singled. Walling hit into a force-out for the second out, but Glenn Davis singled Doran home. Now the Astros were behind, 7–6, with the tying and winning runs on base, and Kevin Bass was at bat.

After the first two breaking balls, it was one and one on Bass, and now I'm in the Mets' clubhouse and already hooked up so I can communicate with Keith Jackson. I had the monitor there in front of me so I could see the game. Keith asked for my reaction. I told him I wouldn't throw Bass anything but breaking balls. As soon as I said that, Orosco threw a fastball. Bass had a great cut. He just missed hitting the pitch out of the Astrodome.

Keith Hernandez immediately ran to the mound, where he met Carter and Orosco. Glaring at Gary, Hernandez said, as we discovered later, "If you call for another fastball, I'm going to kill you!"

Keith didn't have to kill anybody because Carter called for one breaking ball after another until Bass, on a 2–2 count, finally swung and missed, striking out and ending this gut-wrenching game.

Jesse threw his glove so high it seemed to disappear in the warm air of the Dome. The Mets had won the National League pennant in the most staggeringly intense game I've ever seen, played in, or broadcast.

◆ THE WORLD SERIES

The Boston Red Sox were down three games to one against the California Angels, but came back to win the American League pennant.

Their fifth game was comparable to the Mets-Astros sixth game. Dave Henderson hit two two-run home runs. One was for the Angels—he knocked a fly ball over the fence with his glove—and one was for his own team, which tied the game up in the ninth. He also drove in the winning run in extra innings.

Back at Fenway, the Sox blew the Angels out of the last two games. And now it's two titans about to clash on Saturday at Shea.

Rarely in my professional life have I had a chance to go to a game as a fan. This is my opportunity, since I'm not broadcasting the Series. I have broadcast 168 straight games for the Mets; now I'm able to drink beer and I don't have to keep my automatic censor in check. But going into the first game, I wasn't sure I knew *how* to be a fan.

After the first two games, I think most Met fans felt the same way.

Bruce Hurst was brilliant in the first game, and Tim Teufel made an unfortunate error on a ball that went right through his legs, allowing Boston to score the only run of the game. After the incredible tension of the two playoffs, this seemed like the dullest 1–0 Series game ever played.

The second game got advance billing as the ultimate showdown between Dwight Gooden and Roger Clemens. But it ended up as one of those games that would have put patrons to sleep in the middle of the summer. Roger's control was not sharp, and Gooden threw home run pitches to Dave Henderson and the veteran Dwight Evans.

The only controversial part of the game came when Davey allowed Gooden to hit with two on and the Mets trailing 4–2 in the fourth inning. Since Gooden gave up two more runs in the fifth, fans proclaimed that to be the turning point in the game.

But, in my opinion, Johnson wouldn't have removed him during the regular season—so why should he change now?

Either way, it was a moot point. The Mets lost 8–4 and were down 2–0.

On to Boston.

Pressed by the media about every move, Davey Johnson elected to cancel batting practice for the Mets when they hit Fenway on the off-day before the third game. His men, he thought, needed some physical rest and also some surcease from the endless questions. This is sound reasoning. Let's face it—these guys had played 170 games (and the Red Sox 171). Do you honestly think they needed to work out? I think Davey was exactly right. Workouts during postseason play are held strictly for the media.

However, from a strategic point of view, I think that Davey should have started Bobby Ojeda in game two. My obvious thinking is that I'd keep Ojeda away from Fenway Park—where he used to pitch and where his record was never that great. To be honest about it, Ojeda was also Davey's best pitcher during the season. You want him in there as often as possible.

Well, Ojeda survived all the gloomy speculation about his chances with the despicable architecture of Fenway by winning a neat 7–1 game. We were told that he thus became the first southpaw to beat the Red Sox at Fenway in a postseason game since Hippo Vaughn triumphed for the Cubs with a fifth-game shutout back in 1918.

Bobby was aided immeasurably not only by his deft change-ups ("Some of his pitches have the velocity of a falling leaf," said the old word-master Vin Scully), but by Boston's failure to execute a key run-down play in the first inning. The Mets ended up with four runs.

Play has been sloppy for the first three games.

The Mets won the fourth game 6–2. This game didn't turn on miscues but on several missed opportunities at the plate by the Red Sox.

As he invariably does, Ron Darling kept the Mets in the game, defying fate in the early going. Then he clamped down and waited for power from Gary Carter, who hit two home runs, and Dykstra, who hit one.

Manager John McNamara, who has a reputation for handling pitchers with great charm and persuasion, tried to get by with righty Al Nipper (ERA: 5.38, ten losses, twelve defeats) as his starting pitcher.

The McNamara gamble with Nipper drew fire in some quarters. Managers usually don't change their spots, their spikes, or their pitchers who have gotten them there. But Nipper's choice probably reflected McNamara's uncertainty whether Bruce Hurst and Roger Clemens could come back to pitch on only three days' rest.

By the way, Dykstra's home run hit Dwight Evans's glove and popped into the Boston bullpen. That's a play you might see every couple of years—yet now we've seen it twice. Once by Henderson in the playoffs and now by Evans in the Series.

The Mets had had Mike Scott to torment and frustrate them in the NLCS. Now it was Bruce Hurst's turn to play the Scott role, which he did again almost to perfection in game five at Fenway. We were saying that Bruce should change his name to Hearse—because he's really burying the Mets.

Dwight Gooden, on the other hand, almost duplicated his first Series game, in the sense that he never seemed in command of himself or his pitches.

In addition, Marty Barrett, at second base for the Red Sox, was proving that the World Series invariably uncovers for the general public a spate of unsung ballplayers who labor all year without much recognition. Barrett is a reliable hitter, a good fielder without extraordinary range and a capacity to carefully look over pitches before he hits them. He has become the Sox's best hitter in this Series.

The fifth game also marked an intriguing incident in the life and times of Darryl Strawberry. He engaged in a rather lengthy argument at home plate with umpire Ed Montague. As a "reward" the Fenway fans in right field, where Darryl lives during the game, lathered his ears with incessant booing in the final innings. As the fans derisively serenaded him with "Dar-ryl, Dar-ryl, Dar-ryl," almost as little boys in a schoolyard would taunt a companion, Strawberry turned halfway to acknowledge them. He looked like an umbrella stand lifting its cap.

I thought this facetious booing by the Red Sox fans was handled marvelously well and maturely by Strawberry.

Before game six at Shea, you had to be blind and deaf not to have heard the outpouring of complaints from almost everybody—fans, players, press—that the games were starting too late and ending too late. Obviously, television is the culprit. But, I'll tell you, when you pay $100 million a year for the right to televise the games, you should damn well have the final word on when those games start. Plain and simple!

If the sixth game of the playoffs gripped the fans of New York and other parts of the country, it's a certainty that the sixth game of the World Series was at least as compelling—from the first minute, when an itinerant parachutist descended from the heavens over Shea to land not far from Bobby Ojeda on the pitching mound, to the unpredictable last second, when Mookie Wilson's dribbler down the first base line slithered under Bill Buckner's glove to give the Mets a frenetic delivery from the abyss. It's hard to believe how many times I heard people say it was hard to believe what happened. But, you know—it *was* hard to believe! It was Lazarus raised from the dead. For Sox and Mets fans alike it was also hard to watch.

I was there as a fan, as a human being, not as a broadcaster. And as a fan, this game really upset me. And I was joined by millions.

I watched this game in Nelson Doubleday's booth, the WOR booth, and the Sportschannel booth, and I have never seen so many people pacing around. It was like the scene in *Midnight Express* after Billy was sent to the area for the criminally insane.

The reason everybody in Shea Stadium was acting like a nut is because this game was enough to drive everybody crazy. It was comparable to a neophyte art lover's looking at a piece of art and saying, "Yecchhh! Why does Chagall put pigs in a sunset?" But then you learn and appreciate the artistry and the beauty. Well, in game six, the brushstrokes may have been sloppy, but the result was a masterpiece.

Would you believe:

In the ninth inning, with two on, no outs, and a chance to win the game, Davey Johnson had Howard Johnson bunt. The bunt was unsuccessful, Johnson eventually struck out, and the Mets couldn't put the Sox away.

Then, the Red Sox scored two runs in the top of the tenth to take the lead.

Bottom of the tenth, two outs, nobody on, ex-Met Calvin Schiraldi pitching, and two strikes on Carter. Carter singled.

So did pinch hitter Kevin Mitchell—who had replaced Darryl Strawberry in a controversial double switch.

Ray Knight, also with two strikes, singled, too—a dunker to center.

Bob Stanley relieved Schiraldi to face Mookie Wilson. Stanley had thrown only one wild pitch all season. So, of course, he threw one, and Mitchell scored, tying the game.

On the next pitch, Mookie hit a ground ball through Bill Buckner's legs. What, you say? What's Buckner doing in there when he's been taken out for Dave Stapleton in the late innings all year? Good question.

But the ball game was over. And this game will be rehashed and rehashed, the peat for hot-stove leagues for years to come.

So now we were down to the end of the long season of great expectations. Bruce Hurst, with two wins already over the Mets, was Red Sox manager McNamara's choice to go for three, which meant Oil Can Boyd would be shunted aside. A Sunday of rain had forced a one-day postponement of the seventh game, giving McNamara a chance to bring back Hurst with three days of rest. This meant that Hurst would try to emulate pitchers such as Mickey Lolich, Bob Gibson, Lew Burdette, Harry Brecheen, and Christy Mathewson, who, among a few others, had managed to dominate other Series competitions with three victories.

Even though Mets starter Ron Darling had had an extra day of rest, it didn't help him. He was rocked for two home runs in the second inning, one by Dwight Evans and another by Rich Gedman. Believe it or not, Gedman's home run was aided by Darryl Strawberry's glove—the third one of those freak plays in this postseason.

In the fourth inning Davey Johnson called on Sid Fernandez, who had been bypassed in the Series pitching rotation. Little did Johnson realize that this was going to be the key move of the game—and thus the season. Sid kept the Sox at Back Bay until Johnson pinch-hit for him in the sixth inning.

Hurst, in the meantime, was persistently mowing down the Mets through the first five innings.

Then Mazzilli, pinch-hitting for Fernandez, singled. Mookie followed with another single. Hernandez singled to left center for two runs. Score: 3–2.

Teufel walked. Carter nudged a soft line drive to right that Evans had—or seemed to have—and then we could see the ball dribble out of his glove. Backman, running for Teufel, scored the tying run on the play.

Tying the score was important, but it was equally important for the Mets that McNamara pinch-hit for Hurst in the seventh, getting the Mets into Boston's questionable bullpen.

Enter Calvin Schiraldi, who as things turned out, wasn't up to it. Ray Knight lined a home run in the seventh inning to put the Mets ahead 4–3. Dykstra pinch-hit a single and was wild-pitched to second. Santana singled past Buckner and went to second when Evans bobbled the ball, though Dykstra failed to score. Mookie was intentionally walked by Sambito, who had replaced Schiraldi. Backman also walked, and Hernandez connected for a sacrifice fly to center, making it 6–3.

But the Sox were not a team prepared to make concession speeches. They scored two runs in the eighth inning, sparked by Evans's double off Roger McDowell.

This is when Johnson made his last successful move of the

season. Jesse Orosco was called on to replace McDowell—and boy, what a job he did. Gedman lined to second for one out. Orosco fanned Dave Henderson, and Don Baylor grounded out to short.

Two more runs came across for the Mets in the bottom of the eighth, including a towering blast by Strawberry to right.

In the ninth inning Orosco, working inexorably toward the finish that many thought was in the cards going back to spring training, got Ed Romero to pop to Hernandez. Boggs grounded to Backman as an orange smoke bomb dropped onto the field in a premature celebration.

Jesse wasn't going to be denied. Barrett, the best hitter the Red Sox had had in these games, with thirteen record-tying hits, struck out.

"Losing feels worse than winning feels good," said Joe Garagiola, as NBC's cameras invaded the privacy of Wade Boggs's tearful dugout misery.

You couldn't prove that by the 2.2 million people, young and old, who celebrated with the Mets over the next twenty-four hours and with the millions around the country who stayed glued to their TV sets, enthralled by a bunch of guys who refused to be beaten.

As impressive as the season was, perhaps the most impressive element in it was the ticker tape parade on the day after the last game of the Series.

Starting from the Battery, with the impassive face of the Statute of Liberty peering down on us, we wended our way through 2.2 million fans, their adoring faces glowing as we passed by, and the adulation and the excitement seemed to sum up what baseball is all about. The interminable road trips, the controversial calls, the arguments, the loneliness, the fun, the beauty, the thrills—everything came together in one glorious day. It all seemed so worthwhile.

Hell, it *was* worthwhile.

It *is* what baseball's all about.

That's why I love it.

A Glossary of Pitches

Forkball/Split-finger Fastball: The basic difference between these two pitches is that, while both are held between the index and middle fingers, the forkball is held toward the base of the fingers and "choked" or slowed when thrown, while the split-finger fastball is held toward the end of the fingers and thrown harder. Both pitches break similarly, down with a tumbling motion. The effect of these pitches is that they give the illusion of a strike but rarely are. Consequently, they're very hard to catch.

Cut Fastball/Sailing Fastball: Pressure is applied on the middle finger to make the pitch sail away from a right-handed batter—if you're a right-handed pitcher—and in on a lefty. Most hitters determine that it's a fastball, but it's the little dart on the end—the cut—that gets them.

Slider: Very tough on the arm. The Dodger organization doesn't teach sliders. The twisting motion is what makes it so hard on the elbow. It has a horizontal break, moving parallel to the ground, unlike the curveball, which moves perpendicular to the ground. The good slider can usually be distinguished from the bad one by its "dime" or tight spin. (If the spin is a "dime," it's tight. If the spin is a "quarter," it's loose.)

Sinking Fastball: Self-explanatory. It sinks. Usually thrown with the seams, and usually a heavier pitch than the others because of its dead spin. The good ones are impossible to lift. They feel as though you're hitting an anvil with sugar cane.

Riding Fastball: Thrown across the seams to get its riding effect. Not necessary for pitchers who throw this pitch to keep the ball down. Often most effective when up.

Screwball: Thrown with an inverse rotation. You have to turn your hand in and down. Catching it is like catching a feather. Valenzuela is the exemplar.

Curveball: Few pitchers throw the true curve anymore. A dropping breaking ball, which used to be called a "drop" because it gave the appearance of dropping off a table. Known nowadays as the "slurve." Easy to catch. Koufax had the greatest curveball I've ever seen. And Ryan's inability to get it over made him a .500 pitcher until he bridled it.

Change-Up/Palmball: We talked about the illusion of a pitch's being a strike. This is the illusion of a pitch's being there. Batters swing at a pitcher's arm motion. Whatever place a pitcher can hold the ball so he can deceive a batter with his arm motion is where he'll hold this pitch. IMPORTANT: The speed of this pitch compared to the other pitches of a pitcher's repertoire has nothing to do with it.

Spitball: Nobody knows anyone who throws this pitch! Since nobody throws it, it's hard to explain. Blarney! With the help of saliva, grease, slippery elm, or Vaseline, this pitch is a dead spin downer. Heavy like a sinker but breaks much more sharply down. Tough to catch. And tough to throw for a strike, too. This pitch was originally outlawed in 1920 for sanitary reasons. At least we should change the reason for its being banned. I think it should be legalized because all of them add something other than rosin to the ball anyway.

Knuckleball: Inappropriately named, it's rarely thrown with the knuckles. Usually thrown almost daintily with a pitcher's fingertips. Catchers should not have to handle knuckleball pitchers. The guy back there should be a lepidopterist. Bob Uecker once said, "The only way to catch a knuckler is to wait till the ball stops rolling, then pick it up."

TIM McCARVER
Born October 16, 1941; Memphis, Tennessee

	G	AB	H	2B	3B	HR	HR %	R	RBI	BB	SO	SB	BA	SA	Pinch Hit AB	Pinch Hit H	G by POS
1959 STL N	8	24	4	1	0	0	0.0	3	0	2	1	0	.167	.208	1	0	C-6
1960	10	10	2	0	0	0	0.0	3	0	0	2	0	.200	.200	4	1	C-5
1961	22	67	16	2	1	1	1.5	5	6	0	5	0	.239	.343	2	2	C-20
1963	127	405	117	12	7	4	1.0	39	51	27	43	5	.289	.383	5	1	C-126
1964	143	465	134	19	3	9	1.9	53	52	40	44	2	.288	.400	7	1	C-137
1965	113	409	113	17	2	11	2.7	48	48	31	26	5	.276	.408	5	2	C-111
1966	150	543	149	19	13	12	2.2	50	68	36	38	9	.274	.424	5	1	C-148
1967	138	471	139	26	3	14	3.0	68	69	54	32	8	.295	.452	11	4	C-130
1968	128	434	110	15	6	5	1.2	35	48	26	31	4	.253	.350	19	4	C-109
1969	138	515	134	27	3	7	1.4	46	51	49	26	4	.260	.365	1	0	C-136
1970 PHI N	44	164	47	11	1	4	2.4	16	14	14	10	2	.287	.439	0	0	C-44
1971	134	474	132	20	5	8	1.7	51	46	43	26	5	.278	.392	14	3	C-125
1972 2 teams PHI N (45G—237) MON N (77G—251)																	
" Total	122	391	96	13	1	7	1.8	33	34	36	29	5	.246	.338	18	2	C-85, OF-14, 3B-6
1973 STL N	130	331	88	16	4	3	0.9	30	49	38	31	2	.266	.366	39	8	1B-77, C-11
1974 2 teams STL N (74G—217) BOS A (11G—250)																	
" Total	85	134	30	1	1	0	0.0	16	12	26	7	1	.224	.246	43	7	C-29, 1B-6
1975 2 teams BOS A (12G—381) PHI N (47G—254)																	
" Total	59	80	23	4	1	1	1.3	7	10	15	10	0	.288	.400	39	10	C-17, 1B-2
1976 PHI N	90	155	43	11	2	3	1.9	26	29	35	14	2	.277	.432	42	9	C-41, 1B-2
1977	93	169	54	13	2	6	3.6	28	30	28	11	3	.320	.527	36	8	C-42, 1B-3
1978	90	146	36	9	1	1	0.7	18	14	28	24	2	.247	.342	41	8	C-34, 1B-11
1979	79	137	33	5	1	1	0.7	13	12	19	12	2	.241	.314	39	10	C-31, OF-1
1980	6	5	1	1	0	0	0.0	2	2	1	0	0	.200	.400	2	0	1B-2
21 yrs.	1909	5529	1501	242	57	97	1.8	590	645	548	422	61	.271	.388	373	82	C-1387, 1B-103, OF-15, 3B-6
12 yrs.	1181	3780	1029	154	43	66	1.7	393	453	325	285	39	.272	.388	139	31	C-960, 1B-83
LEAGUE CHAMPIONSHIP SERIES																	
1976 PHI N	2	4	0	0	0	0	0.0	0	0	0	1	0	.000	.000	1	0	C-1
1977	3	6	1	0	0	0	0.0	1	0	1	3	0	.167	.167	1	0	C-2
1978	2	4	0	0	0	0	0.0	2	1	2	0	0	.000	.000	1	0	C-1
3 yrs.	7	14	1	0	0	0	0.0	3	1	3	4	0	.071	.071	3	0	C-4
WORLD SERIES																	
1964 STL N	7	23	11	1	1	1	4.3	4	5	5	1	1	.478	.739	0	0	C-7
1967	7	24	3	1	0	0	0.0	3	2	2	2	0	.125	.167	0	0	C-7
1968	7	27	9	0	2	1	3.7	3	4	3	2	0	.333	.593	0	0	C-7
3 yrs.	21	74	23	2	3	2	2.7	10	11	10	5	1	.311	.500	0	0	C-21

ABOUT THE AUTHORS

TIM McCARVER, after a twenty-one-year career as a
major league catcher, has added merriment and insight
to broadcasts of New York Mets games and ABC's
"Monday Night Baseball." He owns a .271 lifetime
batting average and played in three World Series with
the St. Louis Cardinals. Tim lives in Gladwyne,
Pennsylvania, with his wife, Anne, and daughters Kathy
and Kelly.

RAY ROBINSON, a magazine editor and writer, is
currently a contributing editor to *TV Guide*. He has
three grown children and lives in New York City and
Fire Island with his wife, Phyllis, and Penrod, a Norfolk
terrier.